THE UNIQUE AND THE UNIVERSAL

By the same author

THE ORIGINS OF TOTALITARIAN DEMOCRACY
POLITICAL MESSIANISM: THE ROMANTIC PHASE

THE UNIQUE
AND THE UNIVERSAL

Some Historical Reflections

J. L. TALMON

GEORGE BRAZILLER

NEW YORK

To my late teachers
RICHARD KOEBNER
LEWIS NAMIER
R. H. TAWNEY

CONTENTS

7

PREFACE

THE ESSAYS contained in this collection represent an effort to sort out some of the elements of a basic dilemma of modern times. In that sense they are variations on a single theme. They do not claim to offer solutions or to preach a doctrine, for the human condition is not an intellectual problem waiting for a hidden key but an existential situation, the history of which is also its structure and its logic—like the psychologist's case. If laying bare concatenation and association is not a solution nor a cure, it does help us nevertheless to live with our troubles, and adds significance and depth to our lives, even if it does not make us any happier.

These essays are concerned with the quest for identity in a world where on the one hand rationalist modes of thought, technological developments and universal ideologies seem to be wiping out all racial and national differences, but on the other hand nationalist self-assertion is growing more and more intense. The tendency towards oneness, prompted by rational resolve; and the recalcitrance of facts of nature and history asserting their uniqueness: which is more authentic and more potent. The two contending forces have given rise to extreme mass movements of fanatical conviction, Communism and Nazi-Fascism. Some attempt is made in the following pages to examine their interaction.

The present probe has been inspired by the author's existential situation as a Jew who has lived through the traumatic experiences of Nazism and Communism, chose Israel as his home, and who at the same time feels deeply committed to the Western tradition.

The Jew is unable (and unwilling) to shake off his uniqueness, but he can live only in a world based on universal values. In this he is unique, but at a deeper level his problem is really a parable on the human condition in general. In recent times the Jews became witness and whipping-block

9

to the furies released by the unresolved conflict. A part of those who survived the hurricane determined to cut the knot and to be simply themselves. They are now discovering that the problem of identity is staring at them anew, albeit in a different guise.

The collection is thus divided into "general" and "Jewish" essays. Most of them have previously appeared in journals, in the Hebrew or English language, or in both simultaneously, and one ("Experiment in Utopia") in Swedish ("Dagens Nyheter"), and I wish to thank *Haaretz* and *Amoth*, *Commentary* and *Encounter* for permission to reprint the pieces which first appeared in their columns. Several essays grew out of public lectures given at different times: "Uniqueness and Universality of Jewish History" was delivered as the inaugural Hillel Foundation lecture at University College, London, 1956, "The National Brotherhood and the international confraternity" is a much extended version of a lecture given in 1959 at All Souls College, Oxford, and "Herder and the German Mind" was read in the series of lectures on the History of Thought arranged by St. Catherine's College, Oxford for the Academic year 1963-4.

The author is conscious of some repetitions but they appeared inevitable. The reader is asked for indulgence.

Thanks are due and wholeheartedly given to good friends who helped to prepare this collection for publication: Miss Bernadette Folliot, Dr. Jonathan Frankel, Mrs. Efrath B. Kleinhaus, and Dr. Renée Winegarten.

I

The National Brotherhood and the
international confraternity

Nationalism and Socialism

THE TRIBE may be considered as a simple datum, one of
the phenomena of nature. The nation is a product of
both nature and history. Nationalism is a frame of mind, a
type of awareness. At the root of every nation will be found
some tribal-racial nucleus, and almost every nation came into
being through a fusion of tribes. Sometimes one tribe sub-
dued and assimilated its neighbours. On occasion tribes
united of their own free will. There have been many instances of nations emerging from matrimonial-territorial
arrangements between ruling houses, as well as cases of
territorial-political units being split into separate nationalities by dynastic bargains. It was large-scale conquests that
led to the unification, for example, of the Russian people.
The uninterrupted rule of a successful dynasty fused diverse
tribes and distant regions into the single entity that is France.
Though the Dutch and the Flemish spoke the same language,
religious reasons induced the Belgians to prefer the Spanish
rule, while the Dutch Calvinists were fired by a relentless
resolve to secure independence for their convictions and way
of life. Despite the fact that the peasants and burghers of
Switzerland spoke three different languages, a common love
of freedom and the anxiety to make it safe prevented their
falling apart after they had won their victory over the common foe. Historic memories and linguistic differences served
as the media of national self-identification in the case of the

various Slav racial groups, which were intermingled in the same territory. Geographical causes and a sense of partnership in a new venture of universal significance gave vitality to American nationhood. In brief, the factor that lends cohesion to a nation varies from case to case. To become effective it must, however, have a long and relatively unbroken span of time to exercise its influence. One might indeed, call time the Father of all nations.

I

It is when, at a given moment in time, members of a nation wake up to the fact of their forming an all-embracing, and at the same time exclusive entity, a partnership in all things, more real than, for example, a religious faith or social class—that we may speak of the emergence of nationalism.

Such an awareness developed in Western Europe after the various tribes and provinces had been successfully fused into entities by centralised states. Here being, to use the Marxist vocabulary, created consciousness. But the rise and growth of consciousness became in turn a determining factor in shaping the mode of being.

In Eastern Europe nations were born as soon as their members adopted the nationalist creed, or more precisely, became conscious of being deprived of what others possessed —autonomous statehood. In the West union may have been imposed by force from above, and awareness of differences may persist, even after the unitary state has been fully consolidated; yet the lag of time between the early events and the rise of modern nationalism has been long enough to enable the State to achieve the full integration of the various fissiparous elements, and for a community of interests and sentiments to become strong enough to withstand any centrifugal tendencies. The Welsh have for hundreds of years made no attempt to break away from England, nor have the Provençals and Bretons in modern France indulged in anything much more than regional narcissism.

In Eastern Europe, however, Russia, Austria and Turkey failed to bring about the same fusion, or at least close and friendly co-operation, between the various ethnic groups before the upsurge of nationalism. Hence the ardent endeavours of the oppressed nationalities in that area to achieve national states. On the face of it, in Eastern Europe it was consciousness that engendered being; yet even consciousness, however powerful its effects, grew up in concrete conditions and at a certain time.

Some have tried to limit the term nationalism to the aspiration of races deprived of statehood. But this seems to me too restricted an approach. The intense awareness of a common destiny springing from some unfathomable common identity which, it is held, must express itself fully and leave its imprint on anything that members of the entity come into contact with—that is a more valid definition of nationalism. Statehood is treated as the natural vessel for that complete self-realisation, because political sovereignty upon a national territory allows for the untrammelled expression of all the manifestations of the national spirit, and because by severing the nationalities from each other the peculiarity of each nation comes into play, not least through rivalry and competition with other nations.

As can be seen, nationalism is full of ambivalence. It is on the one hand a conservative force, but on the other a revolutionary factor. Nations based on territorial statehood are likely to evolve a conservative variation, whereas nationalities fighting foreign dynasties or colonial powers to achieve independence would naturally tend to be revolutionary. Yet in either case the two elements are confused. Inspiration beckons from the past, while the wish to fulfil some destiny in the future or still more to restore past glories through a dynamic revolutionary effort draws upon a restless passion for adventure and change.

Nationalism is a similarly ambivalent force from the point of view of the struggle for freedom. A factor of release in one place and at one time, it easily becomes a vehicle of aggressive impulses on another occasion. A lever of self-expression and collective free partnership, it easily degenerates into a pretext for authoritarian rule parading as the need for national unity and the concentration of all forces for national defence. It is largely a case of belonging to the haves or have-nots.

As an intense conviction that the nation is the irreplaceable framework and vehicle of collective self-expression, nationalism is a modern phenomenon, dating back only to the end of the eighteenth century. One could without difficulty discern the budding of nationalism in earlier periods.[1] But these stirrings were either frustrated by tribalism, which militated against unified territorial statehood, or were swamped by a constant preoccupation with values derived from the concept of universal unity, especially religious unity, which prevented the idea of national unity and national uniqueness from obtaining supremacy. The Greeks, like the Jews, considered themselves a chosen people, and looked upon all other peoples as barbarians. The enslaved subjects of the kings of Egypt, Assyria, Babylon and other oriental empires lacked indeed the essential attributes of nationhood: not being free and equal partners in a common endeavour they had no notion of a common destiny and no pride in their past. Yet notwithstanding that passionate consciousness of cultural unity and a unique destiny across the centuries, no serious effort was ever made by the Greeks to unite all the city-states into a unitary national state. The bitter wars the Greeks fought with each other paved the way for the unity imposed upon them from above by the foreign conqueror, Philip of Macedon. While this compulsory unification was being carried out, the rhetor Isocrates had already come to the conclusion that the term "Greek" no longer denoted a scion of the Hellenic race but any man, whatever his origin and race, who had acquired Greek culture. Alexander of Macedon allowed himself to be guided by Isocrates rather than by the counsel of his teacher, Aristotle, who urged him to consider the conquered peoples of Asia as born to be slaves and barred for ever from sharing the freedom which was the unique inheritance and destiny of the Greeks.[2]

The history of Rome too is an example of the advance from tribal-national exclusiveness (in a sense more restricted than that of fragmented Greece) towards a supra-national

[1] Hans Kohn: *The Idea of Nationalism, A Study in its Origins and Background*, New York 1945, is very instructive about the pre-history of nationalism.
[2] Hans Kohn, *op. cit.*, pp. 52, 58.

empire in which all men, without distinction of race, enjoy equal rights as citizens, receive equal protection from a system of law considered to be the embodiment of universal justice, and not the fruit of any one people's national spirit, and are partners in one civilisation held to be *the* civilisation of mankind.

If the Roman Empire wished to serve as the fatherland of all civilized men, Christianity offered a spiritual motherland to all who shared its faith everywhere. For many generations tribal and national allegiances were completely over-shadowed by a pattern of ideas, feelings and behaviour which was woven by a variety of strands: Jewish religious experi-ence, Hellenistic philosophy (which thought that racial or national ancestry was irrelevant to the individual's strivings for the salvation of his soul), and Roman legal and adminis-trative forms. The autochthonic spiritual heritage of the medieval nations was also too poor, and their class divisions too accentuated for the emergence of a modern sense of national unity; and the *élite*, like the clergy or nobility, regarded themselves very much as part of the inter-national confratcrnity. To be sure, one could point to instances of xenophobia and contempt for strangers speaking alien tongues in the Middle Ages, at universities, in the Crusades, at Church councils, and of course on the battle-fields where they met as enemies, or even as allies; but hatred of foreigners is not nationalism.

For a while religion turned from a universal and anti-nationalist factor into an influence favouring the growth of the idea of national uniqueness. The German Reformation displayed clear characteristics of a nationalist rebellion against the sway of the universal Church represented chiefly by Italians, just as the earlier Hussite revolt in Bohemia was a consciously national uprising against the German and for the Czech language. All movements of lay piety fell back upon their respective vernaculars in place of Latin. England led the way in the establishment of a national church; Luther-anism and Calvinism everywhere assumed the character of national establishments. The English Puritans found inspiration in the Maccabees, those fighters of the Lord's battle against idolatry: Milton and Cromwell saw the English as a holy people, a nation of priests to whom God turns first when He wishes to reveal a new truth. The Spaniards, for their part, gloried in their mission as the disseminators of Christianity across the seas and as the spearhead of the Catholic Church in its struggle against the Reformation in Europe. On the other hand, in Germany religious division was a decisive factor in the victory of particularism, while in France national unity suffered a near eclipse in the wars of religion, when each side fought the other with the help of foreigners.

The missionary zeal of Catholic Spain, the nationalist ardour of the Puritans in England, and the belief of the age of Louis XIV that France was destined to guide the nations, all seem to suggest that it is often the sense of mission that generates national consciousness, rather than nationalism that gives rise to the idea of a mission. It is important to stress that the mission in every case involves service to a universal ideal rather than the assertion of an exclusive national ethos. The latter was if anything the child of mercantilist theory and practice, namely of the assumption that the natural relationship between states was that of warlike rivalry, while peace was only a temporary suspension of hostilities. An autarkic economic system, protective tariffs and colonial monopoly became powerful instruments of national unity, since they were also accompanied by strong centralisation within the State, which was again favoured by the growth of a national market in place of local small economic units. But this type of *étatisme* lacked the yeast of a collective emotion without which there can be no nationalism in the modern sense. The kind of Shintoism which was fostered by Louis XIV was no substitute for it, especially when the demi-god *"roi soleil"* was followed by an indolent *débauché* like Louis XV or a pathetic weakling like Louis XVI.

II

As a historic force nationalism has been a major factor uninterruptedly since the French Revolution. It has agitated people after people and tribe after tribe, from Ireland to

Indonesia, from Lithuania to Rhodesia, and its dynamism is as yet far from exhausted. The lesson of the last 150 years has been strikingly defined by the British historian, Dr. Gooch,[1] when he pointed out that once a group of human beings is possessed by the idea that it constitutes a nation and ought therefore to have its own independent State, there will be no peace in the world until that group achieves what it desires. It may fail time after time. It is certain to win in the end. The impetus of a national movement may for a while appear stifled and spent, but it is always there, lurking in the background, waiting for the hour of opportunity to strike. You believe it has lost all sting and all armour, you will soon be astonished by its cunning and resourcefulness, its amazing ability to change tactics, to profit from every set of circumstances, and you will be horrified more than once by its totally unscrupulous Machiavellism and terrorist violence.

Nationalism emerged more or less simultaneously with several other great forces which have been making their impact upon the world ever since: liberalism, democracy, parliamentarism, and socialism. Are they different expressions of the same urge—the impulse for liberty: the liberation of the individual, the class, the people? Do they complement each other, or is one built on the ruins of the other? Experience has shown that whenever they are in conflict, it is generally nationalism that has the upper hand. Its propelling force is greater than that of its rivals so that eventually it either makes auxiliaries of them or sweeps them out of existence.

Why did nationalism appear and triumph precisely at the time it did? We may point to three causes: the decline of religious sanction and the weakening of the religious framework; the doctrine of the rights of man and the democratic sovereignty of the people; economic and social processes at the onset of the Industrial Revolution. Despite the great influence of economic forces on the forms of national consciousness and the patterns of nationalist strategy, economic factors alone cannot be considered to have been the matrix of nationalism. Undoubtedly, social mobility

[1] G. P. Gooch: *Studies in Modern History*, London 1931.

which came in the wake of the Industrial Revolution and drove millions of peasants from the country, herding them into vast urban conglomerations, did much to destroy local, social and traditional nuclei and thereby inspired a longing for some new and wider unit of cohesion. In countries with a heterogeneous population and social-racial inequality as, for example, the Hapsburg Monarchy, national consciousness was stimulated by the intensification of linguistic differences occasioned by the movement of masses of Slavs from rural areas to cities where German, Polish or Hungarian was spoken. The new industrial economy compelled the masses to become literate. The new capitalist methods of production created the need for larger economic units, while the development of railways accentuated the absurdity of tariff walls and multiple political division in such an obvious geographical and cultural entity as Italy or a country with a continuous territory and a common cultural heritage like Germany.

Yet, the materialistic explanation does not hold good for a nationalist movement like, for example, the Polish, whose moving spirits were the gentry and whose source of inspiration was the historic past and memories of aristocratic freedom, and hardly an economic grievance against the foreign rulers or the rapid pace of social change. From the economic viewpoint it would certainly have been more profitable for the Greeks to continue to be the chief mercantile class in the Ottoman Empire, the Government of which refrained from interfering with the internal affairs of the Greek community. Nor did urbanisation or industrialisation in the nineteenth century significantly affect the religious and social (agrarian) problems of blood-stained Ireland. The Austrian and subsequently the Austro-Hungarian Empire formed a large economic entity, whose unity was on the whole beneficial to all, in spite of racial frictions, some of which may have had a certain social complexion.

There is something paradoxical about the fact that precisely at a time of such dynamic progress and such staggering changes as the nineteenth century, historic myths, memories of the past and visions of restored old glories should have become a force of such effectiveness as to cause honourable people to fabricate "ancient" documents and "discover" long forgotten national epics (the Czechs). Of the two "spiritual" causes for the emergence of nationalism—the decline of the power of religion, and the rise of the doctrine of human rights and the people's sovereignty—the former was the more important, since, in a sense, it involved the latter. The recognition of the right of the individual to be his own lawgiver, the challenge directed to him to express his personality spontaneously, instead of submitting to godgiven or time-hallowed prescriptions for the expiation of his sins, to work for the triumph of progress on earth instead of waiting for divine judgement—all these were extended to the collective personality of the nation. Moreover, man's own smallness and unworthiness could be sublimated into the greatness and power of the nation, as they were formerly into the glory of the Church.

Modern nationalism seeks to be a substitute for religion. It is, as well as other things, a form of striving for spiritual redemption, a straining for a solution of the contradiction between the urge to break away, and the need to belong; between the desire for self-expression, and the yearning for self-surrender; between the quest for freedom, and the longing for redemption; between the instinct of adventure, and the hope for tranquillity and security; between the impulse to display power and vitality, and the love of justice and the wish for certainty; between hubris, and the sense of sin. These massive experiences are the essence of the human condition, whatever the social order, or the degree of technical development.

The dialectic of uniqueness and universality runs through both prototypes of nationalist philosophy, which received their early outline at the end of the seventeenth century; the French or rational-political trend associated with Rousseau, and the German or irrational, historical, existential variety, propounded by Herder. The motive power of nationalism of the Rousseau kind was the constant, vibrating experience of partnership among equals deliberating jointly on that which was common to all of them, the *res publica*. It sprang from a direct condemnation of a past when the guardians of peoples, kings and princes, treated the lands they ruled as private property, to be transmitted by inheritance and passed from hand to hand like merchandise without any attempt to secure the consent of the inhabitants. This type of nationalism had no feeling for the peculiarity of a given national history, since it was primarily conscious of the fact that the concrete past of every European nation was tainted with monarchy and feudalism. (In his brochures on Corsica and Poland, however, Rousseau struck quite a different note, enjoining the Corsicans and Poles to cultivate most jealously their national customs and traditions and abhor all cosmopolitan debilitating fashions.) Rousseau harked back to a historic myth of a universal appeal, to that of the *polis*, the city State of Greece and Rome, where the citizen was free and equal and at the same time so integrated in his community and so devoted to it as to be always joyously ready to offer his life in its defence. So bound by all the fibres of his soul was the citizen to the life of the community that he never felt any need for a way of his own and individual privacy. Race had no place in this nationalist doctrine. The unifying factor was the general will of those participating in the vote of the hour. Individuals were theoretically free to join or to secede, to set up or dissolve the republic. When after 1870 German historians claimed that the population of Alsace and Lorraine were German by virtue of their German racial origin and language, Ernest Renan countered their arguments in a celebrated brochure in which he defined the nation as the *plébiscite de tous les jours*.[1] It was not the objective factors of race, past and language that were decisive, but the free and conscious will of the individuals in any given generation: concretely, the wish of the people of Alsace-Lorraine to be part of France.

This is indeed the standpoint that has been accepted in the West. No one would think of demanding of the descendants of the Huguenots who found refuge in England or Prussia that they should consider themselves French; nor would anyone accuse the millions of immigrants from many lands who became Americans of being renegades to the nations

[1] Ernest Renan: *Qu'est-ce qu'une Nation?*, Paris 1882, p. 27.

from which they sprang. Nationality in the West (west of Germany) means your passport. In Central and Eastern Europe, with their mixed populations, it means ultimately your race.

The prophet of Eastern-European nationalism, Herder,[1] drew his chief impressions from a border region, Latvia, where various races, tribes and cultures were intermingled and some had not yet emerged from the stage of folklore culture. Wandering blind beggars were still composing epics and chanting them to their audiences; the forests and lakes were still teeming with nymphs and demons. Herder was overwhelmed by the great diversity of language, character and customs which he observed around him. He was also profoundly impressed by the fact that in that primitive society the individual was a part of the whole and had hardly any separate identity of his own. It was this observation which led him to the discovery of collective individuality, the special and separate mode of being of each people and tribe. The rationalistic axiom of the oneness of reason and natural law appeared to be contradicted by the discovery that every people was unique, a compound of such elements as geographical setting, racial characteristics, early traumatic experiences, the marks of time and responses to unforeseeable occurrences, which reactions were by no means fortuitous, since they were conditioned by a certain general disposition, the unique national character. The personality of each people was to be found in its language. Each language was a marvel that occurred only once, and no two languages were the same. Language went to prove that it was not individuals with a conscious will who made a people, but that it was the people that fashioned the individuals. For language was to a most eminent degree a collective achievement. The individual received it, living his experiences and spinning his thoughts through the filter of the collective tongue. Here, then, seemed to be the proof of the superiority of the blind inexorable forces that worked spontaneously, driven by irrational compulsions and with no deliberate scheme. No human being ever sat down to create a language

[1] See below: "Herder and the German Mind".

and work out its grammar. A language was woven in the course of centuries, one might say inadvertently; and suddenly you discover that the mature product was a miracle of order, cohesion and logic. This led to the far-reaching conclusion that man did not subdue nature, and that his understanding and will were not forces directed against nature: on the contrary, man was a part and continuation of nature—man was a compound of blood and soil. Man's thoughts and emotions were a sort of refined manifestation of the life force at work in nature, the same in inert matter and living organism, as in pure ratiocination. Man was a function of race, which was a pristine datum. Race carried within it historic determinism. Implicit in it was the whole of historic development.

Humanitarian and lover of peace that he was, Herder was far from preaching the inevitability of racial strife. He was imbued with a prophetic faith in the sanctity of every people's individuality. Every instance of a people being dominated and assimilated by another stirred him to wrath—to the point of hating the Roman Empire for the imposition of uniform patterns of existence upon nations and tongues. "Kein Vorwurf ist drückender als der, fremden Nationen Unrecht getan zu haben." Protestant minister of religion that he was, Herder lamented the destruction of the original, national, that is to say pagan religions by Christianity. Herder professed boundless admiration for the Bible, the Hebrew language and its poetry. The phenomenon of Jewry seemed to him to be an example to all nations. Here was a people that had for centuries riveted its whole existence to a national principle and dedicated itself irrevocably to the preservation of national unity and uniqueness.

On the other hand, the upsurge of revolutionary French nationalism evoked in the ageing Herder a cry of admiration not unmingled with fear: who should dare to prescribe to a great nation—in his words "an ocean"—how it was to behave? Who should dare to criticize a great people seized by madness? Herder hardly knew what satanic forces he was unleashing. If every nation were to realise itself according to its own unique principle of existence, disregarding the

universal standards of behaviour, and if the test of national
greatness were originality and vitality, surely nations could
not be called before the throne of divine justice; indeed one
should stand in awe before the manifestations of elemental
and amoral forces displayed by the nations.

Solovyev has wonderfully described the dialectic of
nationalism: "the worshipping of one's own people as the
chosen vessel of universal truth; then the worshipping of
one's own people as an elemental force, independent of its
relationship to the universal truth; finally the worshipping
of the historical anomalies and the national particularism
which separates one's people from civilised mankind, i.e. the
worshipping of one's own people on the basis of a denial of
universal truth; these are the three stages of our nationalism,
successively represented by the Slavophiles, by Danilevsky,
and by Katkov and the modern obscurantists".[1]

There is something deeply ironic about the vast influence
which Herder, the German, exerted upon the movements of
national revival among the Slavonic peoples. Herder saw in
the latter examples of authentic unadulterated nationhood,
still unspoiled by foreign influences and not yet debilitated
by blind imitation of alien models. His doctrine gave impetus
to much intellectual activity in the Slav world, such as the
collection of folk-songs, the compilation of dictionaries and
grammars, the study of antiquities, literary creativeness in
general. Initially, there were no political tendencies in this
cultural activity. It was a matter of salvaging the remnants
of expiring cultures, for the upper and cultivated classes of
those peoples already spoke foreign languages and were part
of foreign cultures. There is a story about a party of Czech
and Slovak scholars, all of them poverty-stricken and harm-
lessly impractical, and one of them remarking: "If the
ceiling fell on our heads now, that would mean the end of the
Czech and Slovak nations." Little did he know that far from
being the last of the Mohicans, he and his fellows were really
pioneers. A similar story is told about the Hebrew poet
J. L. Gordon, who lamented all his life that he was the last

[1] Hans Kohn: *Pan-Slavism, its History and Ideology*, Notre Dame, Ind., 1953,
p. 177.

bard of the Hebrew language. One day he was visiting Berlin. It was unthinkable for a Hebrew poet buried in the deepest of the Lithuanian Russian wastes to be in Berlin and not to call upon Professor Leopold Zunz, the author of the monumental *Geschichte der synagogalen Poesie*, a mighty scholar who knew by heart every line of every medieval Hebrew versifier. Zunz had, of course, never heard of Gordon, and had no idea that Hebrew poetry was still being written in the second part of the nineteenth century. The young poet tried very hard to get Zunz interested in his poems, but the old sage was quite unable to grasp that Gordon was talking of himself and his own poetry. In the end Gordon pulled a volume out of his pocket and, trying to pin him down, said to Zunz, "Here is the volume I have published," to which the Professor raised his glasses above the raised eyebrows: *"in welchem Jahrhundert haben Sie denn eigentlich gelebt?"* ("in which century have you actually lived?")

As allies or as foes, each of these two doctrines of nationalism soon became charged with an explosive force. They came into contact with each other in a most fateful manner as early as the French Revolution and the Napoleonic period.

The French felt clearly that with the seizure of sovereignty from the King by the representatives of the people, a new French nation had been born—hence the name "National Assembly" which the representatives of the Third Estate adopted in 1789, emphatically rejecting other designations which were proposed in the course of the debate. Self-determination by the people was the distinct content of French nationalism: the defence of the Revolution's achievements against internal and external enemies became thus the supreme patriotic duty. *Révolution, République* and *Patrie* became interchangeable; a fiery revolutionary patriotism burst forth, comparable only to manifestations of patriotic ardour in ancient times and of religious fervour in the Wars of Religion. It found highly articulate expression in such famous slogans as "The fatherland in danger" and the *"levée en masse"*, and in the new symbolism and pageantry of the nation in revolution and war. One can hardly fail to note that the period of total warfare was opened at the battle of

Valmy, and more generally by the mobilisation of the entire population for battle and war work and the concentration of all available means; and by the releasing of a wave of mass emotion. These were phenomena pregnant with such dangers, that in comparison with them the wars carried on by royal mercenaries in the eighteenth century seem mere child's play.

The gospel of equality proclaimed by the Revolution elevated men to a new dignity. Implicit in it, however, was the demand for his absolute self-identification with the national creed. Hence the Revolution proceeded to denounce and even to destroy its various opponents as schismatics and renegades, worse still—accomplices of the foreign enemy, i.e. a fifth column, rightly to be condemned to be cut off from the body of the nation. Quite soon nationalism and liberalism were shown not to be natural allies.

The French Revolution brought tidings of a new dawn to all humanity. It set out to redeem the individual and to free the nations. The revolutionaries had learnt from Rousseau, as indeed also from Herder and the other thinkers of the Age of Enlightenment, that the natural relationship between peoples was one of peace and fraternity. National hatreds and wars of conquest were due solely to the ambitions of tyrannical and bloodthirsty kings who incited people against people. It was solemnly proclaimed by the revolutionaries that henceforth war would cease to be an instrument of foreign policy. They asserted at the same time that it was their duty to help enslaved peoples achieve the freedoms which the French had won for themselves and which were the natural right and destiny of every nation. Inasmuch as the nations were too backward or too sluggish to respond to the call of the Revolution, the French endeavour to spread liberty assumed the character of forceful imposition of freedom upon slaves who loved their masters and pusillanimously willed bondage. The line of demarcation between the enthronement of a universal ideal and imperialistic expansion was thus blurred. A wave of militant nationalism and a faith in a manifest destiny surged up in France; partly as the result of the pride of victors and their scorn for those who prefer to dwell in darkness, partly as the concomitant of inescapable politico-strategic necessities imposed by a war to the finish. It was on the crest of this wave that Napoleon was swept to supreme power.

The peoples of Europe rose up against France in the name of her own doctrine—the right of self-determination, and in the name of Herder's doctrine—the historic uniqueness of every nation. Revolutionary France and Napoleon sought to establish rational régimes in Europe, to abolish feudalism, to make the *Code Napoléon* sovereign. The peoples' reply was that kings and aristocrats and antiquated laws were part of their historic personality. Germany found inspiration in the memory of the victory of Arminius over Rome, which had sought to submerge peoples in the name of a universal message. It was no accident that Napoleon's downfall began in the most backward of European countries, Spain and Russia. The elemental patriotism of an illiterate peasantry, clinging to their faith and their superstitions, proved stronger than the rationalistic French Empire and the vision of a new European order.

III

All nationalist theories of the first half of the nineteenth century are distinguished by their Messianic character and their emphatic insistence on the idea of the oneness of universal history. Fichte, the German, Michelet, the Frenchman, Mazzini, the Italian, Mickiewicz, the Pole, Russian Pan-Slavism—each of them strenuously endeavoured to integrate the history of his nation into the texture of universal history envisaged as a drama leading to some inevitable dénouement of a salvationist character.

Unless the nation was integrated into an all-embracing and universal totality, it remained suspended in a vacuum. The multiplicity of nations served as proof of the relativity of the values presented by each single and unique nation. The idolisation of History, so characteristic of the nineteenth century, was the outcome of the breath-taking contradictions and antinomies revealed in the French Revolution and the Napoleonic period: the doctrine of the rights of man degenerated into the Reign of Terror; democracy made way

26

for military dictatorship; the hope of world peace and international fraternity was given the lie by the outbreak of wars that lasted for a quarter of a century. These developments undermined the eighteenth century's naïvely rationalist belief that it was possible to reduce all historic and social reality to a struggle between light and darkness, intelligence and obscurantism, and that the progress of light and reason was bound to put an end to evil once and for all. Profoundly disillusioned, great numbers of men were impelled back to religious faith and to religious solutions of the problem of evil. Others found an anchor in the vision of a Messianic fulfilment being gradually unfolded in history. The senseless evil and inexplicable injustice with which history was interlaced were conceived as the inevitable shadows that accompany great light, as the necessary price or the birth pangs from which there is no escape. Nationalism and socialism became the two chief expressions of this Messianic faith.

The nationalist-Messianic doctrines of the nineteenth century may be classified as again deriving from two archetypes, the French (or Latin) and the German. The former school, whose outstanding representatives were Michelet and Mazzini, looked forward to the day when all men would form one federation of mankind, albeit under the leadership of one nation destined for the task by History. The spokesmen of the German trend, like Fichte, Hegel, Treitschke and Bernhardi exalted in one way or another the concept of naturalistic determinism, which makes of each nation a law unto itself and perpetuates inequality and war between peoples and races.

Michelet[1] taught that history was nothing but the story of the struggle between history (spirit) and geography (matter). Geography and matter—that is climate, vegetation, terrain and race—lead to dispersal, diversity, particularism. The spirit begets cohesion and unity. It enthrones a single uniting idea—that of a single law, a single culture. It effects concentration in place of diffusion. Tribes and provinces unite into a single State. Irrational, local customs give way to the

---

[1] Jules Michelet: *Introduction à l'Histoire Universelle*, Paris 1934; *Histoire de la Révolution Française*, Paris 1847 (Introduction).

27

rule of a law that is the fruit of a single abstract idea. A chaotic mass of local autonomous authorities is replaced by a single administrative centre. A class structure based on accidents of birth—that is an irrational natural phenomenon —is replaced by the equality of free men actuated by reason. A universal culture absorbs lower local cultures. After the fall of Rome France had become the standard-bearer of this universal spirit.

For centuries French civilisation and social advance served as the model of progress to all peoples, and France, profoundly aware of its mission, exhibited missionary zeal in spreading enlightenment and assimilating other peoples. This process reached its climax in the French Revolution when French soldiers went forth to impart to other peoples the blessings of progress and social justice.

Michelet thus saw history as a process leading towards the victory of the idea of unity, and freedom as the opportunity for identification with it. Mazzini[1] tried to reconcile the concept of cosmic order and historic inevitability with man's longing for self-expression and self-realisation. History was to him a series of periods and processes that converge into a single drama which was set in motion by a compelling all-embracing purpose. But if all was preordained, what was the place of human freedom? Freedom did not mean isolationism and breaking away, but rather the activisation of every potentiality implicit within the human being. Such self-realisation was possible only when we swam with the tide (otherwise we simply wasted our energies) and when we were participants in a cohesive collective effort like an orchestra, a crew, a team. The greater the degree of integration into the collective effort, the fuller the self-expression of the individual, and self-expression under such circumstances brought with it a sense of happiness, in marked contrast to the malaise and sense of frustration felt when we were deprived of means of harmonious self-assertion.

The natural team within mankind's universal harmonious effort was the nation. The nation was, as it were, an orchestra

[1] Giuseppe Mazzini: *Scritti Editi ed Inediti* (Edizione Nazionale), Imola 1906-43, especially Vols. IV-VII (III-V).

composed of natural data, historic conditions and the unique genius of the nation.

For centuries the Church had impeded the self-expression of man and peoples. The dogma of original sin offered an excuse for the domination of the strong and the tyrannical. Hence the divine right of dynasties—sometimes foreign dynasties—to rule their countries and own them as if they were vast estates. By supporting idolatrous monarchy, giving its blessing to power politics, wars of conquest, and foreign domination, the Catholic Church had forfeited its title to exclusive apostolic succession, while the nations had in the meantime become ripe for the high calling of a people of priests, "a holy nation". History (Mazzini's term for the divine power) had decreed that Rome, which had twice brought about the unification of mankind by first uniting the nations in the Roman Empire and then in the Catholic Church, would now for the third time proclaim the unity of mankind, this time the unity of all free peoples intent upon fulfilling themselves through obedience to the law of History, each in its own divinely ordained manner.

Fichte delivered his famous addresses[1] when Germany had reached the nadir of its political history and the zenith of its spiritual greatness. Napoleon was in complete control of Germany, but at that very time German poetry, philosophy and music blossomed with a splendour that had been equalled before only in Athens at its height and in Renaissance Italy. This was the outgrowth of a period of aggressive German cosmopolitan *Weltbürgertum*, which deprecated patriotic sentiment as an indication of immaturity and condemned nationalism for its negation of the true German spirit, namely, that of unpolitical, spiritual universalism. *"Nur deutsch ist nicht deutsch sein."* There was no more radical a cosmopolitan than the young Fichte who demonstratively expressed his admiration for revolutionary France on every possible occasion and prayed for Germany's defeat in its war with France, since the enlightened man's true fatherland was not the expanse of soil on which his cradle had stood by chance, but the country which was at the moment in the

[1] J. G. Fichte: *Reden an die deutsche Nation*, Tübingen 1869.

vanguard of progress; the face of the enlightened man being turned to the sun. The ideological basis of Fichte's German nationalism may seem to foreshadow the teachings of the Zionist philosopher, Ahad-Haam, a century later. National sentiment meant the concentration of spirit and will, the coming together of all good qualities in place of distraction, listlessness, nihilistic egoism. The German people which in the eighteenth century had been divided into 350 principalities under the rule of petty tyrants, had lost its national consciousness and developed a passion for isolationist apolitical individualism. In the hour of test it found itself without the strength to resist the single-minded powerful egoism of the greatest and most powerful egoist of all—Napoleon. The will of the innumerable atoms—individuals—had to yield to the will of one man. Anarchistic selfishness thereby defeated itself. The German people had to be reborn through a mighty educational effort in institutions which can be likened to Jewish *Yeshivot*, and through unending spiritual concentration and sustained ascetic resolve. But the goal of this national revival and closing of ranks was not military force or political power, and the means were not unchecked imperialist competition with other nations: such ends and means characterise immature peoples, driven by uncontrollable forces and irrational impulses. The German people was a people of the spirit: its mission was to serve as the example of a nation that has succeeded in transcending matter, instincts, passions, and has realised the categorical imperative and attained pure spirituality. For the German nation was the most authentic of all European nations, the only one that spoke an original language, while all the others —English, French, Italian—spoke a Latin jargon. The Germans went straight to the source, the others used borrowed implements. There was about German experience that directness that came from primary impulses, while other peoples copied, imitated or interpreted and produced variations. The Germans were to be compared to eagles that soar high, the other nations to bees that gather honey. The Germans felt the pangs of the mystery of creation, the others merely played, gliding over the surface. Fichte represents thus a curious blend of rationalistic postulates and deterministic naturalism, which ominously becomes the source of a strained mysticism. Universality and uniqueness are strangely blended.

Hegel was not content with pure abstract spirituality. To him spirit had meaning only as it was embodied in institutions and concrete achievements. The spirit of a nation must be incarnate in a State, in a tissue of institutions, in a pattern of power. History was an arena where nations and peoples met and struggled. A nation emerged, accomplished its destiny, and then declined. Another nation then leapt to the centre of the stage to play its part. Spiritual vitality was demonstrated by the effectiveness of the nation's role. If a nation stumbled and fell, that was a sign of its exhaustion: it had spent itself and was no longer worthy of existing. It was thrown on to the rubbish heap of history. This might seem sheer worship of force. But there was a deep and awful mystery here: in its cunning the guiding spirit of History breathed selfish passion into a people and its heroes, but it did it in such a way that while propelled to seek satisfaction of their powerful selfish passions the elect were unwittingly made to further vast impersonal, objective causes.

Hegel and Treitschke taught that nationhood reached the highest point of self-realisation in the convulsion of war. For war called out a nation's energies to the fullest degree and served as the supreme test of capacity for self-sacrifice. War, then, was a noble manifestation of the intense reality of the nation-state. The wheels of history groaned and creaked as they moved on, and they crushed many a delicate and tender flower beneath. It was in this majestic and mysterious mixture of elemental cruelty and pure humanity, of passion and idealism, of the holy and the impure, that man's greatness revealed itself, rather than in the timid superficial optimism which promised itself peace and concord, and closed its eyes to the insoluble massive conflicts of history. Eternal peace was an ignoble dream. It would result in a stagnant pool.

Imperialist arrogance is implicit in the Latin doctrine of mission, in the claim to the right to force the will of one people upon others, in the belief that its will is the voice of pure reason, and its rule will realise the vision of international fraternity. The German attitude is characterised by naturalistic cynicism: a superior power will rule (and indeed destroy) in a Darwinian fashion, since it has greater power of self-adaptation and vitality than others. The end result of the two philosophies is, one might say, substantially the same. Yet in the—if one likes—hypocritical Latin need for reliance upon some universal standards there is something of the tribute that vice pays to virtue. The Latins seek to assimilate, the Germans are driven to destroy or enslave. To a large extent this difference reflects the fact that the Western nations represented great national states of unbroken continuity, whereas the Germans had been deprived for centuries of national statehood, and the impotent Holy Roman Empire was a poor consolation. When national humiliation drove home the lesson of their weakness in spite of their superb achievements in the domain of the spirit, the Germans developed a consuming longing for a national State, indeed a *Machtstaat*. It is no accident that whereas the British speak of "this country", and the French exalt *"la République"* or *"la patrie"*, the German word *Staat* has become imbued with the deepest emotions.

It was due to a peculiar concatenation of circumstances that in the first half of the nineteenth century nationalism became the ally of the revolutionary Left, while in the second half of the century it was made an instrument in the hands of the Right and became entirely identified with it. The feudal-clerical Right did, to be sure, quite early on adopt the doctrine of every nation's historic uniqueness as a shield against the universalist, rationalist ideas such as natural law, the freedoms of man, equality and popular sovereignty—that is against liberalism and democracy. The Napoleonic storm evoked, however, a panic-stricken determination to put an end to the entire legacy of the French Revolution, including nationalism. *"Nation, das klingt jakobinisch"*—the German reactionaries insisted. It suggested the stirring of the masses. And although 1813 was made possible by a genuine and spontaneous national uprising, the tendency in 1815 was to turn the clock back, and base the principle of historic continuity upon royal legitimacy, blocking the road to demagogues who would inflame the mob with slogans of political and national liberation, rule as usurping terrorist tyrants, and embark upon wars of propaganda and conquest in order to divert popular attention. The Holy Alliance was conceived as a sort of United Nations Organisation, rising above the egoistic and arbitrary interests of sovereign national States. (The representatives of the nations in the Alliance were their rulers, the elect of God, the fathers of their peoples.)

There was still another way in which the European reactionary movement attempted to prevent the upsurge of nationalism. It cultivated provincial freedoms, regional and estates representation, with the deliberate intent of thwarting all those centralising tendencies implicit in national con-stitutions and parliaments. For the latter would pave the way for the idea of one indivisible nation of equals, shaping its own destiny and displacing patriarchal monarchy and social systems based on estates and guilds.

Counter-revolutionary legitimists were hard put to reconcile the anti-revolutionary dogma of the supremacy of a unique historic tradition for each nation (which meant of course the *ancien régime* in each case) with the doctrine of universal Christianity and the Christian brotherhood of kings. They took refuge in the idea of a European con-fraternity based on common Christian values in spite of national and class differences. While the Enlightenment and its revolutionary disciples were condemning the old despots and aristocrats for deliberately fomenting strife among nations, the reactionaries were now accusing the French Revolution and its standard-bearer, Napoleon, of destroy-ing the ancient European community through totally un-principled aggression and conquest.

It is not surprising that the nationalist movements in the first half of the nineteenth century assumed the character of a universal, revolutionary camp pitted against international reaction, and that they allied themselves with democratic and socialist trends. Mazzini and the fighters for Polish independence believed themselves to be living in the midst of a struggle for life and death between two camps, the world of yesterday and the world of tomorrow. The liberation of peoples would be possible only as the result of spontaneous, national uprisings started at the signal given by the chosen nation, which to a prophet like Michelet and the French Left in general meant, of course, France. Her feelings of revenge against the Holy Alliance for the humiliation of 1815 could so easily be merged with the passion for the liberation of the oppressed peoples from the yoke of the divine right kings of Russia, Austria and Prussia. To Mazzini, who rejected, not surprisingly, the French claim for leadership, it was inconceivable that the struggle for emancipation should pollute itself by diplomatic, opportunistic co-operation with monarchist, reactionary forces at any stage and in any shape, or should become involved in the chicanery of secret diplomacy. The hour of the uprising would come as soon as one of the great reactionary powers went to war, for the European underground would seize that opportune moment to strike. The Polish exiles in the West—those Don Quixotes of the nineteenth-century European Revolution—prayed to the Lord for a war of nations. Paradoxically, these aristocrats, who in their own country had oppressed and exploited millions of peasants like beasts of burden, appeared on every barricade as the vanguard of the Revolution, soldiers of the crucified Jesus, avenging the first and chief national victim of the Holy Alliance—for it was their joint murder of Poland that had cemented the alliance of Russia, Austria and Prussia. It was indeed the liquidation of the ancient Kingdom of Poland which made Europe aware that there was something unnatural and criminal in depriving a nation of its independence. From there it was not far to the inference that every nation had a right to independent statehood. "The interest of all nations is identical, for freedom is indivisible. He who seeks freedom for Poland, without fighting at the same time for the freedom of all oppressed peoples, is an enemy of Poland," wrote Mickiewicz.

The expectation of a universal liberating revolution, the belief that the era of peoples was destined to enthrone the ideal of social justice—*"le verbe social"* in the words of

Michelet—as the inevitable dénouement of a historical dialectic—were common to both nationalist and socialist Messianism of the first half of the nineteenth century. Nationalist universalism was not invalidated by the insistence on national uniqueness and the rejection of the idea of a universal class war—for one vital reason, and that was the deep faith in the brotherhood of peoples set free.

The Revolution of 1848 was the turning-point in the history of nationalism. It struck a fatal blow to the naïve belief in the natural identity of interests between nations; it destroyed the illusion that there was an insoluble connection between nationalism and democracy. First and foremost, it exposed the profound differences between "historic" and "unhistoric" peoples in areas of mixed population. The Germans were shocked when the Czech historian, Palacky, refused to send a Czech delegation to the all-German Parliament at Frankfurt, and when he insisted that he was a Czech, not a German. Had not Bohemia and Moravia been integral parts of the German Empire for centuries? Had not the King of Bohemia been the first among the Electors of the Roman Emperor of the German nation? And the Hungarians who fought the Hapsburgs for their freedom were furiously angered by the desire of the Croats, Rumanians and Slovaks to be recognised as nations with a historic identity of their own. The Poles would not hear of the Ukrainians being a national unit. Were not the Provençals and the Scots organic parts of the French and British nation-states? Who had ever heard of a Rumanian State? And what was the place of Slovaks in the history of civilisation?

But the unhistorical peoples like Rumanians and the various Slavonic nationalities refused to be convinced. Faced with the uncompromising attitude of the "historic" nations, the Czechs and Croats began to reach the realistic conclusion that it was better for them to remain subjects of an inefficient, supra-national Hapsburg Empire than to be flooded by a German sea or subordinated to the aggressive and jealous nationalism of the Magyars. This was the sentiment behind Palacky's famous remark that had Austria not existed, it would have had to be invented. On the other hand, the

Hungarians were a "nation that dwelt alone", different in race, language and history from all the surrounding peoples. Living in constant fear of being submerged by the ocean of Slavs, Hungary had to be great or perish altogether.

The Slavic peasant peoples came to the aid of the Hapsburg Monarchy, making a decisive contribution to the suppression of the Hungarian revolt and to the stifling of the entire revolutionary, democratic movement of 1848 in Austria, and indirectly also Germany, since a victorious Austrian Monarchy was strong enough to prevent the unification of Germany—that is, a Germany from which Austria was excluded. A union of the multi-racial Hapsburg Empire with Germany was, of course, calculated to frustrate the very idea of a national German State. The tragic failure of German liberalism in 1848 derived in no small measure from its attitude to nationalism. On national-democratic grounds of self-determination, the Assembly in Frankfurt sought to unite all German-speaking populations wherever they were —in Alsace-Lorraine, Holland, Denmark, and elsewhere.

The Polish problem emerged as a test case. For a short period Germany was swept by a wave of pro-Polish enthusiasm. There was intense propaganda for a joint Polish-German alliance against Russia, aimed at setting up a Polish Kingdom and destroying the forces of the blackest reaction, which everyone saw poised to launch a counter-revolutionary crusade. Very soon, however, the Germans discovered that it was inconceivable that the Germans in the Posen area should become the subjects of an inferior race like the Poles. A nation in the process of freeing and uniting itself could not abandon any of its children to live in subjection to a foreign and inferior race. It would be criminal for it to deprive them of their motherland simply because of mawkish sentimentality towards a foreign people which, by losing its independence, proved itself unworthy of freedom. To try to bind nations by precepts of international morality was like trying to catch eagles in cobwebs. The campaign against Denmark was carried out by the troops of the Prussian king, since the all-German Parliament had no armed force at its disposal. The Liberals who were victorious over the monarchy in March 1848 failed, owing to their addiction to the philosophy of social contract and *laissez-faire*, to understand the necessity of wresting from the king control over the army and the administrative apparatus. They thus became the captives of *Junker* militarism. Their weakness was publicly exposed when the King of Prussia, who from the start was very reluctant to fight a brother-king on behalf of *"Demokraten"*, hastened to make peace with Denmark—at the behest of the Powers—without consulting the Parliament of Frankfurt. The violent reaction of the Frankfurt liberals, underlining their aggressive attitude towards other nationalities, undermined their moral standing. Furthermore, when patriotic popular riot broke out, the Assembly had to be saved by Prussian bayonets. Chauvinistic power policies abroad are bound to have a corroding effect on democratic liberalism at home.

IV

The *débâcle* of social-democracy in France during the June massacre; the failure of the French Republic to lift a finger on behalf of Poland; the suppression of Mazzini's Roman Republic by the Prince-President Louis Napoleon; the collapse of liberalism in Germany and Austria; the break-up of the nations' common front—all these combined to free the European Right from its long-standing nightmare of universal revolution. There was no longer need for an international, anti-revolutionary alliance of kings. Moreover, the rulers reached the conclusion that since nationalism was not, after all, an authentically democratic, revolutionary movement, they would do well to foster it and, indeed, take it under their protection. The slogans of national unity and greatness in face of foreign peril would act as safety valves against popular wrath and absorb the social resentment of the masses. This was very clearly understood by the old-fashioned Prussian *Junker*, Bismarck, who in 1848 still branded the idea of German unity as a swindle. Twenty years later he succeeded in intoxicating the liberal German bourgeoisie with nationalist ecstasy so effectively that they forgave the "blood and iron" unifier of Germany his violations of the Prussian Constitution of 1862, acts of anti-constitutional arbitrariness, for which—as Lassalle pointed out—an English king went to the scaffold two centuries earlier. Once 1848 had demonstrated that national, political union could not be achieved with the help of free institutions, unity imposed from above was clearly to be preferred to liberty. Great historic enterprises were not brought to fruition over a tea-table or through argument but rather by confronting one's opponent, whether he be determined or only wavering and uncertain of himself, with a *fait accompli* or a situation which leaves him with no choice but to submit. In the second half of the nineteenth century peoples achieved independence and unity as a result of propitious international constellations, and with the aid of the power politics of the Great Powers. Serbia, Rumania, Bulgaria were aided by Russian imperialism and the Pan-Slavism that went with it; while Cavour united Italy with the assistance of Napoleon III, and Germany's unity was forged in three wars of aggression and conquest.

The tragic disaster of the Polish 1863-4 uprising was the last flicker of romantic revolutionary nationalism. Official Europe looked on as the Poles were being butchered, while the revolutionary European confraternity turned a protest demonstration in favour of Poland into the occasion for setting up the First International. To crown the humiliation, the Czar of all the Russias took the momentous step of emancipating the Polish peasants in order to wean them away from the patriotic nobles, who had never found the strength and determination to liberate the peasants, and thereby turning them into recruits of a great *levée en masse* against foreign oppressors. The nobles were afraid of *jacquerie*, and this paralysed them in their struggle against the partitioning powers.

It could be said that nationalism emerged from the 1848 crucible, "purified" of all association with, and dependence on, values and loyalties extraneous to the principle of "my country right or wrong". A law unto itself, nationalism found powerful support for its urge for exclusive self-assertion in a suitable interpretation of the theories of Charles Darwin.

The Darwinian theory was strenuously applied towards the end of the century by the prophets of imperialism to the relationship between the white conquering and dynamic, empire-building nations and the colonial peoples. In the Anglo-Saxon countries voices were also heard which glorified Teutonic virility and constructive genius, while scorning the decadence and senile feebleness of such Latin peoples as the French, the Spaniards and the Italians. So level-headed and sane a writer as Bagehot could write that the lesson of history is a story of the conquest of the weaker by the stronger and the "the strongest tend to be the best". "The majority of the groups which win and conquer are better than the majority of those who fail and perish, and thus the world grew better and was improved." The Jew, Gumplowicz, the British sociologist, Karl Pearson, not to speak of publicists like Sidney Low or the poet of the "White Man's Burden", Kipling, and such decisive promoters of the "manifest destiny" ideologies as Theodore Roosevelt, Joseph Chamberlain, Lord Milner and Lord Rosebery, preached that out of the fiery crucible of race war there emerges the finer metal in the shape of the fitter—and after the struggle, more steeled—races. They prophesied that the fulfilment of the vision of swords turned into ploughshares would mark the end of progress. The march of the latter was strewn with the corpses of inferior races and the end of war would mean the lifting of all checks on the fertility of the lower races and thus the neutralisation of the law of natural selection, as well as the blunting of the goad which has been stirring higher peoples to strenuous activity and rapturous self-sacrifice in heroic warfare. Shrill Darwinism was moderated and humanised by reference to the civilising and constructive mission of the imperial nations: they were to act as trustees to their wards. "To us—to us, and not to others", wrote Kipling, "a certain definite duty has been assigned. To carry light and civilisation into the dark places of the world, to touch the mind of Asia and of Africa with the ethical ideas of Europe; to give to thronging millions, who would otherwise never know peace and security, these first conditions of human advance." Others spoke of the "unseen superintending Providence controlling the development of the Anglo-Saxon race", which simply commanded the British to resist "with the entire force which they can exert" any rival power trying to frustrate their mission.[1]

Imperialist doctrine developed a social slant which was intended to neutralise and which ran counter to any ideas of international proletarian solidarity. Imperial success was made to appear essential to the well-being of the masses. Monopolistic access to raw materials, and the expansion of the national market were calculated to raise the workers' standard of living, whereas loss or diminution of the imperial assets spelled unemployment and poverty. Hence imperialist rivalry became a matter of deepest concern to all classes. Furthermore, the dramatic character of the race of explorers, travellers and colonial conquerors to plant the national flag on as yet unappropriated territories, as exemplified in the Fashoda incident for instance, stirred public opinion in the respective countries to its depths. Imperialistic nationalism, stimulated by newspapers with large circulations, whipped nationalist feeling to a frenzy of passion. The theoreticians of Nordic racial superiority, who were to become the teachers of Hitler, were part of that atmosphere, and some of the techniques which emerged in the decades of classical imperialism, although very mild in comparison with what was in store some fifty years after, were nevertheless an ominous curtain-raiser.

Towards the late nineteenth and early twentieth century it was nationalism in one form or another that—like Bonapartism a generation earlier—enabled the Right to transform itself from the quietist, feudal-clerical interest of small groups living in terror of the masses and trembling at the idea of any change, into mass movements of a defiantly dynamic and often demoniacal character. In France the anguish of national humiliation of 1870-1 turned the *revanche* ideology into a mass passion, and in the case of Boulangism and the various patriotic Leagues lent a sharp anti-parliamentary edge to nationalist agitation. The par-

---

[1] William L. Langer: *The Diplomacy of Imperialism*, New York 1956, pp. 87-93.

liamentary game and the scandals of corruption attendant upon it were decried because they weakened and split the nation, when the war of revenge called for national concentration under a valiant authoritarian leader. The loss of political as well as spiritual leadership by France caused many of the intelligentsia to turn their gaze inwards. Instead of being proud of the traditionally universalist role of France, writers of the Right came out in condemnation of cosmopolitan individualistic rationalism for having weakened France's fibre and enfeebled the unerring instinct of nationalist egoism.

In Germany pride in the newly won unity of the German Empire, the restless drive of late-comers for a place under the sun, or rather a share in the division of the planet, coupled with the nightmare of encirclement by allegedly jealous and hostile neighbours, produced the nationalist fervour of the various pan-German and colonial Leagues, with their large following and highly-placed patrons. German historians, like Friedrich Meinecke, to whom many liberals looked for guidance, were busily interpreting German history as the progressive victory of the idea of *Nationalstaat* over that of *Weltbürgertum*. The very essence of German history was shown to be in the gradual emancipation of the nationalist conception that every State is a law unto itself, from the trammels of universalistic natural law and atomistic individualism. There was only one step from there to fully fledged racialism.

Nationalism and armed peace led to the erosion of the liberal heritage and to the polarisation of the political life of much of Europe into the extreme mass movements of the Right and the Left. A headlong collision between the nationalist Right, and internationalist, cosmopolitan, national-unity-breaking socialism was inevitable, since internationalism and class war were still more insupportable to the nationalist Right than the individualism or *laissez-faire* of liberalism and the checks and balances of parliamentary democracy. The lower middle class normally chose the Right. The vision of a chosen nation appealed to it, since it granted to the petit bourgeois (despised equally by the aristocracy and the class-conscious workers) membership of a chosen race, instead of a class doomed to extinction in the ranks of the proletariat. It was very flattering to be proclaimed equals with the highest aristocrats of their own stock, and to be able to look down with contempt and self-satisfaction upon the mob of alien breeds, especially the Jews. Furthermore, nationalism of this type developed a social slant. It blamed Jewish international finance and the emergent Jewish chain stores for the evils of capitalist exploitation and made the Jewish spirit responsible for the effects of capitalist liberalism and Marxist socialism as forces disruptive of national unity and spiritual cohesion.[1]

V

The various schools of socialism at first refused to see the nation as an end in itself or an absolute value. In this respect they continued the tradition of Adam Smith and classical liberal economics which accorded primacy to the facts of production and exchange, and considered politics a mere function of economics. The true unit was the world market. Wars between nations were the fruit of violent and stupid competition for monopolistic control of markets and colonies. Adam Smith adopted Swift's famous remark to the effect that "whoever could make two ears of corn or two blades of grass to grow upon a spot of ground where only one grew before, would deserve better of mankind and do more essential service to his country than the whole race of politicians put together".

If Liberal economics held that a mysterious hand would somehow balance supply and demand and ensure harmony between the various interests when the world had become one free market, socialism believed that such harmony was attainable only through the elimination of the universal conflict between the classes, and with the help of deliberate central planning.

Saint-Simon, and his disciples, denied the existence of an all-determining national uniqueness. The prophet of technocracy refused to recognise a French national spirit.

[1] Hannah Arendt: *The Origins of Totalitarianism*, New York 1951.

For him the basic fact was the division into producers (initially including bankers and industrialists) and exploiting parasites, who exacted tolls from the producers for the right of using the instruments of production which they themselves did not know how to use or did not wish to use; and he held the view that the producers of the various countries had more in common than industrialists and feudal idlers of the same ethnic group or State. Among the innumerable schemes which bred like rabbits in the fertile brain of Saint-Simon there are plans for a European Parliament, a union between England and France, and similar visions of a reconstructed and reunited European society.

Saint-Simon and his school dreamed of producers' communities directed by technicians who were at the same time priests and prophets, in a régime not of State coercion but of *"administration des choses"*. Vast industrial schemes on a European and indeed global scale for covering whole continents with railway networks and digging canals such as the Suez Canal, were to unite all Europeans in a common breathless effort which would make them forget their national antagonisms and peculiarities, and even their political ambitions. Fourier sought to organise small collectives, each of no more than 2,000 people, in which direct democracy would resolve the contradictions between communal organisation and the freedom and self-expression of the individual without dependence upon a higher, centralised government. Fourier's chief disciple Considerant was an all-out pacifist, who dreamt of a world federation of these collectives.

But the French socialists, like their British contemporaries, understood little of what nationalism really meant. As citizens of a powerful nation-state they could afford to deprecate nationalist passions, and at the same time, as enemies of every kind of oppression, protest against the subjugation of peoples by foreign invaders or alien dynasties, while taking it for granted that all nations would adopt French ideas. They hardly thought of the national urge as a primary and dominant impulse.

The relation of early nineteenth-century nationalist

doctrines to socialism was, as hinted earlier, ambivalent and subject to dialectical changes. The type of nationalism that could be called Left was marked by a distinct social radicalism. For some time Mazzini called himself a Socialist and was even a member of the First International. Its programme was purposely formulated by Marx in such a way as to make Mazzini's membership possible, although Marx had a hearty contempt for Mazzini's mystic, rhetorical idealism, and called him "Theopompous". The prophets of nationalism looked upon national revival not only as a movement for political liberation but as a token of an imminent and total rebirth. That regeneration was to inaugurate a new heaven and a new earth, purify all hearts and ensure social justice. The aristocrats and the rich were denied genuine patriotism because of their great attachment to their privileges and treasures, which any uprising against a foreign conqueror was bound to endanger. The poor on the other hand had nothing to lose. There was no clash between the interests of the poor and the good of the nation. The redeemed nation would know neither rich nor poor, neither privileged nor exploited: all would be brothers, equal children of one mother—their liberated land. It was alien rule that deliberately fomented class conflicts.[1]

It is difficult not to be impressed by Michelet's touching description of the experience of nationalism which would redeem modern man from his fearful loneliness and from the malaise of living in the impersonal, mechanised world of industrial society. Patriotic solidarity was destined in the eyes of Michelet to absorb and offer a focus to man's religious cravings. Brotherly love was also to make class distinctions irrelevant. This is the reason for Michelet's revulsion against the idea of class conflict, and for his absolute rejection of the vision of international proletarian unity ranged against the international bourgeoisie. A hunger for faith prevented Mazzini from accepting any of the tenets of Marxist materialism. Faith and the duty of self-sacrifice came first, not changes in the modes of production or the methods of

[1] G. Mazzini: *The Duties of Man, and Other Essays* (especially "Faith and Future"), London 1955.

44

distribution. Michelet had too deep a sense of the historic continuity of national history to yield to any abstract scheme of universal class warfare. In brief, the prophets of nationalism fought shy at first of the idea of a conflict between international socialism and nationalism. They liked to treat it as only a temporary misunderstanding.[1]

At the same time the spokesman of economic nationalism in Germany, List,[2] preached the priority of politics over economics. Free trade—he claimed—suited an industrialised State which, like England, had already completed the process of industrialisation, but was fatal to the more backward countries. In free competition these would be flooded by goods from the industrialised Powers, and would never succeed in developing an industry of their own. There was no escape from protective tariffs, and other forms of mercantilism. In the beginning was the nation—not the world market. Industrial development was a prerequisite of military power, and conversely a militarily weak nation was bound to submit to the economic dictates of a stronger country's economic policy. Competition between national units was a law of nature. In order to withstand competition from Britain, the Germans were called upon to unite into a powerful State. After 1848 Mazzini too came to the conclusion that to be free workers the Italian workers had first to become free Italians.

On the face of it, the treatment of nationalism by Marx and Engels is far from consistent.[3] On deeper scrutiny, however, it becomes clear that the shifts and inconsistencies in their attitude derive from their commitment to a sole and all-embracing goal. Everyone is familiar with the slogan of the Communist Manifesto about the proletariat that has no fatherland and the call to the workers of all nations to unite. Industrial production was expected to wipe out national distinctions, reducing nationalism into a superstition or a diversionary weapon of the bourgeoisie. Without a share in

[1] J. Michelet: *Le Peuple*, Paris 1846, pp. 121-3, 129, 223-8, 233.
[2] F. List: *The National System of Political Economy*, translated by S. S. Lloyd, London 1904.
[3] S. F. Bloom: *The World of Nations, A Study of the National Implications in the Work of Karl Marx*, New York 1941.

the national heritage, the workers had no fatherland. Everywhere without property and with no rights, subjugated to the machine, prey to bourgeois exploitation, the proletariat of all countries represented the same universal phenomenon, that of a universal class. That which was common to all its parts far outweighed that which distinguished any one part from the others. The class conflict was being carried on within the confines of existing states, and thus Socialist strategy must take account of the concrete setting; but the workers' struggle in any one State was essentially part of an international front. References to national genius and appeals to distinct national traditions were irrelevant to this universal phenomenon. Marx, it is true, summoned the working class to the Communist party to become strong enough to determine the fate of the respective nations in as decisive a manner as was given in the past to the aristocracy and bourgeoisie, the revolutionary national role of the French Third Estate being given special emphasis. Since the proletariat would put an end to all classes, it would indeed automatically become identical with the nation: from class to nation. The goal, however, was international proletarian unity. Nevertheless, Marx and Engels supported movements for national unity. They considered a large efficiently industrialised and centralised country more progressive than a small backward country, inasmuch as industrial development and a centralised State were prerequisites of the social revolution. As far as Germany was concerned, national unity and radical-social republicanism were in the minds of many Socialists quite inseparable. Only a *"République une et indivisible"* on the French Revolution model, based upon universal egalitarian citizenship and industrialisation on an all-German scale could do away with all the principalities, the social groups, and irrational traditions, which served as props to the princes and princelings.[1]

The teachers of socialism had scant sympathy with the sentimental aspirations of small tribes to preserve their way of life, revive their language and literature, retain their

[1] Karl Marx and Friedrich Engels: *Historisch-kritische Gesamtausgabe*, IIIer Teil, III, pp. 336, 341; Ier Teil, VII, pp. 136-7, 287-317, 68-70, 303, 346-55, 429, 480. Marx, Engels and Lenin: *O Internacjonalizmie Proletariackim*, Warsaw 1958.

customs—in a word, to remain in existence. They did believe, however, that there was an organic connection between national and social oppression. They hoped that in the wake of an uprising against a foreign exploiter and conqueror, the most radical elements in the population—that is, the working class led by its party—would succeed in seizing national leadership. For most of the time Marx and Engels staunchly agitated on behalf of a resurrected independent Poland, and in 1848 and for a while afterwards gave vehement support to the Hungarians, without paying too much heed to the feudal social structure of either Poland or Hungary.

The global strategy of the Revolution determined their attitude to any particular nationalist movement. If in 1848 Marx and Engels ardently advocated the establishment of a Greater Poland with the borders of 1772 and with Stettin as a Polish seaport, it was because the chief enemy of the Revolution and the standing threat to any revolutionary attempt anywhere was black interventionist Russia. For the same reason Marx had no words strong enough to condemn the Czech and other Slavic nationalist movements which in their perverse stupidity sabotaged the international revolution in 1848 and helped Austria and its saviour, Nicholas I, to strangle the Hungarian Revolution and restore the old régime in the whole of Austria. For refusing to yield Schleswig-Holstein to Germany, Denmark too was reviled as a nation that had always been a parasite on German culture and had never created anything worthy of note.

The global strategy of the world Revolution was conceived in a wider context than the actual circumstances. In the last analysis all history was a preparation for the Revolution. From this point of view a distinction must be made between nations that played a progressive role in history and nations that never made any real contribution to the advancement of the Revolution but tended consciously or unwittingly to impede it. There were nations like England and France, with developed industries and a high degree of centralised administration, and there were pastoral nations without political ability or any industrial potential, like the Balkan Slavs. In the course of time Engels' attitude to the Poles reached the opposite extreme. It became clear to him that this nation of aristocrats could not raise more than 30,000 soldiers for the Revolutionary war against Russia. He then remembered the subjugation of millions of peasants by the Polish nobility and the fact that Ukrainians and White Russians were the majority in Eastern Poland. It was not hard for Engels to reach the conclusion that in both the growing industrialisation of Russia and in the tradition of the communal village *mir*, there was promise of an incomparably greater contribution to the world Revolution than in the arrogance and ineffectiveness of the inept Poles.[1]

Once the absolute right of every ethnic group to national existence was denied, and recognition became conditioned on achievement, the civilising mission or role of a people was bound to emerge as a paramount criterion. However harsh his criticism of British rule in India, Marx could not but acknowledge the progressive nature of the British contribution towards lifting—no matter by what means—the Indian masses from primitive squalor and superstititon to rational modes of existence and social-economic organisation. Similarly Lassalle viewed German domination over under-developed Slav territories, and indeed the absorption of German Alsace and Lorraine by France, as an irreversible fact: there was nothing wrong in populations which had not yet evolved a distinct national personality, being assimilated by and into a full fledged nation. As to the aspiration for German national unity, Marx sometimes and Lassalle all the time struck Messianic accents which are strongly reminiscent of the visions spun by the Messianic nationalists. Both saw in the chasm between the soaring advance of German philosophy which had pierced all delusions and illusions and prepared man for the reign of pure reason and justice on the one hand, and the utter backwardness of parochial, pre-industrial, feudal-clerical Germany on the other, a guarantee that the imminent German Revolution would shoot ahead of all other revolutions and effect a clean and total sweep. The Germans, who had for so long groaned under yokes more numerous, heavier and more absurd than all other

[1] Gustav Mayer: *Friedrich Engels, eine Biographie*, The Hague 1934.

nations, would thus be enabled to emerge as the guide to all the perplexed. Deeply steeped in Fichtean teachings, Lassalle succeeded in blending nationalism and revolutionary universalism: since German history had been a *damnosa hereditas*, the liberation and unification of Germany would be tantamount to the enthronement of that universal reason and pure spirituality which has been the distinct mark and glorious achievement of the German *Volksgeist* as represented by the famous Pleiad of thinkers from Kant to Hegel.

Yet, there were fundamental differences between Marx and Lassalle.[1] To the latter the *Volksgeist* was something eternal and of absolute significance, while it had no place in the philosophy of Marx, who ultimately recognised only the universal capitalist class and the universal proletariat. Moreover, Lassalle's attitude to the State was old-Hegelian, while that of Marx far transcended the ideas of the common master. Lassalle's scheme reserved for the State a vital and eternal role as bearer of values, educator and instrument of social progress. Marxist philosophy treated the State as a passing phase, as a tool evolved by class difference and destined to be superseded by administrative councils, once exploitation of man by man was put an end to by a classless society. It was therefore possible for Marx to discriminate between nations and yet to remain a genuine universalist, because whatever the differences in status between nations on the way to Revolution, all these distinctions would become irrelevant in the world of tomorrow, where there would be neither Jew nor Greek nor Gentile. Not so Lassalle. If the *Volksgeist* was a primary datum and imperishable, and if it found its embodiment in the State, and consequently states were to remain distinct and separate entities forever, then clearly the criterion of superior merit asserted through struggle implied perpetuation of national rivalries and wars.

It was most galling that the unification of Germany was carried out by the Junkers of Prussia with the arch-Junker,

[1] Ferdinand Lassalle: *Gesammelte Schriften*, edited by Eduard Bernstein, Berlin 1919: Vol. I ("Der italienische Krieg"); Vol. VI ("Fichtes politisches Vermächtnis und die neueste Gegenwart; Die Philosophie Fichtes und die Bedeutung des deutschen Volksgeistes"). Hermann Oncken: *Lassalle*, Stuttgart and Berlin 1923, pp. 154-79, 360-73.

Bismarck, as the great national hero, as if to spite and confound all the calculations and tidy schemes of Socialist and radical theoreticians. There was nothing to do but to accept the *fait accompli*, with the consolation that in the long run Bismarck, by uniting and industrialising Germany, had been working for the Socialist Revolution; and that with the tragic collapse of the Paris Commune and the general weakening of isolated France, the torch of proletarian leadership had after 1870-1 passed to the rapidly growing Social-Democratic party of Germany.

With the unification of Italy and Germany, the emergence of the new Balkan states and the disappearance of the Polish question from the international arena after 1863, nationalism and socialism found themselves face to face as rivals and enemies, especially since nationalism was in most states espoused by the bourgeoisie. What should be the attitude of the Socialists to national defence (or aggrandisement) and war in countries like Germany, France and Italy? What stand should Socialists of oppressed nationalities, like the Poles, Czechs, Ukrainians, and others, take in relation to the national aspirations of their peoples in the Austro-Hungarian and Russian Empires? It was no longer true that the proletarians had no stake in their country. They had votes, deputies, social legislation, powerful organisations and institutions. Few French Socialists were indifferent to the Jacobin type of patriotism and impervious to the idea of *revanche*. The fear of being branded by the patriotic bourgeoisie as national traitors was very deep. The German Social-Democrats were condemned by the Kaiser himself as aliens and national traitors, which they certainly were not. Both parties were pledged to internationalism and anti-militarism on principle, as well as out of calculation that the army was the most potent weapon of the capitalist State after the age of barricades had gone. They had learned from experience that patriotic agitation in an hour of real or imaginary national emergency were powerful props of the existing régimes and could cause electoral disasters to Socialists preaching anti-militarism. The Socialists were against war, but not only were they at heart good patriots, they were bent upon winning the votes of the petty bourgeoisie, to which nationalism appealed so strongly. The idea of violent revolution having been abandoned, the winning of votes in elections became the paramount consideration outweighing purity of doctrine. The dilemma of the German Social-Democratic party was poignantly expressed in the juxta-position of two slogans: "to this régime not a single Pfennig" (hence the policy of voting against the army budget), and "we will not abandon our fatherland in its hour of need".

The Socialist conscience was somewhat eased for the French Socialists by the aggressiveness of the traditional German enemy and robber of French lands; but that was offset by the French alliance with despotic Czardom. The latter in turn was a help to the ailing conscience of the German Socialists. The abolition of standing armies and their replacement by national militias seemed to Jaurès a solution to both the danger of standing armies and the need for national defence.[1] The Social-Democratic spokesmen condemned the old Prussian military system and called for a democratisation of the army—ironically enough—as a measure designed to modernise the fighting forces and make them more effective. The more radical Socialists, like Hervé in France, or Liebknecht and Rosa Luxemburg in Germany,[2] tried their utmost to compel the International Socialist Congresses to adopt resolutions which would make the workers answer a declaration of war (or imminent prepara-tions for it) with a general strike, refusal to join the colours and sustained active sabotage—"*plutôt l'insurrection que la guerre*". It is pathetic to follow the agonies of irresolution of the Socialists in the fatal days of the summer of 1914, the frantic, yet half-hearted attempts to "do something", and the relief that events had decided for them! A striking and moving description of that state of mind is found in the confession of a former radical Socialist, Konrad Haenisch: "The conflict of two souls in one breast was probably for none of us. May the author try to overcome a certain inner embarrassment and speak for a moment of himself . . .?

[1] Jean Jaurès: *L'Armée Nouvelle*, Paris 1911.
[2] Rosa Luxemburg: *Die Krise der Sozialdemokratie*—"*Juniusbroschüre*", Berlin 1919.

Well then, I'd like to say: not for the whole world would I like to live through those days of inner struggle again! [On the one hand] this driving, burning desire to throw oneself into the powerful current of the general national tide, and on the other, the terrible spiritual fear of following the desire fully, of surrendering oneself to the mood which roared about one and which, if one looked deep into one's heart, had long since taken possession of the soul. This fear: will you not also betray yourself and your cause? Can you not feel as your heart feels? [This it was] until suddenly—I shall never forget the day and the hour—the terrible tension was resolved; until one dared to be what one was; until—despite all principles and wooden theories—one could, for the first time in almost a quarter century, join with a full heart, a clean conscience and without a sense of treason in the sweeping, stormy song 'Deutschland, Deutschland über Alles'."[1]

"The Socialists will do their patriotic duty and their Socialist duty at the same time. In face of aggression they will accomplish their duty to the full, to their country, the Republic, the Revolution" (in alliance with the Czar)—cried Eduard Vaillant, the old Communard leader, and ardent Socialist, who in the memorable sitting of the Chamber of Deputies in the afternoon of the 4th of August, 1914, demonstratively shook hands with Comte Albert de Mun, the veteran Rightist, and one of the butchers of the Commune, to whom he had in the past vowed never to speak.

"Oh, I can see still M. de Mun, the representative of the past, and M. Vaillant, the embodiment of the Revolution, the two old men who saw 1870, approaching each other, the French Revolution and the Crusades, the whole of immortal France symbolised in them"[2]—Viviani, the renegade Socialist Prime Minister recalled the scene eight years later.

The Socialist leaders, Guesde and Albert Thomas, joined the French War Cabinet and the militant anti-nationalist pacifist Hervé changed into a chauvinist overnight; and the Social-Democratic faction in the Reichstag voted for war

[1] Quoted in Carl E. Schorske: *German Social-Democracy, 1905-1917*, Cambridge, Mass. 1955.
[2] Maurice Dommanget: *Edouard Vaillant*, Paris 1956. Annie Kriegel and Jean Jacques Becker: *1914—La Guerre et le Mouvement Ouvrier Français*, Paris 1964.

credits, the party's declaration being read by Hugo Haase, of the anti-war wing, so as to emphasise the unity of the party in face of national peril, and also to save it from suspicion and reprisals by the military government. The Socialists were no longer the untouchables they had been, but partners in the national effort, fighting the unspeakable Czar, and his allies, the French Socialists. The latter on their part fought the lackeys of the Junkers and Prussian militarism. Both worked to further the cause of the Revolution.

VI

The establishment of the dual monarchy in 1867 after the *débâcle* of 1866 gave the Hungarians more than they had asked for in 1848. It granted them not only an autonomous status equal to that of Austria, but a preponderant influence on the foreign policies of the empire, which produced disastrous results, for, whereas Austria was quick to grant wide cultural autonomy to the various racial groups, Hungary championed repressive policies towards its own national minorities and aggressive actions against the Slavs outside Austria-Hungary. The victory of the Hungarians was bound to stimulate the national aspirations of the Czechs, Croats and others. The quick urbanisation and industrialisation of the Danubian Monarchy brought large peasant masses of Slav stock to towns, and there the language differences between them and German, Hungarian or Polish officials, foremen and workers acted as a strong irritant upon both. The oppressed felt still more injured, the dominant races gravely endangered. The workers of the various nationalities were exposed to the opposing claims of socialist solidarity and national brotherhood.

It is difficult to determine whether the attitude of Eastern European Socialist thinkers in the multi-racial empires to the problem of nationality was inspired by a nationalist instinct stronger than Socialist awareness, or whether it grew out of the conscious and rational conclusion that the nationalist question was a grave obstacle to the unity of revolutionary workers and the class struggle in its classic form, and that the obstacle must therefore be removed first.

In any event, the means quickly became an end in itself: first national freedom, and then socialism. At times one receives the impression that the socialism of the aspirants to national freedom was more the fruit of the spirit of the time than a basic propelling force. Rebellious nationalism found an ally in socialism, the revolutionary movement of the time.

A comparison between the nationalist doctrines of the Austro-Marxists, the attitude of Rosa Luxemburg, and the Bolshevik nationalities theory is most instructive.[1] Otto Bauer and Karl Renner tried to solve the national problem in Austria-Hungary on two levels: territorial autonomy for territorial minorities, and "personal autonomy" for members of minorities dispersed in the midst of a population of a different culture and language. They were to be granted the right to have their own schools and their own institutions. The extra-territorial communities suggested by these thinkers as the means to satisfy the cultural needs of extra-territorial minorities (for example, Czech labourers in German Austria) are very reminiscent of Jewish self-government and of the doctrine of Jewish autonomy held by the "Folksists" and, to a certain extent, by the "Bund". The Austrian Socialists rejected the idea of the dissolution of the Hapsburg Monarchy into independent political units. The united monarchy was not only a historical fact, but an economic whole, and the Czarist Russian giant lurked in ambush, ready to spring upon the small peoples of the empire, once they were free but unprotected. Furthermore, a policy of total political severance was calculated to be interpreted as a defeatist admission under the same government. National uniqueness would thus be granted a higher degree of reality than socialist universalism.

Austro-Marxist policy and its Jewish version were bitterly opposed by the Bolsheviks, particularly the theoreticians of the national question, Lenin and Stalin.[2] The latter insisted

---

[1] Otto Bauer: *Die Nationalitätsfrage und die Sozialdemokratie*, Vienna 1924.

[2] Lenin: *Selected Works*, 12 vols., Moscow-Leningrad: Vol. II ("The National Question in our Programme: Does the Jewish Proletariat Need an Independent Political Party?"); Vol. IV (Part IV—"The National Question in the Period 1908-1914"; Part V—"Problems of the International Revolutionary Movement in the Period 1908-1914"). J. Stalin: *Marxism and the National and Colonial Question*, London 1942.

on the right of subjugated peoples to break away from the great empires. There would seem to be a contradiction in this, but the inconsistency is only apparent. In the first place—Lenin argued—it was politically unwise for Socialists of dominant nations to deny, or even to question, the right of national self-determination to national minorities. It played into the hands of Czarism and its henchmen. Recognition of the right to national "personal" autonomy carried with it acknowledgment of the primacy and the permanence of national individuality as an objective end in itself. The "Bund's" demand to be recognised as the spokesman of all Jewish workers in the Russian Empire, whatever their native language (and not only Yiddish) was strenuously resisted by the Bolsheviks. If religion was ruled out, territorial concentration was not asked for, no solidarity with the Jewish bourgeoisie was permitted and race was irrelevant, what reason, they asked, was there for Russian- or Polish-speaking workers of Jewish ancestry, already assimilated to another culture, to be grouped together and isolated in a Jewish party? The "Bundists" were called Zionists who feared sea-sickness. And indeed there was a case here of *"le cœur a des raisons que la raison ne connait pas"*. The preservation of Jewish identity assumed the character of a paramount goal, an end in itself. Stalin quite rightly pointed out in 1913 that the Austro-Marxist doctrine implied reformism and gradualness, and eschewed revolutionary violent change, whereas the Bolshevik theory was wholly permeated by the vision of total dissolution and complete transformation.

The recognition of the right of all peoples to become independent states was consistent with the anticipation of an eventual universal federation of free, Socialist republics. For the right to national self-determination was not preached as an obligation, only as a right like divorce: it was permissible, but not obligatory. It was made explicitly conditional upon the circumstances and the requirements of revolutionary strategy. In so far as it was certain that the struggle of subject nations for their freedom weakened the power of Czarism, it was certainly to be encouraged. The Bolsheviks were to argue after the October Revolution that once the Revolution had won in Russia, any attempt on the part of one of the peoples to break away from the Socialist union of nations must be considered as nothing but counter-revolutionary bourgeois chauvinism. The only truly thorough-going internationalist on the eve of 1914 was Rosa Luxemburg, who bitterly fought Lenin's views on the nationalities problem. A Polish Jewess, she had "no room for the ghetto in her heart", since it was throbbing with compassion for the sufferings of all the poor and the persecuted the world over. And although she became, through a fictitious marriage, a German citizen and the most prominent leader of the radical wing of German Social-Democracy, she continued to regard herself as a representative of the Polish workers, though she staunchly fought the majority Polish Socialist party's nationalist programme of national independence. The gathering momentum of the revolutionary proletarian movement in Russia—she claimed—had removed the need for unconditional support for Polish independence as a means of weakening Czarist Russia. The Polish workers were now called upon not to break the unity of the all-Russian proletariat in its effort to achieve an imminent revolutionary break-through. Needless to say she won the eternal hatred of such patriotic Polish socialists as Pilsudski, Daszynski, Mendelson and Perl.

It is no exaggeration to state that it was the attitude to war and the national interest that constituted the line of demarcation in the final split in the European Labour movement. Those who felt themselves first and foremost part of their national community, like the majority Social-Democratic party in Germany in 1918-19, quite naturally put the legitimacy of the nationally elected Parliament above the dictatorship of the Workers' and Soldiers' Councils (in Russian nomenclature, Soviets). Having assumed responsibility for national survival and revival, they were driven to persecute as saboteurs those who fomented class hatred and civil war, and to seek allies to help them to suppress sedition in the Left—*Reichswehr* and *Freikorps*. Those who regarded themselves as fighters of the international proletarian confraternity saw their heaven-sent chance in the bankruptcy and disarray that befell their country as a result of defeat. The hour seemed to have struck for the great reckoning of the international proletariat with the universal class enemy who had plunged the world into the bloodiest of wars and finished by reaping chaos and misery. And after all, a beginning had been made. Someone had shown by 1917 that it could be done, and a tremendous myth had been created. To the believers in world Revolution the "social patriots" appeared as worse than the out-and-out reactionaries. The famous Manifesto issued by the First Congress of the Third International hardly mentions national Communist parties. It speaks only of the world Communist movement under the most highly centralised direction of the Moscow centre, and proclaims the national state an economic and strategic impossibility. The Comintern was the Socialist World Republic on the way. The not less famous nineteen points of 1920 go so far as to order national parties whom to accept into and whom to expel from their ranks, naming renegades who are to be damned forever. The platform of the Second International as revised after World War I foreshadows a loose federation of national parties. There is a world of difference—all the difference in the world – between an international confraternity with legions in various countries receiving their marching orders from a G.H.Q. situated in the seat of a Great Power, and a loose congeries of national parties which meet occasionally at international congresses, extend fraternal greetings to each other, rejoice in each others' victories or lament each others' failures, but fundamentally consider themselves separate and independent entities with interests and traditions of their own.

The Bolsheviks in the early days not only firmly believed that they were merely the spearhead of the European or even World Revolution, and that the Revolution was about to spread at once at least to all Central Europe. They were profoundly convinced that the October Revolution could not survive unless a revolution in the Western countries brought down the capitalist governments. For surely the latter would never rest till they had destroyed the Communist hydra in Russia. It worked out differently. The limitation of (victorious) socialism to one country led on the one hand to a growing emphasis upon Russian antecedents and Russian uniqueness, on the other—as a result of the isolation and the state of siege in which the U.S.S.R. felt itself to be—to a situation where, in the words of Léon Blum, the Communists of the various countries became "the nationalists of a foreign Power".

At the end of World War II the Soviet Union surrounded itself with a belt of "safe" states, the governments of which owed their existence to the victorious Red Army. Stalin was the supreme mentor in the science of socialism at work, exacting blind obedience from the faithful throughout the world. His enormous prestige, the frightful tensions created by the cold war, and the shadow of the American monopoly of the atom bomb combined to maintain the state of permanent mobilisation in preparation for some imminent universal break-through, and with it the conditions of iron discipline, leaving no room for nationalist deviation or isolationism.

The passing away of Stalin and the process of de-Stalinisation which set in soon after, opened all dams. If the supreme teacher could have been guilty of so much error and arbitrariness, surely the whole doctrine of the absolute necessity of a unified global command needed a thorough revision. And so emerged the theory of different roads to socialism, and the formerly unspeakable heresy of Tito found followers in Poland, Hungary, and elsewhere, especially of course in countries which had for centuries regarded Russia as their hereditary foe and whose economics at the end of the war were "adjusted" to the requirements of socialist reconstruction in the Soviet Union. The process gathered momentum with Russia coming into the possession of nuclear weapons. A global ideological war became an impossibility. The nations in both camps no longer felt the compulsion to range themselves around the banner of the Big Brother. They were free to indulge in nationalist deviation. And so we have lived to see Communist parties openly criticizing, and even disavowing the Kremlin.

VII

Engels and his faithful disciples had already perceived the danger of "federalism" at the end of the nineteenth century. Growing gains and an unrevolutionary atmosphere were beginning to create powerful vested interests of strongly entrenched national parties in each country, and, as a result of the victory of parliamentary methods, the chief preoccupation of Socialist leaders became, as said earlier, vote catching instead of doctrinal purity. The theory of imperialism as the final stage of capitalism appeared then as a sheet-anchor. At the end of his life Engels proclaimed that the relationship between capitalism and the proletariat, as he had described it in his youth, had become transformed into the relationship between imperialism and the colonial peoples. At home Western capitalism had become more gentlemanly, since a more humane attitude to the working classes had become possible owing to the huge profits reaped by the rapacious exploitation of the peoples of Africa and Asia. In the colonies capitalism was unabashed and unrestrained. While pretending to expand the national patrimony and to plant the flag of the fatherland in the four corners of the earth, the capitalists were treacherously dragging their countries into selfish ventures, and forcing the hands of governments to defend their investments and secure those huge profits, which they could no longer expect in the metropolitan countries. The armies designed to protect colonial conquests had become the praetorian guard of the propertied classes against the proletariat at home. As Marx had prophesied half a century earlier, the class struggle had now reached universal dimensions and the hour was therefore ripe for a world explosion. The colonial peoples had become the most exploited part of the world proletariat. The revolutionary movement was therefore called upon to feed the wrath and aspirations of the colonial peoples for national freedom, which in the circumstances would be tantamount to social emancipation. The conflagration that would start in China or Africa would spread and revive the dying embers of the European Revolution. The route to Paris led via Peking. The downfall of capitalism and the triumph of socialism would begin in Asia and Africa.

Events have proved much less tidy than the Marxist forecast. It will long be debated to what extent the movements of national liberation in Asia and Africa were the result of social revolt which in turn awakened a dormant national spirit and a desire for national self-assertion in the form of independent statehood, and to what extent they were due to the influence of European nationalist teachings and models. If the latter be the case, then the relatively short age of imperialism may in the perspective of history appear less as a period of barbarous oppression than as apprenticeship for national independence, however remote this eventual outcome was from the minds of the high priests of imperialism. Whether national liberation has been achieved at the end of a bloody war as in Algeria, a long drawn-out political struggle as in India, reasonable compromises as in the case of most other colonial countries, whether it was granted under duress or accorded by enlightened statesmanship, the former colonies find themselves in the same situation as the trade unions: persecuted in the past, and decried as hotbeds of trouble and riot, they are now assiduously courted and flattered by all.

Little doubt is left as to whether communism or nationalism is winning in the two vast continents. To the extent that there has been an alliance between the anti-colonial movements and communism it was a marriage of convenience because of the common foe, like the alliance between nationalism and the revolutionary or liberal movements in the first half of the nineteenth century. In both cases the emancipatory nationalist parties sought help from the most oppositionist tendencies of the age. Leaders of backward countries, without a democratic tradition, may also be tempted to see in Communist dictatorship and centralism the best and shortest method of accomplishing that industrial revolution which is the *sine qua non* for both raising the standard of living (in due course) and building up military might. The Socialist myth may serve nationalism as a welcome antidote to tribalism, and vast schemes of economic-social development such as dams or power stations are calculated to become levers of national cohesion and expressions of nationalist pride. One may already venture a forecast that the new states in Asia and Africa, far from being free from the virus of militant arrogant nationalism, are destined to go through the same phase of nationalist self-assertion and power politics as the European nations. There is no longer, if ever there was, an Afro-Asian fraternity of nations. But this does not exclude the unification of the former colonial peoples by force under the aegis of a paramount power, e.g. China, where Communist proselytism fed by American intransigence may easily coalesce with the age-long almost instinctive conviction that China is the sole civilisation, and all foreigners barbarians, and with the rankling resentment at having been kicked around for so long by lesser breeds from across the seas. If China were to see its destiny in acting as an avenger of all the victims of imperialism, and as it were, wrest the palm from the hands of the U.S.S.R., which has grown too contented and too lax, the problem of universality and uniqueness might enter upon a new metamorphosis of incalculable consequences in a world divided into the have white races and the have-not coloured races.

The Marxist vision of a war of Armageddon on a global scale may be realised, but it would hardly be a world struggle between universal capitalism and the indivisible proletariat of all countries, but rather a war of races, however strong the social aspect of the struggle might be—and the more dangerous for that. Who would have believed only a short while ago that an ideological schism would immediately be followed by territorial claims of Red China upon the country of the October Revolution—treated as the heir of imperialism? This brings us back to that part of the world from where it all started—Europe.

The post-1918 settlements were intended to satisfy the national aspirations of all European peoples and thereby to put an end to aggressive nationalism. There could hardly be a more striking case of sowing dragons' teeth. It was objectively impossible to sort out the nationalities map of Europe so as to enable each nation to have its own State coterminous with the racial composition of the territory. Political, economic and strategic reasons of the victors gave rise to policies of aggrandising some and correspondingly enfeebling other states. The Versailles peacemakers left behind them a cauldron of nationalisr fury. The young, often too inflated, states fostered nationalist cults and oppressive attitudes towards national minorities, which very often led to gravely reactionary social policies, such as the abandonment of agrarian reforms, since the peasantry of the given area was of foreign stock, whereas the gentry belonged to the majority race. On the other hand, the opportunity was given to Hitler, the Hungarian revisionists and Italian Fascism to whip up frantic nationalist passions at home, and by bringing up the slogan of national self-determination to undermine the resistance of many conscience-stricken liberals in the West. In that atmosphere of nationalist tensions and war scares the tender plant of liberal parliamentary democracy and international economic co-operation could take no root in Central and South-eastern Europe.

Prima facie, ultra-nationalistic Nazism and Fascism were the extreme expression of old type nationalism. Everything was to be subordinated to the central impulse. In the name of the categorical imperative of the national interest everything deviationist and sectional, such as class war and party divisions, was to be extirpated, and only the pure expression of the national genius was to be tolerated in the life of the spirit. Yet such is the dialectic of doctrines stretched to their extreme conclusions that the very opposite is achieved from what is desired. At first class reconciliation is urged on the grounds that our own nation as a whole and all its classes and components are threatened by foreign states or alien interests, and that class hatred and party struggle are artificially fomented by plotters from outside in order to sow confusion. An exclusive *élite* party of the pure arrogates to itself the role of spearhead in the struggle for national revival or grandeur. The pioneer soon turns overlord, the "beneficiaries" become vassals and victims.

In fact the Nordic "philosophers" like Rosenberg and Himmler thought in terms of a medieval nobility destined to rule. In their weird dreams of an artificially reared international Nordic *élite* of the racially fittest and purest, they really went far beyond the classical ideal of a German *Nationalstaat*.

Some uphold the hope that World War II has seen the eclipse of nationalist passion, and still more—its wild excrescence, racialism, in Europe. They point at the Common Market which is bound to lead to a Western European community, and above all o the genuine *rapprochement* between France and Germany. It is too early to say whether the Common Market is the expression of a spontaneous urge for wider unity in place of outworn national rivalries or a defence reflex of a group of proud ancient peoples, with a glorious past, in face of the emergence of vast powerful blocs, and a means of reasserting Europe's greatness on the morrow of its withdrawal from other parts of the globe. In which case a new type of nationalism is in the making.

General de Gaulle dreams of being another Charlemagne and of uniting Europe, or at least Western Europe, into a Holy Roman Empire. One cannot help reflecting that for well over 1,000 years the French and the Germans have been fighting each other for the title of being the true heirs to the great emperor—in history books as well as on battle-fields.

2

Uniqueness and Universality of
Jewish History

A mid-century revaluation

THE EPOCH-MAKING changes that have taken place in recent Jewish history have caused more than one Jewish historian to re-examine the basic assumptions of earlier writers. Not only does the extirpation of Jewish civilisation in Eastern and Central Europe mark a decisive shift in the distribution of the Jewish population of the world, it appears to negate Simon Dubnow's view that the essence of Jewish history lies in the urge for full Jewish self-expression through autonomous institutions.

The Western Jewries that lived most of their lives within non-Jewish patterns seemed to the Dubnovist school a pale reflection and dry limb of the real Jewish existence of Eastern Europe. Today these Jewries may have come to represent a primary datum, a culminating point, rather than a peripheral and secondary manifestation of Jewish life. And in view of the decline of Jewish cohesion and unity that has taken place in both the democratic West and the Communist East, under circumstances of real or merely formal civil equality, it would seem doubtful whether the historian will be entitled to apply the same terms of reference to the diaspora history of the future as he did to Jewish history in the still not too distant past—terms like "the community of a special fate", "identifiable modes of Jewish self-expression", "a corporate Jewish contribution or ingredient".

The emergence of Israel has vindicated the Messianic-nationalist vision and laid for the first time in 2,000 years the foundations for a wholly integrated Jewish life. The fact, however, that the majority of Jews, though powerfully affected by the resurrection of Jewish statehood, show every intention of continuing to live outside Israel is bound to bring about a revision of that strenuously dynamic conception, wholly dominated by the category of "becoming", which treated all of diaspora history as one long preparation for the Zionist consummation, and hardly acknowledged the force of the inertia of mere "being" here and now.

The main question the future historian must resolve for himself is this: Is it right to consider the problem of Jewish nationhood in Israel, and the problem of the Jews living in the diaspora among other nations, as one subject?

There are people in the Western dispersion who, afraid of being accused of a dual loyalty, claim that the State of Israel is to them just another little state, the only difference being that most of its inhabitants profess, at least nominally, the Jewish religion. There are some cocksure Israelis who proclaim that the sovereign State of Israel, a country like any other, stands in no special relation to Jews outside its borders. But even if there were no religious or cultural ties between Israel and the diaspora, this attitude would still be completely at variance with reality. It is just not true that Israel and the diaspora are becoming so dissociated in the consciousness of Jews and Gentiles as to do away with the deeply ingrained habit of associating all Jews everywhere in a common responsibility. Should one of those calamities with which Jewish history is punctuated overtake the Western diaspora, above all American Jewry, the State of Israel would be shaken to its foundations. On the other hand, should the Jewish State be engulfed by a catastrophe, the legal status and economic position of Jews elsewhere might not be affected at once, but the blow to their self-confidence, the loss of the vicarious prestige which Israel had bestowed upon them in the eyes of the world, and the general dis-enchantment would be too great to be sustained for long.

Nor can Israel claim that as "an independent state like any other" she has placed herself beyond the reach of those special laws to which the unique Jewish destiny has been subject for so long. The ultimatum addressed by the Soviet leader at the time of the Suez crisis to Ben Gurion was an eloquent comment on the fact that the handicaps besetting Israel have a dimension additional to and different from the limitations under which other small states live in our days. In a note to Libya, Sudan, or Haiti, the Soviet leader would never have hinted so darkly yet so directly about their very right to exist as states. The Jewish right to Israel is not taken for granted. One is reminded of the famous words of General Bonaparte about monarchical Europe's non-recognition of the French Republic—"France is like the sun, she needs no one's recognition, she is there in blinding splendour". But Israel needs recognition as no other political entity in a world where the existence of a state is, under international law, proven solely by the fact of its recognition by other states.

Thus, at a deeper level, Israel is still involved in the problematic ambiguity attaching to Jewish existence everywhere and at all times. Abnormality, insecurity, ambiguity, absence of full and unequivocal matter-of-factness and recognition continue to haunt her existence; the refusal of the Arab states to recognise Israel seems a parallel to the European-Christian treatment of Jews as late-comers and aliens. The bitter disillusionment of Israelis with the recent policies of the United States was not a little offset by President Eisenhower's emphatic statement that since 1948 he had never contemplated that Israeli-Arab problems could be dealt with without accepting Israel as a historic fact and as a country whose problems were like those of any other.

Jews of the liberal persuasion were less shaken in their convictions by the Jewish catastrophe under Hitler, in spite of its enormity, than Jews sympathetic to communism have been by Soviet anti-semitism. After all, the Dreyfus affair and the persistence of discrimination amid conditions of legal equality had accustomed Jews to the limitations of their situation even under the most liberal of régimes. It was Communist Messianism that inherited in our time the fervent hopes of the early Jewish liberals that a general cure for the evils of mankind would do away with every vestige of the peculiar Jewish predicament.

Many a non-Communist was prepared to overlook the fact that totalitarian Messianism, insofar as it asserted an exclusive doctrine embracing every aspect of human life and social existence, was an uncongenial setting for Jews, who are nothing if not non-conformists. Even those to whom the unity of the Jewish people was an article of faith were willing to accept the separation of the Soviet Jews from the rest of world Jewry on the grounds that, as a church militant surrounded by the city of the devil, the U.S.S.R. could not permit any part of her population to maintain contact with an international community that had a kind of foreign policy of its own. These "tolerant" Jews knew, of course, that Jewish life shrivels when it is deprived of free channels of communication for ideas, aid, sympathy, and a general sense of kinship, and that it can prosper only in an open society. But the atrophy of Jewish life did not seem to them too high a price to pay for truly equal status.

Events have given the lie to the claim that a Communist régime would do away with the disposition of the non-Jewish world to bracket all Jews in a joint responsibility and guilt by association. The Moscow "doctors' plot", the execution of Jewish writers and artists, and other manifestations of official and social anti-semitism in the Soviet world are, like all other evils, now blamed by the Communists on Stalin or Beria. But this is to evade the fundamental issue.

It used to be confidently said that the triumph of socialism would not only eliminate all the conditions making for social and racial conflict, but that it would inaugurate the reign of fully scientific and deterministic laws of social development under which human arbitrariness and individual or group perversity would be ruled out. If such terrific effectiveness is now ascribed to the personal arbitrariness of one man, surely this is to deny the fool-proof scientific determinism of the Communist system and to open the door to all those psychological and other influences which remain conditioned, but are rarely negated, by social and economic factors. And it is indeed these influences which constitute the core of what has been called the Jewish problem.

Those historians whom faith in dialectical materialism or

left-wing sympathies had led to ascribe all anomalies of Jewish existence to its peculiar socio-economic structure, and therefore to hope that these would be conjured away in a classless society, may well now come to see that the top-heavy socio-economic structure of the Jews was ultimately itself an outcome of their initially exceptional character. The Jews were different and were regarded as such, and therefore went—and were driven—into special occupations. In a sense, the experience of the Communist countries goes to confirm a "law" of Jewish history: a new society, régime, or economic system welcomes Jews as pioneers, but thrusts them out unceremoniously as soon as the "natives" are ready to take over the Jewish functions. This was the case in the early days of urban colonisation in Europe, in the first stages of *laissez-faire* capitalism, and the same development appears to have taken place in Russia since the October Revolution.

Under the most dissimilar historical circumstances, the Jewish fate remains very much the same. At the end of World War II the Soviet troops were bound to appear as saviours to Jewish survivors emerging from the forests, bunkers, and caves of Eastern Europe. The Jews had every reason to co-operate with the new régimes, and could offer them cadres of trained personnel and even leadership. But then came the Stalinist drive against "cosmopolitanism", against Jewish intellectuals and Jews in general; and the resurgence of the Poles, the Hungarians, and others under Soviet Russian domination hit Jews from the other side insofar as they were regarded as collaborators of Stalinism. In brief, fate seems always to prove more potent than any human resolve to change things by imposing new, man-willed and man-guided laws.

The historian need not be ashamed to use so heavily charged a word as "fate". The fate of a nation, like that of a person, may be the working out of the traumas of early childhood, the outcome of some basic and decisive experience. The Jewish psyche received a traumatic twist when the Jewish belief in chosenness sustained the terrible shock of national disaster and exile. This made most Jews impervious to the assimilating influences of hellenism and Rome. And they could hardly be absorbed by the amorphous barbarians in whose midst they found themselves in the early Middle Ages. Not only were they the bearers of a higher and more ancient civilisation, by then they were burdened with the charge that they had killed Jesus. Their status as never wholly assimilable strangers in the midst of the European nations was thus determined for centuries to come, and there is little evidence as yet that in the New World, where all are strangers and newcomers, the Jew has ceased to be regarded as more alien and more different than all other newcomers.

What will be the subject matter of the Jewish historian of the diaspora of the future, when Jewish life will have lost its old cohesion and the individual Jew will be living most of his life within non-Jewish patterns; when religious observance will often have been reduced to a minimum or ceased altogether, and Jewish learning will have assumed the character of a philological and antiquarian interest; and when communal activities will not amount to more than care for synagogue and cemetery, charity balls, and youth clubs?

How shall we pick out the slender threads which weave themselves into a Jewish collective pattern distinct from the so much more salient non-Jewish patterns? How shall we detect, in the behaviour and actions of seemingly unconnected individuals, features significantly Jewish? To what extent shall we be justified in pronouncing these a Jewish contribution or ingredient?

We are here confronted with that supreme difficulty which Chaim Weizmann used to call Jewish "ghostliness". The world is scarcely large enough to contain the Jews and they are said to possess all the wealth of the earth, and yet when you strain every nerve to fix them in a definition they elude you like a mirage. It seems impossible to lay a finger on anything tangible and measurable in the Jew's Jewishness; yet an ailing, all-devouring self-consciousness comes like a film between him and the world. Not taken into account when things are normal and prosperous, he is seen as ubiquitous, all-powerful, sinister when there is blame to be apportioned. I believe the links holding Jews together—in the words of

Edmund Burke—to be as invisible as air and as strong as the heaviest chains, and the Jewish ingredient to be as imperceptible to the senses yet as effective in results as vital energy itself. Such things, however, are too subtle for the historian's customary crude techniques and his far from subtle instruments.

Jewish impulses and reactions, attitudes and sensitiveness, Jewish modes of feeling and patterns of behaviour call for the intuition of the artist, and indeed can only be intimated by symbols, conjured up by poetic incantation, and communicated by the art of the novelist. In brief, the Jew is part of a collective destiny, even when he does not know it or is unwilling to share in it. To consider as Jews only persons who explicitly affirm their Judaism by positive participation in Jewish activities would be tantamount to approving the statement made in the 1920's by a German Jewish Social-Democratic leader: he maintained that he was no Jew because he had sent a letter of resignation to the Berlin Jewish community—upon which he was asked by a Gentile British friend whether he thought that Jews were a club. Even when they live their entire life in a non-Jewish milieu and have little contact among themselves, Jews still bear within them the imprint of a centuries-old community whose members were regarded by themselves, and by the outside world, as responsible for one another: a community that lived apart, within a hermetically closed framework of laws and regulations, climatic conditions, and economic pursuits, and that was imbued with an intense self-consciousness because it believed in its own special destiny on the one hand, and was discriminated against and persecuted on the other.

Nevertheless, the Jewish historian would be quite mistaken to direct his attention to every single Jew, even one who had never had any ties with Judaism, on the assumption that all the activities and associations engaged in by every person of Jewish extraction came within the purview of Jewish history. Nor should encouragement be given to the presentation of Jewish history as a collection of biographies of persons of Jewish ancestry who made good in the world. History addresses itself to social patterns; the individual—whatever the ultimate uniqueness of every human being—is significant as a representative type. In the absence of an all-embracing Jewish life of the kind that existed in Eastern Europe, the historian's attempt to isolate specifically "Jewish" associations and activities such as attendance at services, charity campaigns, intercession on behalf of suffering brethren abroad, absorption of immigrants, and even Jewish scholarship (of mainly philological or antiquarian character) will prove depressingly unrewarding and jejune.

When the elusive yet extremely potent Jewish patterns of thought, feeling, and behaviour that have crystallised around an extremely tenacious nucleus of race and religion no longer receive—outside Israel—integrated and limpid expression in autonomous and closely knit communities, the nature of these patterns will perhaps best be brought into relief by constant confrontation with general, non-Jewish patterns, and by turning our attention upon the encounter between Jew and Gentile. The earlier historians were naturally inclined to pursue their quest for meaning in Jewish history from within. The future historian of the Jews may prefer to operate from the vantage point of general history. The older historians were impressed by the uniqueness of the history of a people dwelling apart. The newer ones are likely to be struck by the paradox that it is precisely in the uniqueness of a clannish, marginal community dispersed around the world that the secret of the universal significance of Jewish history lies.

An attempt to sort out the elements of an interpretation of Jewish history from the point of view of world history must nowadays take cognisance of two facts. One is of far-reaching significance: the shift of balance which has been taking place between the West and the non-white civilisations. The other is of a more topical and probably ephemeral nature: the treatment of the Jews in Arnold Toynbee's *Study of History*, the most ambitious world-historical synthesis so far undertaken in the twentieth century. The two facts are, in my opinion, closely connected.

I believe that the lack of respect and the air of irritation, if not downright hostility, which mark Professor Toynbee's approach to Jewish history are on a par with his violent reaction against Europe-centrism, and that both are derived from a deep sense of guilt toward the colonial peoples and a corresponding collapse of European self-confidence. What a distance divides Toynbee from Macaulay, who was so cheerfully sure that "a single shelf of a good European library was worth the whole native literature of India and Arabia", and to whom the peoples of the East were simply candidates for admission to Western civilisation!

In Western Christian civilisation's vision of history, the Jew occupied a vital or at least a unique place. To the multitudes of Eastern and South-eastern Asia, Jews are an unknown, incomprehensible, and negligible factor. The Jew in the West might be persecuted, reviled, despised, expelled, and massacred, but he was indissolubly connected with the central event in the history of Christendom. He constituted a terrific problem. He embodied a great mystery. Immense effectiveness was ascribed to him, for good or evil. He appeared to be a factor of significance out of all proportion to his numbers.

The Jews have a long, terrible, and blood-stained account with the Christian West. I venture to suggest, however, that the rise of non-European powers is already beginning to make the record look somewhat different and less straightforward than was the case even in the recent past. For one thing, no Jewish historian, whatever his evaluation of the various factors involved in the restoration of Jewish statehood, can ignore the fact that Zionism would never have had a chance of success if centuries of Christian teaching and worship, liturgy and legend had not conditioned the Western nations to respond almost instinctively to the words "Zion" and "Israel", and thus to see in the Zionist ideal not a romantic chimera or an imperialistic design to wrest a country from its actual inhabitants, but the consummation of an eternal promise and hope. The Far Eastern civilisations, however, show no trace of Jewish associations. Their record is clean of anti-semitism—but it is also empty of Jews.

The whole centuries-long relationship of the West to the East is made to appear by Toynbee as one of sustained aggression, motivated by insatiable avarice against essentially contemplative and pacific civilisations. Church militant, European nationalism and racialism, modern imperialism, acquisitive capitalism, and—in some of its aspects—revolutionary communism are only phases and versions as it were of the sin of self-centred pride and arrogance. Far from having its cause in intellectual or spiritual superiority, the victory of the West over the Eastern and other non-European peoples, Toynbee believes, is due to one single factor—technological mastery. The Western absorption in techniques is evidence that Western man was much less anxious to know the truth than he was eager to turn discoveries and inventions into instruments of self-aggrandisement and dominion. The Chinese fathomed some of the mysteries of science long before the Europeans, but remained indifferent to the possibilities of science's utilitarian application.

The sin of pride has always carried its own punishment with it. *Hubris* prepares its own undoing. Greed expanding and conquering generates irreconcilable social cleavages and antagonisms within the victorious society, and bitter resentment among the conquered. The internal proletariat, alienated from the body politic, feels a common resentment with the external proletariat of the enslaved nations. Together they evolve a system of values—a new religion—to match and oppose the values of the conquerors and to act as a sublimating compensation for the enjoyments from which they are debarred. Dominant society, which has waxed fat and sluggish and succumbed to the malaise of the satiated, is pervaded by the new religion and simultaneously destroyed by the combined blows administered from within by the internal proletariat, and from without by the external proletariat. Western civilisation—with communism corroding it from within and closing in on it from the outside—having now reached this stage, it can be saved only by a new universal religion based on a synthesis of the four great creeds—Christianity, Islam, Buddhism, and Hinduism. Such a universal religion, Toynbee holds, will redeem it from the cancer of aggressive egotism by enabling it to achieve blissful reconciliation with the eternal order of things.

Toynbee[1] appears to trace the original sin of the West, self-idolatry, back to the "arrogant" Judaic idea of a Chosen People. Hebrew society was according to him only a parochial, marginal community within a much wider Syriac civilisation. Judaic religion evolved in the encounter between the Syriac exiles in Babylon and the proletariat of Mesopotamia, just as Christianity arose out of the meeting between the Jews oppressed by Rome and the proletariat of hellenistic-Roman society.

That the tribal god Yahveh, and not any one of his so much more powerful rivals within "Syriac civilisation", came to be accepted as the One God of the Universe is attributed by Toynbee to the all-devouring jealousy of Yahveh, who would not brook other gods and incited his believers to destroy all idols and images.

Obsessed by its tribal exclusiveness, Judaism failed to seize the chance, offered it by incipient Christianity, of becoming a universal religion, and instead rose against Rome in a nationalist uprising. When the Jewish revolt was crushed, Judaism's role was played out. The subsequent 2,000 years of Jewish history represented the meaningless perdurance of a fossil. The Jews' only response to the challenge of exile and persecution, Toynbee says, was to maintain a hermetically closed, highly intricate ritualistic framework, and to accumulate great financial power.

At the end of this long period of fossilised existence, Zionism marked another outburst of tribal arrogance. Yielding to the essentially Western passion for archaisation, the Jews, instead of keeping their hopes fixed on miraculous Divine deliverance, launched an attack on the Arab inhabitants of Palestine, succeeded in expelling them, and set up a tiny statelet of their own which in its crude aggressiveness combined all the disagreeable features of a military garrison and the Wild West.

Imbibed by the Christian West, the Judaic spirit acted as a potent evil factor in the history of Western civilisation. The

[1] Arnold J. Toynbee: *Abridgement of A Study of History* (made by D. C. Somervell), Oxford 1960, pp. 8, 22, 135, 310, 361, 380, 388-9, 509, 640, 729-31, 739, 816.

intolerant militant exclusiveness of the Church—a primary
Judaic legacy—was in due course transformed into the self-
idolatry of parochial nationalisms like the English and the
French. Taught by the example of Joshua's extermination of
the pagan Canaanites, Puritan settlers felt no qualms about
annihilating the Red Indians. Believing themselves to be the
heirs of the Jews to whom the earth had been promised as an
inheritance, European imperialist nations went out to conquer and enslave the non-European races. Having turned
their backs on the One God, they abandoned themselves
completely to Mammon: all their energies were applied to
perfecting the means of accumulating wealth and reaching
the highest degree of rational utilitarian efficiency. In brief,
the West underwent—in the words of Toynbee—a process of
"Judaisation".

At the other end of the scale, socialism and communism
were nothing but a version of the Judaic apocalypse, except
that the final consummation was again looked for, not in the
intervention of the Almighty, but as the result of social
cataclysm and a violent uprising of men.

So much for Toynbee's definition of the Jewish ingredient
in Western civilisation. How will the Jewish historian, coming from general history, define it?

There is every justification, it seems to me, for the view
that finds a distinctive Jewish ingredient at the very core of
Western civilisation. This is the measure of the paradox: an
essentially marginal group said to be the most clannish of all
communities, the Jews have in their tribal seclusion in
Palestine as well as in their worldwide dispersion, as spirit
and as flesh and blood, played a powerful part in making a
collection of tribes, communities, and countries into a
civilisation. Needless to add, they were not alone in the field
and their influence has not been invariably beneficial.

I shall not labour the obvious: that Judaism was the
parent of Christianity, and that therefore almost the whole
of Jewish history till Jesus, and on into the first centuries of
Christianity—the period in which the latter received its
shape either within the Jewish community or in the course of
debate with Rabbinic Judaism, and spread through the

Jewish communities along the shores of the Mediterranean—
it constitutes a vital chapter in world history. One can well
imagine a future Israeli historian undertaking to write the
history of Western Christian civilisation as the story of the
Judaic kernel in its encounter with Greek philosophy and art,
the mystery religions of the Orient, the institutions and laws
of the Roman Empire, the Germanic traditions, the facts of
European economy, etc., etc.

I shall take up only the one idea which Professor Toynbee
thinks to be the most distinctive and effective Jewish ingredient in world history—the idea of a Chosen People. I
agree as to its paramount importance. But my reasons for
thinking that Western civilisation (and consequently
universal history) would not have been the same without it
are altogether different from his.

To Dr. Toynbee, the whole concept of chosenness signifies
mere tribal exclusiveness and a conceited claim to racial
superiority. He omits the attributes of "a holy nation", "a
people of priests". I believe that the uniqueness of ancient
Judaism did not consist so much in the monotheistic conception, traces of which we can find among neighbouring
peoples, or in moral precepts whose similitudes we can find in
Greek philosophy and the teachings of the Stoa—it consisted
in the idea of a whole people's recognising, as its sovereign,
God alone. The laws under which it lives are not dictated
by a ruler, are not derived from the will of the people, are
not a utilitarian contrivance. Hence what Matthew Arnold
called the Hebraic passion for right acting, as distinct from
the Greek passion for right seeing and thinking in order to
know, experience, and dominate the world around.

Here we have the secret of the victory of parochial Yahveh
over Helios, the god of the sun, and all the other pagan
deities, and indeed over hellenistic philosophies like the
Stoa. The uniqueness of Judaism did not lie, as Toynbee
says, in the devouring jealousy of Yahveh, but in the total
and one-sided absorption of a whole people—not a sect of the
chosen or a monastic order—in the service of an impersonal
idea. The teachings of other Near Eastern religions were
more tolerant, more open to sweetness and light—and left

very many things outside their scope. This is why they failed
to revolutionise history. The hellenistic systems are incomparable in their broad humanity, but they were addressed to
and absorbed by individuals as counsels of personal perfection. Not conclusions of close discursive reasoning, but the
living model and the all-absorbing passion proved so effective
in the Jewish case. From that point of view, Toynbee's
attempt to dilute the sharp identity of the Judaic source by
pointing to a wider Syriac context of ideas and beliefs is
hardly relevant.

What distinguishes mature Christian civilisation from
other civilisations is to be sought not so much in particular
tenets of Christianity, to which parallels of some kind may be
found in other religions, but in the fundamentally and
peculiarly Western relationship between Church and State.
There was no example of it in antiquity, and none to my
knowledge in Islam or the Eastern Asiatic civilisations. And
this ingredient is substantially Jewish. The Church means
in this respect the universality of believers, "the people of
priests", and not merely the hierarchy. The members of the
ecclesia are actuated by a consciousness that, as a "holy
nation" and a "people of priests", they belong not to the
earthly State alone, but to a community of transcendental
laws and aims.

The permanent tension between Church and State, as
long as neither proved able to absorb the other, is to my
mind the source of the essentially Western obsession with the
problem of the legitimacy of power. It is not enough that the
law is promulgated by the authority which is recognised to
have power to legislate. King, Parliament, the sovereign
people, even pope and council, must all the time exhibit their
credentials in the face of divine or natural law. Natural law,
is, of course, of hellenistic and Roman provenance. Yet it is
fair to say that without its being amalgamated with divine
law, it would have failed to become the great formative
influence that it did.

One should not underestimate the other factors which have
shaped Western ideas of State, law, and legitimacy, such as
the Germanic traditions, feudalism, the guild system, the

changes in methods of production. Yet I believe with Lord Acton that none of these was so effective as the tension between Church and State, which was the greatest and most important vehicle of ideas and controversies and which, as it were, enveloped all the others and set the tone. When political theorists of the West spoke of Oriental despotism, what they meant was that the Orient did not know the problem of the legitimacy of power. Power to them was a datum, a fact of nature, an elemental, amoral force to be taken for granted like sunshine and rain, storm and plague. It need not always be tyrannical and malign, it might be as benign as one could wish. But it is given, it is there, and we have to bow to it.

Now it is the tension between Church and State, based on the idea of a chosen holy people, that gave the history of European nations its highly dynamic quality in comparison with the early stagnation of the non-European civilisations. Thanks to the Judaic concept the papacy never could, and perhaps never really wished to, reduce the body of lay believers to mere receivers of grace through the instrumentality of sacramental mystery and miracle. The task of realising the Kingdom of God was never restricted to the *ecclesia docens*. It always continued to rest with the *whole* body of believers. Hence the sense of dignity and awful responsibility of a Christian nation. It could not accept easily an evil king any more than a corrupt pope. For Christianity could never quite be reduced to a matter of personal ascetic discipline and unworldly holiness, and it could not divest itself of all responsibility for this world on the ground that its kingdom was wholly of another. It was thus bound to feel the permanent challenge to realise its high calling here and now. If this be true of the Catholic Church at all times, it is especially true of Calvinism and the Puritans in Britain and America.

There is, I submit with Dr. Toynbee, a direct line from the Church Militant permeated with the Judaic idea of a holy nation of priests, to modern nationalism with its ideology of a chosen people. We are only too painfully aware in the twentieth century of the terrible ravages wrought by nationalism run wild. Yet it would be wrong for the historian to forget that in the first half of the nineteenth century, the national idea in the mouth of a Mazzini, and indeed even of a Fichte, not to speak of the Polish Mickiewicz, was a prophetic clarion call for spiritual regeneration. Far from proclaiming tribal war on neighbours thought inferior, it imposed a special mission, a particularly strenuous obligation on one's own nation within the scheme of mankind's endeavour towards higher things and universal freedom. It is indeed most strange to read today Fichte's boast that the German nation, the *Urvolk* of Europe, would not demean itself by joining the general bloody scramble for territories and colonies, and would take no part in the squalid game of political and mercantilist rivalry. The only truly original nation in Europe, since all others had their thoughts and feelings shaped by an acquired language—whether Latin or German—the Germans were destined to maintain, with brows furrowed and spirits keyed to the highest pitch of concentration, a special communion with eternal values.

Everyone is familiar with the religious, Messianic overtones of Mazzini's philosophy of nationalism, with such slogans as "God and the people", "nationality is a mission", "nation means sacrifice"; with Mazzini's conception of patriotism as a counterpart to selfish utilitarianism and moral self-indulgence; with his vision of a federation of free peoples, each with its own mission, under the inspiring guidance of *Roma Terza*—Rome of the people—the first Rome having been that of the emperors and the second that of the popes. Mickiewicz, like Mazzini, consciously drew on biblical ideas and imagery in describing Poland as the suffering Remnant of Israel, destined to atone for the sins of other nations and redeem them through her self-sacrifice.

Professor Toynbee wrings his hands over the horrors wrought by modern nationalism and its evil offspring imperialism, seeing in them nothing but irredeemable evil, pride, and *hubris*, which stand in such crass contrast to the broad, quietist tolerance of the Eastern religions and civilisations.

It seems to me that in his prostration before the East and

self-flagellation as a Westerner, Dr. Toynbee has missed a truth of awful import, a mystery of tragic grandeur—the ambivalence with which the whole of the Western achievement is charged from the start. It is an infinitely tragic fact that great good is somehow always mixed up with terrible evil, that the worst seems always to be the degeneration of the best, that some Hegelian *List der Vernunft*, a trick of Universal Reason, complicates in a sardonic manner the yearning for self-surrender with the craving for self-assertion.

Professor Toynbee is filled with reverence for those Eastern civilisations whose religions are a syncretistic synthesis of various, often heterogeneous, strands, and are ultimately the concern of the individual only, and whose churches know no intolerant militancy. He is attracted by those vast conglomerations of men who are not primarily political animals at all, and whose passion for power is held back by a highly developed capacity for contemplative communion with the invisible world and the attainment of that peace which passeth understanding—a peace for which we all strain in vain, and of which only very few in our midst ever catch a glimpse.

Nearer home Dr. Toynbee selects the Ottoman Empire for special commendation. That was a system in which racial, linguistic, and religious communities lived as *millets* side by side on a completely non-political basis. He is not worried by the fact that the Turkey of the sultans was a byword for despotism, corruption, and bribery, that even the Ulema, the supreme Moslem court of experts in Islam, was most of the time unable to restrain the cruel vagaries of personal despotism; that under such a régime there could be no individual rights and no corporate consciousness or self-respect; that only a palace plot or the assassin's dagger, and at a lower level bribery and flattery, could avert the pure arbitrariness of brute power; and that consequently complete stagnation overcame all cultural endeavour and spiritual vitality under the Ottoman Turks. In the vast empires where there is no political life and no popular passion, the individual may at times attain a very high degree of personal, unworldly perfection. But it is at the cost of the vitality and the moral advancement of the body social.

It is a curious thing that a man so sensitive to any sign of arrogance and pride, and who over acres of self-analysis recording his visitations makes such tremendous efforts to be humble, should at the same time be so fascinated—as Dr. Toynbee is—by colossal dimensions, the mighty barbarian conquerors wading in blood up to their knees, building sky-high pyramids of the skulls of their slaughtered foes. England and France, on the other hand, Professor Toynbee again and again calls parochial, puffed-up little countries.

The finest flowering of culture never occurred on the vast expanses of steppe and desert but in tiny, overcrowded, noisy, and proud communities such as Athens, Jerusalem, Alexandria, Florence and Amsterdam. Why damn vitality by calling it arrogance? The truth of the matter is that an ambitious undertaking like Toynbee's to embrace all ages and all civilisations in one system, with the help of tidy schemata, sweeping generalisations, and quantitative measurements, can afford little room for the understanding of the unique phenomenon, the local idiom, and the particular concatenation of data and circumstances; little room for the exquisite miniature; and nothing of that feeling for the specific situation, limpid and throbbing with real life, which comes from long meditation and loving immersion in it.

In the last two centuries Western history has indeed become universal history. The non-European civilisations, sunk in languor or atrophy, have had their fate shaped by the expansion of Western capitalism, which turned the whole world into one economic and cultural unit. In our own day the essentially European ideologies of nationalism, democracy, and communism—not the organic growth and inner dialectic of their own heritage—stimulated the Asiatic and African peoples to assert themselves and seek self-determination.

I agree with Dr. Toynbee that in the forging of the various instruments for the unification of the world by the West—or if one prefers, by Western imperialism—the Jewish ingredient played the role of a powerful catalyst. Jews as living men, and not merely the Jewish spiritual legacy, moved on to the centre of the stage of world history in the

81

nineteenth and twentieth centuries. One need not belittle the part Jews played in maintaining international trade almost alone in the early Middle Ages, in interpreting and transmitting for Christian scholarship the classical wisdom preserved in Arab translations, and as a lever in early urban colonisation. Whether you call them rapacious usurers or bankers—as one calls the more respectable because richer Christian Medicis and Fuggers, Lombards and Templars—whether the Jews went into business from their own choice or because all other avenues were closed to them, they kept up through centuries a rudimentary credit system in Europe.

Nevertheless, I hold the somewhat chilling view that the history of most European countries, with the exception perhaps of Spain, Poland and Holland, would not have differed very significantly had there been no Jews—but only the Judaic heritage—in Europe between the end of the Crusades and the eighteenth century. Indeed, for most of that time they had been expelled from a number of the European countries. The living ghetto commanded too little respect to influence directly a society so highly stratified as European society was for centuries.

Only in the last 150 years was it again given to Jews to affect the structural framework of universal history.

I believe it legitimate for the universal historian to call the age ushered in by the French and Industrial Revolutions the "era of industrial civilisation based on contract". This formulation takes account of the two most salient features of the period—industrialism and democratic growth. Furthermore, it implies that capitalism and the various forms of socialism and communism are only two poles of the same development, and not phenomena on different planes. The formulation postulates a type of spiritual-cultural superstructure evolved from the essentially universal and cosmopolitan character of industrial civilisation. The main point to be borne in mind is the transformation of a society based on status and on more or less rigid patterns into a society based on contract—in other words on individual and social mobility. This meant an entirely new situation for Jews, and one of unlimited possibilities.

Nuanced thinking and formulation are required here in order not to overstate our case. None of the early inventors of the industrial revolution was a Jew, and there were to my knowledge hardly any identifiable Jews among the early captains of industry. Werner Sombart's[1] attempt—in imitation of Max Weber's connecting of the Puritans with the rise of capitalism—to make the Jews of the seventeenth century bearers of early capitalism has long been discredited. Yet it is true that in the building of the sinews of the modern international capitalist economy, the part of the Jews, especially on the Continent, was that of pioneers and catalysts *par excellence.* International credit, banking and exchange, joint-stock companies, telegraphic news agencies, railway networks, chain stores, methods of mass production and mass marketing, the media of mass entertainment, experimentation in new techniques—in brief, the lifelines of a universal economy—were in very many cases laid down and set working by Jews, who thus played, in the words of Joseph Addison, the part of "pegs and nails" in the world economy.

The abstract, rational nexus holding together concrete, disparate detail was grasped more quickly by people with a long training in intellectual speculation. Not place-bound, the emancipated and de-tribalised Jew was unhampered by routine and conservative attachments, and his international connections helped him to forge the hinges of new artificial frameworks. It is in the nature of a marginal community, especially one living in metropolitan centres, to acquire the refined sensitivity of an exposed nerve and to be the first to detect the trend and shape of things to come. Hence the disposition and the courage to experiment. Emancipated formally, but not really or fully admitted as equals, lacking the prestige of lineage and long establishment, while eager for a place in the sun, and restless and ill at ease as people in ambiguous situations are, the Jews threw all their pent-up energies into the two avenues of power open to them: economic activity and intellectual prowess. Centuries of disciplined living and sober calculation prevented ambition from dissipating itself in a haphazard, chaotic manner.

[1] Werner Sombart: *Die Juden und das Wirtschaftsleben*, Munich 1928.

Vitality turned into a strictly rational instrument of power designed to obtain maximum results at the lowest cost.

As for the Jewish ingredient in revolutionary Messianism, the other pole of industrial civilisation, I have come to the conclusion on somewhat closer study that it was to a large extent the Jewish Messianic vision of history that made the industrial revolution appear not merely as another crisis and another bad spell, but as an apocalyptic hour leading to some preordained final dénouement. It was the Jewish Messianic tradition that was responsible for the fact that the social protest of the victims of the industrial revolution did not take the form of another desperate, elemental *jacquerie*, but became part of the preparation for a Day of Judgement, after which justice and peace would reign supreme and history really begin as it were with all conflicts and contradictions resolved.

The earliest prophet of socialist transformation in nineteenth-century Europe, Saint-Simon, was quite explicitly linked with the Jewish Messianic expectation. Jews were the leading spirits in his fascinating and influential school, and they emphatically voiced the conviction that they were carrying on the perennial Messianic mission of Judaism. Their future city of universal harmony was to be guided by technicians and bankers who were at the same time artists and priests, and was to rest on a universal religion of humanity, *Nouveau Christianisme*, with the old division into State and Church, matter and spirit, theory and practice done away with for ever. It is most significant that Jewish Saint-Simonists, the Rodrigueses, Pereiras, d'Eichthals, should have in the course of time become the architects of France's industrial and financial revolution and of much of Europe's banking and industry.

The deeply ingrained experience of history as the unfolding of a pattern of judgement and deliverance makes it almost impossible for the Jew to take history for granted as an eternal meaningless cycle. Time must have a stop. History must have a dénouement. At the same time his lack of roots in a concrete tradition, with its instinctive certainties and the comfort of smooth, almost automatic procedures, combines with the absence of experience of practical government to turn many a Jew into a doctrinaire and impatient addict of schemes of social redemption. When he is of a prophetic temperament, as in the case of a Karl Marx, a torrent of relentless denunciation issues forth. A terrific, fiery over-simplification reduces everything—human laziness and thoughtlessness, the weakness of the flesh and the hetero-geneity of impulse, peculiarity of tradition and complexity of situation—to greed, falsehood, and hypocrisy, a kingdom of the Devil that will be overthrown in the imminent future by a kingdom of God. Suspended between heaven and earth, rejected and excluded, tormented by the humiliations, complexities, and ambiguities of his situation, many a young Jew threw himself with the deepest yearning and passion into the arms of the religion of revolution.

We all know the inhumanities practised by capitalism at the height of its imperialistic expansion, and the perverse denial of traditional morality and of man's freedom and dignity which accompanies the attempt to satisfy the Messianic longing for salvation by a totalitarian system. This erosion of ideals has no particular relevance to Judaism as such, for it is rooted in the tragic condition itself of man, in the essential ambivalence of things human and social—as the Christian would say, in original sin. It is at the same time not to be denied that the fact of a surplus of intensity among Jews, such as is peculiar to a marginal minority in constant need to justify its separateness by self-assertion, has its own polar ambivalence: besides idealistic self-dedication to causes and things of the mind, there is a particularly harsh, shrill and unscrupulous style of Jewish self-seeking.

We come now to the Jewish ingredient in the universal or cosmopolitan culture characteristic of an industrial civilisa-tion based on contract instead of status, and sustained by media of mass communication.

It is one of the commonplaces of Jewish apologists to emphasise that Jews have enriched the life and culture of every country in which they have lived. Yet, as I have said, I do not believe that the culture of England, France, Italy, or even of pre-nineteenth-century Germany would have been significantly different if there had been no Jews in those countries. Modern universal civilisation is, however, unthinkable without Marx, Freud, or Einstein, who have moulded the consciousness of modern mankind.

Isaiah Berlin has given an acute explanation of the contrast between the superb achievements of Jews in the sciences and music, and their rather inferior showing in literature. Jewish writers have excelled in biography and the biographical novel (André Maurois and Stefan Zweig). They have written in highly stimulating fashion on the complexities and dilemmas of the contemporary human situation (Arthur Koestler, Arthur Miller, and Ilya Ehrenburg). In this they were helped by their psychological acumen, which their race acquired from its agelong need to understand and adjust to others, as well as by their being at the very nerve centre of metropolitan life and at the same time detached and over-sensitive. Yet, while being often stirring and provocative, their writings in no sense represent great literature. It is not enough to be able to penetrate, even lovingly, the inner springs and hidden recesses of men and societies. Vigour and intimacy come to the novel from subtle, almost unconscious and automatic associations, which are not acquired with the algebraic language of science but are imperceptibly experienced within a concrete, long-established tradition. This is why Yiddish literature has such vigour as well as warmth.

The literature produced by Jewish writers in non-Jewish languages in centres like old Vienna—where Jews as producers as well as consumers often formed a nucleus of the most cosmopolitan vanguard—served despite its lack of greatness as a barometer and stimulant of universal significance.

On the political level, the passionate patriotism of a Benjamin Disraeli, a Walter Rathenau, a Léon Blum had perhaps greater intensity and depth than the devotion of an ordinary British, German or French statesman to his country. It was conditioned by an agonised yearning for something romantically idealised which was not a simple datum to be taken for granted. This kind of Jewish patriotism betrayed a deeper and more articulate understanding of the national tradition and its peculiarities than could the patriotism of a "normal" leader, for whom the national tradition was a matter of spontaneous reflexes. And the patriotism of Jews was always more universal (or more imperial, as in the case of Disraeli) in its awareness.

Far from lending support to any doctrine of race in the biological sense, our argument has been concerned, throughout its latter part, with a spiritual legacy and the facts of history and social psychology on the one side, and the individualistic mobility of industrial civilisation on the other.

Indeed, the fate of Jews under Hitler may in this respect be seen as a focal point of twentieth-century history—and not merely because of the enormity of the crime and sufferings inflicted on them with the help of scientific long-term planning and execution, and not only because the mass violation of the sanctity of human life was not calculated to stop with the Jews but was bound to undermine the most vital foundations of our civilisation and initiate general race slaughter. Hitler's racialism signified an attempt to reverse the main trend of modern Western civilisation, and to return from individualistic contract to deterministic patterns of race, caste, and tribe through a denial of the unity of mankind. It is no accident that nazism found it necessary to reinterpret the whole of history as a permanent life-and-death struggle between Nordic Aryanism and the Jewish spirit, attributing to Jews a significance and effectiveness which the most extreme Jewish chauvinist would not dream of claiming.

Some of my readers may have begun to feel a certain surprise that there has been relatively little reference so far to Israel in this survey. Our theme has been Jewish history from the point of view of universal history. Although the Palestine problem has been one of the focal points of international politics, and albeit that little country of such strange destinies is once more a centre of world attention, it is still too early to say whether the return of Jews to Zion (which coincides with the general retreat of Europe from Asia: an extraordinary fact, highly charged with symbolism) will mean more than the establishment of another little state among the dozens of new states which have come into existence in the twentieth century.

In Professor Toynbee's[1] violent condemnation, Zionism figures as an integral part of Western imperialistic rapacity. The music of Messianic hope kept alive for 2,000 years; the saga-like quality of the return to Zion; the historic perspectives and vistas opened by that event; the awful tragedy that the restoration of Jews to Israel had to be effected through a terrible conflict with the Arab world—all this fails to strike a chord. We have instead Dr. Toynbee's nonsense about Jews taking over the Western "heresy of archaisation"; his tasteless, sermonising censure of Jews for not trusting in God's miraculous deliverance, and for demeaning themselves with such unworthy things as a state, a flag, an army, and postage stamps; a selective method of presenting facts which amounts to untruth—as, for instance, the failure to mention the decision of the United Nations, as representative of world conscience, on partition, or to refer by a single word to the invasion of Palestine by five Arab armies. We then get the horrifying comparison of the treatment of the Arab population by the Jews with the extermination of six million Jews by Hitler, and finally the crowning sanctimonious blasphemy: the prophecy that on the Day of Judgement the crime of the Jews shall be judged graver than that of the Nazis.

There are one or two pointers to be borne in mind by the universal historian meditating on the future of Jews within the scheme of world history. There seems to be something almost providential in the way in which the two new centres, Israel and the United States, were as it were prepared just on the eve of the catastrophe which put an end to European Jewry's history of some 1,500 to 2,000 years. There is also a striking analogy between the present relations between Israel and the Anglo-Saxon Jewish communities, especially American Jewry, and the relations that obtained at the time of the Second Temple between Jewish Palestine and the Mediterranean Jewish communities of the Roman

[1] A. J. Toynbee, *op. cit.*, pp. 735-7.

Empire on one side, and the Jewish conglomeration in Mesopotamia on the other. It is a fact of very great importance that English has come to be the language of the majority of the Jewish people.

The problems that faced the Palestine-Mediterranean axis were very similar to those of the Israel-Anglo-Saxon axis today, including all those needs which had to be met by an annual United Jewish Appeal, the problems of assimilation, mixed loyalties, and so forth. The encounter of Judaism and hellenism, and the synthesis of the two in the Alexandria of Philo, paved the way for the triumph of Christianity. Is it too fanciful to suggest that the New York of today may be destined to play the part of a Jewish Alexandria of the twentieth century? There is much food for speculation in the fact that tiny Israel, on the troubled eastern shore of the Mediterranean, has a kind of counter-part in what is the most vital country in the world today, and the one which seems destined to set the tone in the years to come.

If it was given to the Jews to make some mark on world history, it was not because God, as someone has said, was kind to the Jews, in scattering them among the nations, but because they had fashioned their real contribution—the Judaic heritage—in their own country, and were dispersed only after they had been moulded into a unique phenomenon. . . .

No historian, I believe, can be a complete rationalist. He must be something of a poet, he must have a little of the philosopher, and he must be touched just a bit by some kind of mysticism. The sorting out of evidence, the detective's skill in ferreting out inaccuracy and inconsistency, are of little help when the historian strikes against the hard residue of mystery and enigma, the ultimate causes and the great problems of human life.

The Jewish historian becomes a kind of martyr in his permanent and anguished intimacy with the mystery of Jewish martyrdom and survival. Whether he be Orthodox in belief or has discarded all religious practice, he cannot help but be sustained by a faith which can neither be proved nor disproved.

89

I believe that notwithstanding all the vexations and entanglements caused by emergency and inescapable necessity—all so reminiscent incidentally of the times of Ezra and Nehemiah—Israel will one day be spiritually significant and, in conjunction with the Jewish diaspora, spiritually effective in the world.

History would somehow make no sense otherwise.

3

Herder and the German Mind

LATE IN May 1769, the twenty-five-year-old Lutheran pastor and budding man of letters Johann Gottfried Herder left the Baltic city of Riga on his sea voyage westwards.

I

The *Journal* which the traveller composed during his journey, if it was not actually the model for the famous opening monologue of "Faust", as has been suggested, might well have served as an inspiration to Goethe. A clarion call of the *Sturm und Drang* movement, the *Journal meiner Reise*[1] has come to be regarded as one of the earliest and most significant symptoms of that vast ferment, out of which emerged such powerful currents as Romanticism and Nationalism, the classicism of Goethe and Schiller and the tremendous philosophical achievement by the Pleiad of thinkers from Kant to Hegel, and finally historicism and the evolutionary sciences.[2]

The *Journal* is indeed an extraordinary document. The reader will search in vain for description of scenery or accounts of meetings, characterisation of people or record of incident. He is from the outset subjected to the hot blast of confession, his entails are torn·by having to witness Promethean wrestlings and Faustian self-questioning, and he is then heavily imposed upon with a detailed blueprint for the total re-education of mankind.

Rousseau's influence is unmistakable, and is indeed

[1] *Sturm und Drang—Kritische Schriften*, ed. E. Loewenthal, Heidelberg 1949, pp. 289-397.
[2] H. A. Korff: *Geist der Goethezeit*, 4 vols., Leipzig 1949-57.

acknowledged. Instead, however, of that passionate rejection of a world that has gone irretrievably wrong through having stifled man's innocent spontaneity, the experience which informs Herder's *Journal* is the feverish urge to conquer the world, the whole world and to refashion everything in it in accordance with the author's deepest own truth. The intensity of the conquering impulse seems much greater than the certainty about the nature of the inner truth.

Who am I? What are my real wishes and my genuine convictions? What is my own authentic truth; not what I have read and learned, and acquired or accepted. As it did to Friedrich Nietzsche a hundred years later, bookish learning appears a snare and almost a demoralising factor. It makes one accept truths without having experienced them directly; it incites one—to strive to embrace all things, until nothing is genuinely and fully one's own; and under its impact one becomes more afraid of missing external occasions than anxious to let one's own self unfold.

If we may now substitute for learning rationalist Reason—Rousseau would have said civilisation—we are led to conclude that truth is personal experience and not conformity to some objective pattern. And if this be so, then the vehicle of truth is not mathematical ratiocination, but the spontaneity of individual feeling. Authenticity of experience is to be sought not in later stages of development, when one's own truth has already been criss-crossed by all manner of heterogeneous influences, but at the source, in the early immediacy and purity of the pristine state.

But, as already said, Herder is not out to discover his authentic identity by withdrawing into undisturbed solitude away from all the distorting and corroding intrusions; he is consumed by a desire to do things. It is not that he can discover himself only by coming into contact with all possible situations, and thus inevitably through reading and study; he wants to create. Not to formulate abstract ideas by the way of a *Tintenfass* (ink-pot) scribe, but to stir up experiences in others, and mould patterns of life; to play in short the role of the great Rousseauist Legislator à la Solon and Lycurgus. Herder is excitedly scanning the horizon for possibilities in that direction. Why not become the Father-teacher-Legislator of his adopted Hanseatic city of Riga? Surely, with his good connections, he could also obtain the ear of the Great Kaiserin Catherine of all the Russias, the sovereign Lady of that German island, in a sea of Latvian primitive peasantry, for centuries previously the bone of contention between the ancient kingdoms of Poland and Sweden. He might thus become a tremendous influence in that rising, mighty empire, very rude still, but full of fresh-ness, impelled by elemental forces and destined one day—the father of German nationalism speaking—to lay down the law to unauthentic, enfeebled, decrepit Europe, and turn the Ukraine into another Greece.[1]

And the best way to go about that is, of course, to write a great, a very great book, encompassing the history of all nations and the lessons of all ages, a book which would constitute a ready *vade-mecum* for all men on how to experience things and how to behave in every contingency.

To be one's own lawgiver, a law unto oneself and a legislator of nature—we know that Kant put to himself the same postulate on the epistemological plane in his revolt against naïve dogmatism as well as mere sensual receptivity, and on the ethical plane—in his rejection of a morality based upon external authority, religious, traditional or social, or mere natural impulse. We are familiar with the Kantian solution which reconciles the autonomy of every human person with the idea of the essential sameness of all men. In the case of Herder the quest of authenticity seems to develop from the wish of the individual to become a law unto himself into a desire to become a law to others. Such a form of self-expression is motivated not only by ambitious craving for power, but also by a fear of remaining alone in the midst of an infinite variety of selves. Mastery over others enables you to preserve your own self, and to keep all the others with you, or rather under you, at the same time.

The parallel with Rousseau is no less instructive.

Although Herder's ideas were destined to evolve into no less explosive a force than Rousseau's, and to emerge as the

[1] Rudolf Haym, *Herder*, 2 vols. Berlin 1958, Vol. I, pp. 258, 357, 362.

foci of vast power complexes and the sinews of compact institutional structures, Herder, with all his hankering for power, soon veered away into prima facie totally unpolitical regions, whereas the morose recluse, without any political ambitions for himself, at once became the astringent political legislator of incomparable immediate effectiveness. Whence that difference?

No longer was a universal Church able to offer fulfilment to the stirrings of ardent young hearts in preaching and teaching, apostolic zeal or worldly influence, mystical contemplation or administrative activity, while embodying at the same time a most comprehensive and coherent *Weltanschauung*. Young talented plebeians all over Europe were filled with an impatient hatred for the traditional, authoritative and hierarchical patterns as unnatural, contrary to reason, oppressive and degrading. With the growing consciousness of man's worth went the growing horror of human waste. The old curbs appeared as not only a violation of man's dignity and liberty, but also as a standing attempt on authenticity. In France the frustrated angry young men were destined to become Marats and Dantons, and the clerics among them were to turn into Sieyès and Fouchés. Social-political revolt and revolutionary action were ruled out in Germany. The 350 principalities and operatic tyrannies of Germany could evoke no passionate, proud loyalty or even engender interest in politics. A Pauline-Lutheran tradition upheld the primacy of the inner light over external conditions, treating the latter as irrelevant, and thus in fact yielding to evil. Hence such astonishing discrepancies as that between the size of Weimar—a townlet of 6,000 inhabitants, in which it was still forbidden to carry mirrors in the streets for fear of frightening the cattle, and the world-shaking conquests of Goethe and Schiller, Herder and Wieland; between soaring flights of fancy and intellect on the one hand, and feudal stagnation and civic timidity, on the other.

Long before he fled the domains of the hated King of Prussia in order to escape military service, the precocious boy Herder had shot ahead of, and become estranged from, his hymn-singing pious artisan family and all the other 2,000 humble dwellers of the little East Prussian townlet of Mohrungen in the shadow of the medieval Teutonic Knights' fortress. The indignities of an equivocal status which he experienced in adolescence as half assistant-copyist, half servant-messenger boy to a vain pedantic scribe were to be repeated more than once in later life, especially during the period when he held clerical office at the Court of Graf Wilhelm von Lippe-Schaumburg, a dazzling, yet absurd prince, a knight-errant who had served in or commanded most of the European armies of his day, who turned his own tiny force into a Spartan host, and from a Puritan destroyer of images evolved into a model of a Renaissance prince and enlightened despot. Notwithstanding the latitude of the enlightened Herzog Karl August von Sachsen-Weimar, the chapter on government in Herder's *magnum opus* had to be rewritten by the high ecclesiastical dignitary of the Principality four times, and many Weimar manuscripts were left unprinted. Herder often said of himself that being so deeply convinced of his own worth, he bitterly resented injuries, but could never muster the strength to revolt or break away. Hence his extreme touchiness, and bottled-up rancour. He was always weighed down by a general malaise—"I am like Prometheus chained to the cliff and like Lazarus in the grave." "Nothing drives and oppresses me here but my inner man, but he oppresses me very much and makes me opposed to other human beings." "I have too little reason, and too much idiosyncrasy."[1] He would find refuge from this unhappy and unhealthy state in wild dreams of glory, transports of ecstatic elation or trances of idyllic bliss. To such a split personality, the concrete and immediate was bound to appear as something transitional, a pale shadow, a murky imitation of the truly real, that is to say the imaginary, and the longed for. A most remarkable disposition for the prophet of the authentic and concrete, and enemy of all abstraction and generalisation.

It is easy to see why Herder nowhere felt at home or at

[1] Quoted in Robert H. Ergang: *Herder and the Foundations of German Nationalism*, New York 1931, pp. 71, 74.

ease. He had, for instance, become utterly miserable in that Scythian outpost, Riga, where he had in fact every reason to feel free, welcome and successful, and was filled with longing to get away from its cramping and stultifying conditions into the wide world. No sooner had he put his foot on board ship when, frightened by the limitless expanse of sea, he is seized by tender regret for that warm grove Riga, for the sense of fixedness and permanence which his well defined position and duties had given him there. Herder was always subject to agonies of indecision. This explains his obsession with signs, omens, auguries, destiny and fate, the inner Socratic daimon and unerring instinct. Herder was prone to get into bad trouble with promises, or half-promises given, retracted, changed. He was always waiting for circumstances to decide, to place him before a *fait accompli*. Evasions and equivocations on top of an envious mocking disposition, led to dishonest actions and quarrels with closest friends—a situation aggravated by a big mouthed and loud voiced wife, with a large bevy of children, a conviction that her husband was the greatest man on earth, and with never enough money. Wieland wished for the Pyrenees to separate him from Herder.[1]

The insatiable hunger which precluded firm commitment and which could never be assuaged by a feeling of safe possession or a sense of achieved power found relief in Herder's extraordinary capacity for—the word was coined by him—*Einfühlung*[2]—the ability to get under the skin of other people and become immersed with imaginative sympathy in diverse situations and moods, and distant civilisations. "*Welch ein Werk über das menschliche Geschlecht! den menschlichen Geist! die Kultur der Erde! aller Räume! Zeiten! Völker! Kräfte! Mischungen! Gestalten! . . . Universalgeschichte der Bildung der Welt!*"[3] He could not own all things; he was at least allowed to experience all things vicariously.

From another angle this genius for *Einfühlung* was a compensation for other gifts denied to him. Herder was

[1] Ergang, *op. cit.*, p. 76.
[2] Friedrich Meinecke: *Die Entstehung des Historismus*, 2 vols., Munich and Berlin 1936, Vol. II, p. 385.
[3] *Sturm und Drang*, p. 298.

essentially a *poète manqué*. He could respond and reflect, but he could only agonisingly watch the spontaneous elemental welling up of poetic experience and its instant transformation into marvellous shapes and forms in his friend and pupil Goethe. He was also at bottom a cerebral type, and of course much too self-conscious. No wonder he felt acutely uncomfortable in the presence of such powerful natures and utterly uninhibited eccentrics as the outsize Master of Bückeburg, except when on the crest of swelling eloquence in the pulpit. On the other hand Herder lacked the philosophical rigour and perseverance for consistent syllogistic reasoning. While capable as very few have ever been of epoch-making intimations and premonitions, which explains his rhapsodic style and the abundance of sudden incantations, Herder's writings abound in bewildering inconsistencies, with moods and *tableaux* held together by the most tenuous links. His most important books were in fact left unfinished. Herder stopped writing fairly early, partly because he simply burnt himself out.

There is a most revealing and painful admission in one of his *cris de cœur*: "What in my past has made me deserve this, that I can see only shadows, instead of feeling real things. . . , Always that swollen imagination that runs ahead, that diverts me from the real things and kills all joy, dulls and lulls my sensibility to sleep."[1] He would be straining in anguish for the experience to seize him. When the visitation came upon him, the experience would turn not into the direct immediate thing at all, but into a shadowy affair. The effort of anticipation had been too great, and the act itself inevitably became an anticlimax. "What in my past state has made me deserve this"—significant words, betokening a vague haunting memory of some break, of some traumatic experience, perhaps of guilt, as a result of which real things turned into shadows, full-blooded life into dim recollections or only objects for reflection. In this fallen state Herder is possessed by the never-stilled nostalgia for the innocence and spontaneity of childhood.

[1] Quoted in Meinecke, *op. cit.*, Vol. II, p. 385.

II

Reason, natural law, the natural order of society, happiness and justice—universal, eternal, objective criteria, interconnected like Platonic ideas into a systematic totality: Herder's rejoinder to this basic postulate of eighteenth-century rationalism was made in the significantly called *Auch eine Philosophie der Geschichte*, 1774,[1] the title defiantly offering an alternative to the dominant philosophy of the age. It may be summed up in the idea that everything has a history. Instead of asking—is it absolutely true or false, right or wrong, one should enquire how, when, where, and in what context did it arise, happen, take place, what came of it under the impact of circumstances. All value judgements are then suspended, on the assumption that, granted the conditions, this or that was bound to happen or could not take place.

Man is essentially the sum total of impacts exerted upon him by forces, and his reason is made up of his modes of responding to them. In this respect reason is not an autonomous or isolated faculty at all. Furthermore, when disentangled as power of ratiocination and calculated choice, it is the feeblest of all instruments, the least safe of guides, and the most unauthentic of man's characteristics. Do not speak therefore of reason pitted against irrational elements, of morality opposing passions. These have meaning only as the peculiar combination of vital forces and habits with which concrete man copes with real life. Herder follows here in the footsteps of his teacher and friend, Hamann, that strange harbinger of romanticism.

The truly powerful forces are, to use Burkean language, the deep massive sentiments which shake, overwhelm, impel or hold in thrall. And this is why the age of childhood in man, tribe, race or nation is all-important. Appearing for the first time the phenomena seem outsize and have an overpowering effect, and experiences lived in early age have all that intensity of the deep feelings of awe, fear, delight, trust and hope that accompany initiation and discovery. We are

[1] *Sturm und Drang*, pp. 579-670.

all at first drunk, and only gradually grow sober, and poorer. This is why song or chant has always preceded speech. Men danced before they began to walk steadily. Science grew out of mythology. Poetry—Herder adopts the idea of the English pre-Romantics and Hamann—was the original language of mankind. Myth and ballad, epic tale and ode, folk-song and proverb are the record of young mankind's first encounter with nature and life, and of enchantment with them.

The early imprints, shocks and traumas if you like, are decisive for the whole future in that they engender dispositions, shape responses to stimuli. This predetermined mode of reacting to impressions, which in themselves are occasioned by purely fortuitous circumstances, constitutes fate. Fate is thus a matter neither of pure chance nor of wholly deterministic necessity. It is not capricious, it obeys a law, only a law all of its own, unique in each case.

We catch Herder experiencing at one moment a wonderful premonition of modern psychology. We see him watching birds flying around the ship's mast. His thoughts wander to some ancient Greek sailor upon an unknown sea, a fugitive from his country who—Herder is musing—had committed some heinous crime, had perhaps killed his father. At the rumblings of the oncoming storm the sailor is anxiously scanning the sky, the stars, the moon for signs and omens. At dawn he suddenly beholds birds—the sure token of land, the message of a shore shrouded to the fearful wanderer in dreadful mystery. That may have been the birth of ancient augury and Greek mythology—exclaims Herder. Does a moment come when reason takes over and mythological imagining makes room for rational analysis? Herder seems to deny such a sharp break and such a passage into pure rationality. He says indeed in one place that mythology and science follow the same procedure in that they set out from hypothesis, and make discoveries under deep emotional stress. Science is refined, sophisticated myth.

If the genuine, the true and the authentic is what is directly experienced, with the intensity of a new discovery, then the more private the experience, the deeper the truth.

99

No experience can in fact be lived twice, not even by the same person, let alone by others. Nothing therefore is more absurd and false than to hold up some classical model of perfection to be conformed to or imitated. Such an attitude suggests that the life springs have dried up, and abstract formulae, ritualistic recipes taken over, commanding mechanical obedience. Herder pours scorn upon his contemporary *raisonneurs* who sit in judgement upon bygone ages and distant nations, according praise or apportioning blame for coming up to or falling short of the exigencies of Reason, or models of artistic perfection, which in fact are their ideas of reason or artistic excellence, and blame the ancient Egyptians or medieval Englishmen for not being Greeks of the fifth century B.C. and youthful tribes for not behaving like polished Frenchman of the *grand siècle*. The very concept "barbarians" should be banned from our vocabulary. Herder goes out to provoke his contemporaries on the eighteenth-century touchstone, despotism, that omnibus term, like capitalism a century after, and imperialism, 200 years later, for all the evils and absurdities of mankind. In its time, in its place Oriental despotism was an answer to the needs of young, tender humanity for fatherly protection, and was brought into being by the same sentiments of trust, devotion and awe, that went out to an omnipotent deity. Those who sneer at founders of religions calling them impostors or grow eloquent on the evil cunning of Oriental despots, simply lack the imagination to understand the mainsprings of young nations. They are totally oblivious of the underlying factors, landscape, climate, the economic conditions, and fail to see that despotism flourished in regions where the flow of water was held to depend upon the course of the moon high above and had to be centrally regulated by an all-powerful agency down below.[1] The life of nations does not obey the rules of mathematical evidence and is not a reasoned argument, but a half-pragmatic, half poetic response to a unique concatenation of circumstances. The biblical stories are represented in Herder's magnificently imaginative book on *The Spirit of*

[1] *Sturm und Drang*, pp. 302, 584ff., 590ff.

Hebrew Poetry[1] neither as chronicle nor as Divine parables, but as poetry like the poetry of Homer or the Nordic bards, and he has nothing but contempt for the clever rationalists who treat them with an air of infinite superiority as barbaric tales or tissues of childish absurdities.

Everything in its place, and in its time. Christianity could not have appeared earlier or later. Although it was of course in the Books of Almighty God—it had to be called into being when mankind had reached a particular stage of development, and in answer to circumstances and needs. Furthermore, to Herder the Christian religion of the eighteenth century was hardly the same as that of the twelfth, and the creed of Spaniards something very different from the Catholicism of the Slavs. Herder's treatment of the Middle Ages in his first essay in the philosophy of history was an epoch-making event. He calls the period *einzig nur sich selbst gleich*—"solely like itself". It was an age of fermentation of human forces, with strong vital impulses and passions erratically, violently interlocked, and yet of unsurpassed cohesion maintained by the corporate spirit and the code of honour which informed all medieval institutions, chivalry and the monastic orders, guilds and estates general: "An instrument in the hands of Time . . . sustained by the heart and not by the head . . . not with sickly thoughts."[2] Nothing rouses the ire of Herder more than the eighteenth-century addiction to what we would call today digests, encyclopaedias, universal codes of morals, compendia for all men in all countries and of all times, where man is treated as an algebraic cypher, human situations as mathematical equations. All this is *Papierkultur*, and has no relevance to all the untidy reality of existence. Like a member of one set of dons belabouring another set of dons in the second part of the twentieth century, Herder pours scorn upon philosophers presuming to lay down political principles and teach statesmen their business. They believe they can think out an ideal commonwealth and could sit down to put the pieces together. Little do they know that "the formation and development

---

[1] *Sämtliche Werke*, 33 vols., ed. B. Suphan, 1877-1913, Vols. IX-XII.
[2] *Sturm und Drang*, pp. 614-20.

of a nation are never anything else but the work of fate; the result of a thousand contributing causes". There is the unbridgeable gap between the abstract general rule and the recalcitrance of mixed-up things to which the general propositions and systems are meant to apply. Political wisdom—as in Athens—is gained solely in contact with concrete realities and forces, within a narrow and compact, most concrete setting, which no one had deliberately chosen to create, but which evolved, unique, inimitable, unrepeatable. Even good old Montesquieu, although acknowledged as a fine guide, comes in for a trouncing. He tried to subsume all infinitely diversified reality under some three or four headings. The classical unities of French drama, the formalisation of human behaviour, even of wit, those writers who first think out the general moral to be conveyed, and then contrive the story to get it across—all that stands condemned. Herder exalts Shakespeare for not merely throwing all conventions to the winds, but letting primary, turbulent, contradictory passions break forth in situations which are unique, and yet force upon the reader a tremendous human truth. *Herz! Wärme! Blut! Menschheit! Leben!* "Heart! Warmth! Blood! Humanity! Life!"—exclaims Herder, not anaemic abstractions and the lifeless universal benevolence of calculating machines which treat man as a cypher.[1]

III

If every experience is unique, and no concatenation of circumstances is ever the same, then surely no generalisation is at all possible, and nothing can perhaps ever be communicated. *The Ego and His Own* by Max Stirner springs indeed to mind. There is a wonderfully moving passage in Herder's *Auch eine Philosophie*: "No one feels the futility of general characterisation more than I do. You describe a whole people, an age, a whole region—whom have you depicted? You try to sum up the flow of nations and ages ... like the waves of the sea—what have you painted? ... What an inexpressible thing is the peculiarity of a person ... what depths in the character of a nation."[2]

[1] *Sturm und Drang*, pp. 629-631, 637ff., 652ff.   [2] *Ibid.*, p. 600.

As against the rationalist concept of the individual, who partakes in the same universal reason, claims the same rights as all other individuals, and therefore could be fitted into a mechanical whole, Herder raises the idea of *Individualität*, individuality, which is, in the words of his disciple Goethe, ineffable, and ultimately defies any common criteria. Later writers have commented upon the strange fact that in spite of his wonderful talent for *Einfühlung* and his obsessive awareness of the uniqueness of every person, Herder never came to grips with a concrete individual. They tried to explain the riddle by pointing to Herder's own diffuse personality; a bundle of impressions and intuitions, without a firm centre or clear contours.[1]

Whatever the reason, Herder chose to make his powers to bear upon collective entities, and in comparison with his achievements in this field all the eighteenth century earlier philosophising on *esprit de siècle*, *esprit général*, types of social-political systems, and effects of natural conditions on society, appear trivial indeed.

The great paradox of Herder's approach is in the way in which for him human individuality rapidly loses its autonomy of a self-directing person, and assumes the character of something evolved, and of a function of environment.

There are no two identical individuals, as there are no two identical trees. But the study of the tree has to start with the nature of the soil upon which it grows, the rainfall in the area, the access to sun and so on. Once upon this track, Herder is driven on to the confines of materialism, Darwinian evolution and biological-organic nationalism, not to say racialism.

The Germans have claimed for themselves the credit for a Copernican revolution achieved by the age spawned by Herder and Hegel. Envisaged till then as a mechanism, the workings of which could be ascertained with the help of mathematical-physical tests, nature was given by Herder and Goethe a historic dimension as an organism, which evolves, grows, casts out and assimilates elements, and creates its own faculties in the course of the struggle for existence. At a certain stage of the natural evolution man was

[1] Meinecke, *op. cit.*, Vol. II, pp. 404ff., 433.

thrown up. Herder devotes the first part of his four-volume magnum opus *Ideen zur Philosophie der Geschichte der Menschheit*,[1] published in the years from 1784 to 1791, to the history of the universe, regarding it as a prolegomenon to the history of mankind. Herder explicitly rejects the idea of man's descent from the ape. But although he was a *deus ex machina*, man could not have come into being, had not the earlier stages of evolution intervened. The phase of crystals, plants, animals: each phase served as a condition for the other, and was, as it were, absorbed into the other. Human intelligence is in a sense only a vastly refined version of the reactions of plants and animals, and man's reason is no more than a superior replica of the phenomenon of organisation, which may be discovered in every phase of evolution and in every element in nature. It is wrong to describe the relationship between man and nature as that between an active subject and a passive object. It would be no less wrong, however, to see man as just a passive extension of nature or a creature merely obeying natural impulses. Nature acts upon man, but man acts upon nature, which from the point of view of man has meaning only insofar as it impinges upon man and is acted upon by man. Nature evolves under the impact of man's endeavours, and man changes with the change of environment, which he has to a large extent himself effected. The relationship between man and nature is thus dialectical: both are in a state of evolution, and shape each other all the time. Truth is in a state of flux. Everything is fluid. Herder, the theologian, has considerable difficulty with the place of man in nature. He gives at times the impression of accepting the religious idea of a Divine fiat, which brought the unique soul- and reason-endowed creature, man, into being. Yet he devotes all his energies to proving man's uniqueness to be naturally evolved. What put first man apart from all animals was his erect posture. That left his hands free to shape tools, a faculty all unique to man. The erect posture opened to man a widely extended field of vision, in comparison with the narrow track of the animal. It deprived him of the unerring

[1] *Sämtliche Werke, op. cit.*, Vols. XIII-XIV. Use was also made of the *Ideen*, ed. E. Kühnemann, constituting Vols. IV-V of *Herders Werke*, Stuttgart, *ca.* 1890.

instinct of the animal but compelled him to employ reason and make choices. Moreover it brought to bear a great multitude and diversity of impressions, while the animal on all fours remained earthbound by its urgent animal needs. The multitude of impressions, and the need to learn engendered the unique gift of man, speech. In his little work of genius, *On the Origins of Language* of 1772,[1] Herder uncompromisingly rejects the old theories of speech as a Divine ready-made gift, it having pleased God to endow man with reason made articulate and fully organised. The origins of speech are to be sought in the exclamations which were at first hardly more than physical reflexes, with which primitive man responded to the sight or sound of objects, in fear, pleasure, wonderment, or simply in obedience to the instinct of imitation. When man saw the sheep for a second or third time and, identifying it as the same, greeted it with the ejaculation which imitated the noise made by sheep, a name was born, ready to be communicated to others. Language became the repository of the experience of the tribe, in a sense the mirror of its landscape, in another sense the unique mode of the tribe's grappling with nature.

There are no two identical languages. Language is not a contrivance of reason deliberating, but something like a force breaking through. The closer to nature, the richer, more limpid, warmer the language, abounding in metaphor, colour, imagery, idiom, proverb, and it is then truly unique. The more logicised and abstract a language becomes, the less idiomatic, the poorer and more lifeless, lacking the distinct flavour of genuine, authentic experience.

Natural instinctive spontaneity produces thus a cohesive whole that is unique. And it is not the instinct of the individual man, but of the group. The tribe, the nation on the one hand created the language, and on the other hand are shaped by it. The individual derives his reason from his language, in other words his reality from the race, tribe, the nation. The nation is not a heap of stones, but a living organism and a physico-spiritual personality. Herder was blissfully unaware, and remained so to the end, that he was forging

[1] *Sturm und Drang, op. cit.*, pp. 399-506.

the most dangerous dynamite of modern times. Under the stress of discovery Herder accords to the nation an all-determining significance. No two nations can ever be compared. Each nation is self-sufficient, like a circle with a centre of happiness, a principle of existence that is all its own. Herder goes on to praise nations for their insensitivity to the values, we may say the music, of other nations, and he does not shrink from approving mutual dislike and reciprocal contempt among nations. You call it "prejudice" (*Vorurteil*), "*eingeschränkter Nationalismus!*"—"narrow nationalism". Prejudice is a good thing, "in its own time: it bestows happiness". A prejudice-ridden nation is of a piece, wholesome, sure in its instincts, overflowing with authentic original creativeness. Receptivity to alien ideas and aspirations is "a disease, a flatulence and an unhealthy saturation foreboding approaching death." Some 150 years later, men took these teachings for an encouragement to burn books and pictures by artists of alien extraction or *Weltanschauung*, although Herder himself was really no more than actuated by a neurotic need for authenticity and stability. Only in the second place was he concerned with discovering a collective common denominator other than the oppressively inhibiting institutions of class, Church, dynastic State. Insofar as he was consciously nationalistic in the modern sense of the word, Herder's interest was predominantly spiritual-aesthetic: he was fighting the cultural and literary predominance of France, and politics hardly entered into the problem.

But once the unique nation had been proclaimed the most decisive phenomenon in human history, there was no escape from this question: if every nation is absolutely unique, how is a universal history of mankind possible?

Is it possible—asks Herder in the closing part of his essay on the philosophy of history—for all that to be "without a goal (*Zweck*) and with no purpose (*Absicht*)"? There must be some providential design at the back of it all.

At the moment Herder is still full of aversion for both the tidy schemata of optimistic rationalism and the sterile supercilious pessimism of a Voltaire dismissing history as a tissue of evils and absurdities. He is above all awe-struck at the thought of the tortuous ways of Time. "The march of Providence passes to its goal over millions of corpses." The vast changes effected by the great doers leave behind them a trail of ruin and misery, and far less obvious an increase in human happiness. The seemingly beneficial reforms are carried out to the accompaniment of so much that is positively evil, cruel and mean.

"Fate works change" through great spirits who "cannot be measured with the yardstick of average souls". These "exceptions of a higher order" through whom "almost everything remarkable in the world takes place" are like comets: they descend to the lowest pit in order to soar out of sight. They are not conscious agents at all. They are instruments of history, like the nations which "gang up to take their place in the workshop of history, without knowing whence and where. Fate summons them to their business in the vineyard."

Like Luther, for instance, they are agents of tremendous revolutions, without ever having intended to be. And there had been Luthers before Luther, but they fizzled out. The age was not yet ready for one. Just as there is no predictable relationship between design and result, so there is little connection between merit and effectiveness. Vast preparations ensue in nothing. Tiny beginnings, like the needle of the compass, produce incalculable transformations. And a little cavity in the skull at the dawn of time may determine the nature of a civilisation for millennia. So man is only a mouse upon a vast wheel, scurrying backwards and forwards upon it, while he thinks he is making free decisions. "I am nothing, the whole is everything", exclaims Herder.[1]

Instead of feeling crushed by his own insignificance, "I who am hardly a small letter in . . . the great Book of God that spans worlds and ages . . . and can see no more than three letters in it", Herder experiences a deep sense of elation. He is carried by that jubilant feeling, as Meinecke rightly says lost to us, of being part of a solemn, Divine fulfilment. Herder had assimilated in a way all his own the teachings of Neo-platonism, Spinoza, Leibniz and Shaftesbury about a

[1] *Sturm und Drang op. cit.*, pp. 607, 647, 651, 668-70.

God unfolding through time and space, entering into every particle of reality and turning it into an aspect of the great Totality, with everything impelled to fulfil itself, and to evolve from matter into force. Everything is unique, and all partake in one grand universal design.

IV

In the *Ideen zur Philosophie der Geschichte der Menschheit* Herder set out to show upon an enormous canvas the uniqueness of every nation and age, and place it into the context of the grand design of the whole—as Hegelian an undertaking as the one undertaken by the great systematiser himself a generation later.

Marvellous as are Herder's insights into what makes a given civilisation tick, and how its various aspects are interconnected; perceptive as is his comparison of the ages of the world and of single nations in it to the ages of man; imaginative as is his vision of the one great Chain of Being, in which one nation takes up where another had left off, with the seed having wandered a long way and a long while, before giving new birth—in the end the postulate of the oneness of Mankind, which Herder could never give up, leads him, especially in his last writings, to a complete repudiation of the early revolutionary anti-rationalist tenets, and to the full espousal of the position of his first opponents, till we think we are reading not Herder, but Condorcet.

The reason for the volte-face was, as we shall still see, the insoluble nature of the dichotomy itself, as well as a fundamental ambivalence in Herder's make-up, an ambivalence which has dominated modern German history.

Herder's revised doctrine is formulated in the famous fifteenth book of the *Ideen*, and is elaborated with endless repetitions in the *Briefe zur Beförderung der Humanität* and *Adrastea*,[1] which appeared in the last decade of the eighteenth century and in the first few years of the nineteenth century.

The purposeful harmony prevailing in nature must have

---

[1] *Sämtliche Werke, op. cit.*, Vols. XVII–XVIII, XXIII–XXIV.

its replica in a natural social order, otherwise the God who first implanted in man the vision of and the hope for a harmonious social order, and then abandoned him to vagaries and evil, would be either impotent or cruel. The existence of the natural order is proved by reason and is attested by all history, with the precision of mathematical truths. It is based upon an irreversible correlation between reason, equity, and happiness. Reasonable conduct is the condition of purposeful organisation, and in a well-organised society everyone receives what is due to him, and while contributing dutifully to the well-being of others, reaps private happiness and contentment. There is a natural balance of society, which may be and is occasionally disturbed, but which is sooner or later redressed. The punishment for upsetting this rational order is pain-inflicting disorder, which in turn becomes a lesson and stimulus for self-improvement. For every excess brings upon itself sooner or later its nemesis. A passion propels men violently, an opposite one goes into action, till the pendulum returns to the centre. Progress is achieved precisely through one generation reacting against its predecessors.

The natural order is obeyed "not through the will of a sovereign, or the persuasive power of tradition, but through natural laws on which the essence of man reposes". Through the possession of reason all men share the same humanity, and there is wonderful agreement among the noblest minds of all civilisations and nations on the fundamental tenets of rational morality, from Socrates to Confucius, Plato, Cicero and Zoroaster. By the light of reason and equity the troglodyte or Negro would be enabled to obtain a polity no less advanced than the polished Greeks.

That there are dissimilar and unequal achievements among nations is part of the grand design whereby a single nation or age is called upon to evolve a maximum of a certain potentiality. The maxima of the various entities fall sooner or later into meaningful collective patterns and symmetries.

Humanität, humanity, is the substance and the goal of history. It is a very vague term best rendered as rational benevolence, resulting in harmony and concord. Like Adam Smith, and in later days Saint-Simon and Auguste Comte, Herder was heartened by the conviction that discord and wars were gradually giving way to peaceful and mutually profitable intercourse in trade and commerce. The malignant poisons would all be turned into beneficial forces, just as fire and powder had been. To use somewhat anachronistic language, Herder felt confident that military civilisation was about to be replaced by an industrial society. The inventors pursue their individual curiosity, and have no conception of what will arise from their discoveries, but such is "the general connection of things that no attempt, no discovery, can be made in vain . . . (and) every good employment of the human understanding necessarily must and will, at some time or other, promote humanity."

The former poet of the glory of the Middle Ages, who had ridiculed the detractors of that age of chivalry and sincerity, now defies "monks, sybarites, and tyrants . . . it is no longer in their power, to bring back the night of the Middle Ages". And in the confident hope that men have learned the rational calculus, he even looks forward to a time when we shall be able to prophecy the future.

This rationalist optimism inevitably destroys the historian in Herder. Not only does he turn moralist, drawing lessons, and unconsciously looking for samples and proofs for his preconceived thesis, he cannot help dismissing recalcitrant irrationality, inexplicable evil, the triumph of violence as insignificant, temporary aberrations, nonsense, non-being.

Humanitarian individualism silences Herder's deep awareness of the reality of collective entities, since he now sees only mankind and individual men as possessors of reason. The newly won rationalist optimism closes his mind to any dichotomy of collective destiny and private happiness, reason of State and individual morality. "Nature does not take account of sovereigns and states, but of the welfare of man", because laws and governments exist only for the individual's "more pleasing and freer enjoyment of life, undisturbed by others".[1]

[1] *Ideen* (Kühnemann), pp. 608, 615-18ff., 628ff., 636, 640.

It is one of the ironies of history that Herder evolved this brand of extreme atomistic utilitarianism in the course of his polemic against Kant of all people. Both protagonists were driven by injured feelings to overstate their respective cases. Herder had been deeply hurt by Kant's contemptuous review of his *magnum opus*, in which the Koenigsberg philosopher advised the morbidly sensitive younger man to write poetry instead of engaging in scientific speculation; whereupon Herder brought upon himself a measure of poetic justice by writing a review of the *Kritik der reinen Vernunft*, after merely —as he told a friend—"running through it": some run! Kant restated in a secularised form the medieval theory of the dual character of the State, as a punishment for falling away from the precepts of pure morality and as an instrument for man's re-education—with the help of coercive curbs upon men engaged in strife—towards pure autonomous morality. As might have been expected of a thinker who would never equate human dignity, based upon unconditional fulfilment of duty, with felicity or bliss, Kant drew a sharp distinction between the perfection of the species and the happiness of the individual.

Herder, who had no political experience, and saw only big despots or petty tyrants, primitive economic conditions and simple relationships around him, failed to acknowledge in the modern State anything other than a mechanical contrivance imposed upon men by usurpers. It was not an organic entity to him at all. International relations, especially war and conflict, appeared to Herder as just a game engaged in by ambitious intriguers. On the very eve of a period of violent national conflicts and wars, to the unleashing of which he was destined to make no mean contribution, Herder, the prophet of national uniqueness, rejoices in the thought that perfection in the techniques and arts of war would soon put an end to all national wars. Old heroics no longer being possible, and men having become too enlightened for nationalist pride, and nationalist hatred—both according to Herder signs of the most abominable barbarism—war would be left to the handful of professionals. In the midst of the total indifference, or hostility of the masses, the war lords would soon get tired of their game.[1]

That every nation should have a state of its own Herder considered most desirable, but it would not have occurred to him to incite subject races to revolt or to proclaim a crusade for the dismemberment of multi-racial empires. He considered the latter monsters, destined in the course of time to fall apart because of indigestion. So incomprehensible to Herder was the phenomenon of imperial conquest that he blessed the confusion of the Tower of Babel: the multiplicity of languages was surely a barrier to conquest of nation by nation. And no latter day opponent of colonialism could have equalled Herder's wrathful denunciation of imperialism. The Roman Empire and medieval papacy stand condemned for having imposed a single language upon all dependencies. Not only was thereby authentic native creativeness stifled. The cleavage between Latin-speaking upper classes and the vernacular-speaking lower orders split nations into hostile social classes and prevented the emergence of nations.

Nothing is more revealing for the absence of any self-reliant, self-assertive German nationalism than the ode which young Herder addressed to Czar Peter III, calling him the modern Cyrus for having saved Prussia from extinction by suddenly changing sides in the Seven Years War: a very Judaic, pre-Israeli sentiment—not by its own exertions will the nation be saved, but by an alien Saviour!

Herder felt no inconsistency in being a proud patriotic citizen of semi-republican Riga ("*unter russischem Schatten beinahe Genf*") in sincerely professing passionate loyalty to the Russian Czarina, in fighting for the purification of the German language from foreign ingredients and the intellectual life of Germany from French influence, and in collaborating in a plan to set up an all-German Academy of Sciences and Letters as a substitute for a national all-German Parliament. It was not German life or German philosophy

[1] *Sämtliche Werke*, Vol. XIII, pp. 322, 476. Yet under the impact of the French Revolution Herder gives vent to a feeling of awed admiration for a "nation's madness . . . a frightening word. Something that has once struck roots in a nation, that a nation has come to know and to value; how could it not be true (*Wahrheit sein*)? Who can doubt that?"—quoted in Meinecke, Vol. II, p. 473.

that inspired Herder's conception of a nation. The Herderian idea of national uniqueness was born in him in a flash when he attended one night a semi-pagan equinoctial festival in a Latvian village, celebrated with dance, song and ballad. He stood awe-stricken before the same Latvian serfs, against the relaxation of whose serfdom his German baron friends had petitioned the Russian Government as late as 1765 on the ground that the existing serfdom "was not a result of barbarism, but was due to the natural disposition of the Latvian-Estonian nation, and may well coexist with humanitarian principles". In other words, that they were born to be slaves, and the Germans were destined to be their masters. "But they are like cattle"—one can almost hear the Teutonic Knights making an innocent matter-of-fact statement. It is no mean paradox that the anti-German nationalism of the Slavonic peoples should owe so much to Herder. In the spirit of Herder and at his behest Slav nationalisms started as movements for salvaging folkloristic remnants of a tribal past in danger of obliteration.

On the philosophical plane Herder's change of view marked a victory of ethical values over the aesthetic approach and a vindication of the superiority of reason over nature. It implied thus the subordination of impulse to free resolve. We have to return for a while to the psychological aspect of Herder's *Odyssey*.

Earlier on we tried to explain Herder's obsessive preoccupation with authenticity and instinctive certainty by his perplexed inability to cope with life that had lost stability. It was not given to Herder to win self-assurance or effect a firm commitment. In that treacherous twilight that is—he says—worse than total darkness, he fell back upon the idea of a rational order.

Herder, as we saw, had an insatiable craving for power, but could muster no strength. Too timid and too weak to fight, he evolved the comforting and protective vision of universal concord and harmony. And so in spite of his strong awareness of the material substratum of every civilisation, and in spite of his fine insights into the role of irrational passion and recalcitrant forces in history, Herder's great History became as the Odyssey of mankind's soul, a survey of patterns of thought, feeling and behaviour, rather than the drama of institutionalised values interlocked in bitter strife.

In this failure to understand the phenomenon of power, and in this inability to face the tragedy of demoniacal compulsion and insoluble conflict, Herder is a true son of the Enlightenment.

In a good Herderian fashion we tried at the beginning of our quest to see Herder grow out of the soil of mid-eighteenth-century Germany. It is time now to try to see the tree growing up in the midst of the German forest, and to throw a glance at the fate of the seed sown upon the German, indeed European, soil by Herder.

V

How are we to explain the evolution of *Sturm und Drang* iconoclastic, anarchical individualism into that ultra-conservative and ultra-reactionary cult of feudal-clerical medievalism and Divine right monarchy? What caused the romantic religion of spontaneity to make way for the worship of the power of the State?

One is familiar with extraordinary vagaries of the author of the *Blaue Blume*, that poem of *Sehnsucht*, nostalgia, without bounds and without object or form. In his political writings Novalis calls himself often on the same page a republican monarchist and a royalist republican, extols the glory of medieval tradition and sounds the clarion call of revolution, yearns for Christian universalism and sings the praise of Teutonic originality.[1]

This *Polarität*, this playing with contradictions has been described by historians of German romanticism as a way of obtaining harmony: one type of onesidedness is redeemed by another type of onesidedness.[2] The root of the matter is really a neurosis of choice.

While Novalis and the other romantics were swaying in

---

[1] Oskar Walzel: *Deutsche Romantik*, 5th edn., Leipzig 1923.
[2] Henri Brunschwig: *La Crise de l'Etat Prussien à la fin du XVIIIe siècle et la Genèse de la mentalité romantique*, Paris 1947.

all directions, German states and populations were being shuffled and reshuffled by an alien master, and her centuries-old laws and institutions were being changed by the stroke of his pen. A highly centralised State machine and a reputedly invincible army collapsed under the first blow administered by a resourceful enemy. Years before, the disappearance of their prime mover, Frederick the Great, had left a leaderless population bewildered and unprepared to fend for itself. As a result a wave of irrationalism swept Prussia, giving rise to occultism, mesmerism and on a higher plane mystical and romantic moods. The nostalgia for pristine innocence and perfection won such dominance because reality was no longer experienced as natural and self-evident.

As a *Kulturnation*, the Germans sought an anchor in a unique spiritual originality, with at first no thought of political power and political effectiveness. Spirit and power were entirely dissociated.

The French Revolution and Napoleon revealed what a mighty force ideas might become, while the nation of poets and thinkers proved itself impotent, and indeed characterless under the sway of France.

It was under the impact of these traumatic events that original uniqueness came to be seen by the Germans as a quantum of force. This discovery was at a much later date defined in terrifyingly defiant words by Nietzsche: "to expect that strength will not manifest itself as strength, as the desire to overcome, to appropriate, to have enemies, obstacles, and triumphs, is every bit as absurd as to expect that weakness will manifest itself as strength. A quantum of strength is equivalent to a quantum of urge, will, activity."

The revolutionary period and Napoleon taught the Germans that a nation can assert itself only as a State. The State was thus invested with the dignity of embodying a unique principle of existence, and was called upon to realise it in a way all its own, with no regard to abstract and universal standards. Herder treated the individual as one aspect of an organic nation. This view was revised to mean the subordination of the individual to the State, its particular ethos and destiny.

The State and the great doers of history were absolved from the moral restraints binding ordinary flesh and blood after the French Revolution and Napoleon had so signally proved how tortuous were the ways of history, and how inseparable were historical change and progress from the catalystic action of violent passions.

These discoveries were immediately erected into dogma, almost a religion. The authentic *Volksgeist* embodied in the State became a god, because it was not the kind of real and cherished possession that the British Constitution was to Burke. The Machiavellian philosophy was assimilated into the conception of the truly German State: Herder's struggle for an authentic German literature, free from the tyranny of French classicism, was transformed into a Teutonic revolt against the denationalising influence of the allegedly French ideology of natural law.

All these reinterpretations of Herder received a truly magnificent systematic elaboration in Hegel. Hegel was only one in the long string of German thinkers and historians from Frederick the Great to Friedrich Meinecke and Gerhard Ritter who could never shake off the fascination of the great Florentine thinker.

It would be an over-simplification to claim that this philosophy gained exclusive dominance in Germany, and was alone responsible for the terrible self-assertion of racial uniqueness. The truth is more subtle than that.

In their majority the German thinkers and writers were no more able to tear themselves away from the natural law tradition and the idea of the unity of mankind than was Herder. The opposite philosophy however gained a tremendous hold on them, enjoying the prestige both of a distinctly German national *Weltanschauung*, and a creed tested by history.

This is why German historiography, even in the case of the most liberal exponents, has been so preoccupied, half-lovingly, half-guiltily, with *"Macht"*, *"Wucht"*, *"Gewalt"*, *"Kraft"*, *"Leidenschaft"*, from Ranke's *"Grosse Mächte"* to Gerhard Ritter's *"Dämonie der Macht"*, and with the problem of the exceptional man, the demoniacal hero, the great doer, a Frederick the Great or Bismarck, to whom no natural law or ordinary moral criteria must be applied. These would never be treated by German historians with the irony which English historians, with all their affectionate respect and admiration, reserve for a Gladstone or Disraeli.

One is hard put to decide when reading German historians whether they deplore all this or are awe-stricken by the unfathomable, deep mystery of it. In fact, the historians themselves would be unable to give an unequivocal answer. A very great and professedly liberal historian like Meinecke devoted the greater part of a long life to the victory of the idea of the *Nationalstaat* which is a law unto itself, owes no allegiance to natural law, and shares no common plane with other States, over the traditions and habits of thought rooted in natural law philosophy and *Weltbürgertum* universalism. So fascinated was he by the spectacle of powers driven by demoniacal compulsions and interlocked in mortal combat that the reader will search in vain for the word *Arbeiter* or the social question in his major works. He had no mind and no time for such trivialities, except in his publicistic writings.

When the *Macht* philosophy appeared to score triumphs, the inner resistance of German intellectuals would be completely undermined, and they would be overwhelmed by a feeling of deep awe. When the going was bad, they would tear their hair in an orgy of remorse. On the morrow of 1945, Meinecke wrote *The German Catastrophe*, a most powerful indictment; but in 1941, when the going was very good indeed, his essay on Machiavelli was published in a de luxe edition, although paper must have been short in Germany. Success had resolved all doubts, power had proved its justification. When in doubt, we all look for omens. What more clinching proof than *fait accompli*? *Weltgeschichte ist Weltgericht*. The trouble is that it is for ever an unfinished story. One would have thought that the awareness of ceaseless change and of infinite diversity would engender a humbly, if not a nihilistically, resigned acceptance of historicist relativism. With their strange and dangerous hankering for the absolute, and their humourless habit of seeing things more than double their size, the Germans, like the Marxists incidentally, turned the relative into a horrible, compelling absolute. The cultivation of national folklore ended in murderous race theory. Strange, exciting and terrifying are the adventures of ideas.

The dichotomy of the unique and the universal has been a basic fact of the human situation for a long time. While it has had a most fructifying effect on such disciplines as history, sociology and the arts, it has been eating away at the very foundations of our self-assurance, and—as we all know so well—has also unleashed orgies of unprecedented destruction. Not only is the dilemma still defying solution on the intellectual plane; it has now become, with races and civilisations pitted against each other, a matter of life and death.

We cannot ignore the fact of uniqueness evolved in time. We dare not do without the assurance of universality grounded in the timeless.

4

Mission and Testimony

The universal significance of modern anti-semitism

I

"**D**EADLY JEWISH POISON". These are the very last words in Hitler's testament. "National Socialism deserves eternal gratitude for having eliminated the Jews from Germany and Central Europe." "It is not true that I or any one else in Germany wanted war in 1939." "The people who wanted a war and engineered it were international politicians of Jewish extraction or those who worked on behalf of Jewish interests." . . . "That race—Jewry—were the criminals responsible for this murderous struggle."[1]

Hitler's will was written against the background of a ghostly drama, the horrors of which surpassed the apocalyptic visions of Dante's Inferno, and were more terrible than the *Götterdämmerung* which Wagner's imagination had conjured up. The city of Berlin was no more than a heap of burning rubble. Soldiers of the Red Army were venting upon it the fury and the thirst for revenge which had accumulated in their breasts over the years. In the Führer's bunker final preparations were being made for the grand suicide. Hitler no longer needed the Jews to undermine the resistance of his opponents at home and abroad whom he wanted to destroy. Nothing could have saved him at that stage. Hitler's raving against the Jews can in no way be dismissed as mere political opportunism or deliberate demagogy.

[1] H. R. Trevor-Roper: *The Testament of Adolf Hitler*, London 1961, pp. 109, 105.

On one side, the groaning of the mighty war machines of vast empires interlocked in mortal combat; an Armageddon struggle of Gog and Magog for world mastery. On the other side, the dust and ashes of millions of defenceless Jews, who after having been tortured beyond endurance, humiliated as no humans have ever been, were put to death with all the refinements of modern science. If such a lack of proportion as demonstrated in Hitler's testament is a token of madness, what is the secret behind the success of that possessed demon who cast an evil spell over one of the most developed and advanced countries in the world, conquered the whole of Europe and came to the threshold of world conquest?

How can this horrific tale fail to drive one to a despairingly nihilistic contempt for those who seek some logic in the maze of happenings that we call history?

Some years ago *The Observer* conducted an enquiry among a number of writers and artists on the relationship between art and social reality. One of the questions was concerned with the failure of the post-war artist to give adequate expression to the Jewish tragedy during World War II. Among those interviewed were two Jews, Arthur Miller and Lionel Trilling. Their answers to this particular question were not given, perhaps because the interviewer thought it would be better not to put it to them so as to spare them embarrassment. But three answers by non-Jewish writers are worth quoting.

Mr. Graham Greene confined himself to quoting a woman, with whom he had spoken recently on a flight, who had told him that she was convinced that all the stories about the destruction of European Jewry were mere propaganda. "Isn't it awful", Mr. Graham Greene commented, "that there are still people like that about?" The playwright, artist and film producer, M. Jean Cocteau, gave a truly shocking answer. To him the death of six million Jews had no general significance. It was just an act of revenge committed by a particular private individual—Hitler—who wanted to avenge himself on the Jews because they had refused to buy his pictures. M. Cocteau was apparently blissfully unaware of the enormous insult that he was throwing at the Jewish people. By contrast, the reply given by the great French Catholic author, François Mauriac, touches the very depths of one's feelings. Since the holocaust in Europe, he said, nothing in the world would ever be the same as before, for the world had been shaken to its very foundations.

Jewish nationalism and racist anti-semitism both attribute great significance to the Jewish phenomenon, although they do so of course from opposed viewpoints. While recognising the importance of the Jewish contribution, the liberals are reluctant to single out the Jews for special attention. The Jewish issue can in their view be summed up in terms of tolerance or intolerance, in the context of the struggle between liberty and tyranny. During the war a good old liberal confided to me that he was worried about the way the Jews tended to isolate their own problems. This, he feared, was indirectly a help to Hitler, and he wanted the Jews "to be like all the rest of us".

Racial anti-semites like Houston Stewart Chamberlain dubbed the nineteenth century "the Jewish century". They considered the entry of the Jews into the public life of Europe, following their emancipation, a crucial event in world history. To the liberals the achievement of equality for Jews was just another milestone on the road of human progress in general. The enemies of the Jewish people declared the destruction of the Jews a turning-point in history, but in the eyes of the liberals the holocaust was seen as an unfortunate, but only temporary, relapse into intolerance. The intentions of the liberals are good. But in one sense their attitude is at best superficial, and at worst somewhat offensive to Judaism. The majesty attached to a unique fate is impaired and the awesome grandeur of an apocalyptic tragedy is wholly missed.

The optimistic belief in man's reasonableness and in the logic of history which characterises the believers in progress boggles at the notion of fate, for man is supposed to be endowed with the power of controlling the course of events and shaping his own environment. It is only natural that this belief should make its adherents oblivious to demoniacal forces and cause them to recoil from deep insoluble contradictions. Eternal curses, incurable diseases, unfathomable and irreparable tragedies have no place in the scheme of universal progress. Evil is only seen as the absence of goodness, and there is no place for a kingdom of Satan that is always at war with the kingdom of God.

II

The intention of these pages is to try to show that the fate of the Jews during the last 200 years is indissolubly connected with issues which form the very core of the condition of modern man. Jews played so important a role in modern history, not because they had a mission to carry out (though this aspect should not be belittled), but because it was their fate to serve as a testimony, as a living witness, a touchstone, a whipping block and symbol—all in one.

The whole gamut of relations between Jews and Gentiles calls for an examination in terms of a relationship between stimulus and response, where the reacting party is conditioned to experience the way in which the other side impinges upon it as an acute irritant. The intensity of the reaction is determined more by the condition of the reacting party than by the nature of the stimulus. The latent tension between the two was in the past punctuated by waves of persecution culminating in bloody outbreaks, but it was for most of the time held in check by the institutionalised inequalities of a society based on status on the one hand and the firm setting of belief, tradition and custom on the other. The new society based on contract rendered the Jewish irritant ubiquitous, while the collapse of traditional forms and spiritual certainties shook the balance of the modern world to its foundations. The arrival of the Jews was associated, indeed identified in very many minds with the arrival of the evils besetting modern bewildered man and a world adrift. The general malaise was fastened by them upon the Jewish irritant.

If the French Revolution may be considered as the beginning of an era that has not yet come to an end, we can view the 1880's as the beginning of a historical wave—with anti-semitism as one of its motive forces—which may for all we know not yet have been brought to a halt in 1945. Jewish emancipation in the French Revolution was an off-shoot of the triumph of rationalism and the idea of the rights of man. More than that, it sealed the complete victory of these values, since the Jews were a marginal case. The anti-semitic rage that boiled up in Europe eighty years ago was not a by-product, but the point of departure and focus of a vast political and ideological movement. From its Archimedean point of anti-semitism that movement was driven on to repudiate everything affirmed by humanist rationalism, and indeed everything taught by its parent, Christianity.

Between the tendency for unity and the stubborn fact of peculiarity, history steers its course. The postulate of unity, on the basis of the oneness of God, the oneness of reason, the brotherhood of men, natural law and the moral values that are held to be eternal and universal, is all the time thwarted by those stubborn facts which can give no other ground or justification for their existence than that they are there and will not budge—the uniqueness of every man, the uniqueness of every human situation, the peculiarity of a national character and tradition, race, the irreducible facts of geography and climate, the particularity of the particular interest; in brief, recalcitrant, obtuse, exasperating; if one likes, unreasonable and irrational forces. The unique refuses to be swamped and swallowed up by the universal. It sticks out as a hurdle, an obstacle, an immovable wall.

The tragic paradox of the Jews in modern times has been the fact that their existence and success have been dependent upon the triumph of the idea of oneness as represented by liberal democracy and socialism, while the very phenomenon of Jewry is an unparalleled demonstration of the enormous power of the element of uniqueness. The Jews did not want and could not escape the fact of their uniqueness, the Gentiles would not and could not be made oblivious of it.

The liberal State which accorded full rights to its Jewish citizens on the same basis as to all others, including freedom of economic pursuit, a share in the running of the nation's affairs, took its stand on the theory of a social contract concluded between men of reason. Racial origin, religious affiliation, social class, and all those deep but elusive differences, rooted in and exemplified by habit and custom, reflex and prejudice, instinct and frame of mind, disposition and manner of reasoning, which separate and isolate men, were considered irrelevant, when compared with the forces of conscious deliberating reason. On the other hand, the texture of the liberal State was limited from its very inception to a legal framework. Outside it, the citizen was free to follow his own judgement. Such a régime was ideal for the Jews: but to their misfortune it never even came into being. Liberalism came to the fore partnered by nationalism. The universalist principle of common citizenship replaced the feudal structure based upon class and caste distinctions, but the new national brotherhood strove after homogeneity which would mark it off from all the other national communities.

From the very day when the nation-State appeared on the scene of history it began—as does every vital institution—to develop an ethos of its own by trying to enrich and deepen its own contents. Every nation went out of its way to stress its own uniqueness based on blood, common memories, common symbols of a remote past in which the Jews had no share and which very often only served to remind them of past persecution, and to emphasise their status as aliens. Already during the honeymoon of emancipation after the victory of the French Revolution, the slogan was coined: "Everything for the Jews as individuals, but nothing for them as a nation." And if the Jews were unfortunate enough to be irrevocably committed to the preservation of a national identity and their historic uniqueness, they would have to be expelled, for there was no place for a State within a State. Napoleon did not merely compel the Jews to forget Zion and the Messiah who, the Jews believed, would some day come to redeem Israel. He went further, planning to force the Jews to intermarry with Gentiles "so as to dilute their blood".

In Western Europe there were ancient nation-States with developed economies, a balanced social structure, a rich and varied cultural heritage, and small Jewish communities. The Jews soon abandoned their separate language, became assimilated to the culture of the environment, and discarded most of those religious observances which served to separate them from their neighbours. They still nevertheless tended to congregate in certain districts and neighbourhoods and to associate with fellow-Jews, maintaining only loose contacts with the non-Jewish population that surrounded them. Moreover, even those families that had converted to another faith often continued to maintain their social connections with one another and in some cases would only intermarry among themselves. In some countries there grew up a literature written by Jews, the subject matter of which was not always specifically Jewish, but the readers of which were nearly all Jews. Many Gentiles became "Judaised" through frequenting the salons of the rich or intellectually eminent Jews. Yet, ease, directness, genuine, unforced intimacy between Jew and Gentile was rare. "After 6 p.m. I don't have any Christian friends", used to say an American Jewish millionaire who was also a noted Jewish communal leader a generation ago. The Gentile colleagues of a Jew who held a very senior post as a minister in several governments in one of the Western European countries would accept invitations to dine at his house, but they would not bring their wives. They were prepared to talk "business" but not to pass the time pleasantly in that relaxed atmosphere of intimate personal friendship. "You are the first and the only non-Jew with whom I feel absolutely no tension whatever," was the astounding and tragic confession made to a Gentile friend, after decades of close friendship, by a Jew who had spent his life in the very centre of the political and intellectual life of his country.

Genuine intimacy is not something that comes easily even to members of the same race, the same culture and the same milieu. How much more difficult it must be for people of different races, bred on different traditions. It is well known that the majority of Englishmen prefer the company of Germans to that of Frenchmen, although Britain and France have been allies for more than sixty years, whereas Britain and Germany have fought one another in two bloody wars within living memory. The real test of the unconscious, and therefore deeper and more decisive, thoughts of a people can be found in its folklore and its proverbs. In the dictionaries of every European language we find the word "Jew" defined as synonymous with thief, cheat and usurer. Even a verb has been coined from that noun. The Jews repaid in kind.

Many Jews became of course totally assimilated and disappeared from the fold without a trace. Many others assumed the colour of their surroundings so that they lost almost all distinctness in the eyes of their Gentile neighbours. The process of assimilation was continuously disturbed by waves of Jewish migrants from the Eastern-European pale. Special circumstances prevailing for centuries in that part of the world had kept the latter apart as a separate entity, with its own religion and culture, special social functions and self-governing institutions. A rising national-social ferment was sending them now in mounting waves westwards. Their arrival in the West infused new blood and new vigour into the enfeebled veins of the local Jewish communities, while the image of the alien Eastern Jew was transferred in the minds of many Gentiles to all Jews, including the assimilated or half-assimilated ones. It is enough to recall the description in *Mein Kampf* of Hitler's first encounter in the streets of Vienna with an Eastern-European Jew with a long beard, sidelocks, caftan and so on. Earlier contact with "assimilated" Jews had left no special impression upon him, he assures his readers.[1]

III

The murderous assault did not come from the side of the conservative, feudal and clerical forces which were opposed to equal rights for Jews because the "arrival" of the Jews was in their eyes a symbol of a libertarian repudiation of all traditional values, the overthrow of hierarchical order and the end of the Christian State as it had existed for centuries. Nor did it come from those who in the name of national homogeneity demand that the Jews should become totally assimilated.

The attack came from men who started as devotees of the

[1] Adolf Hitler: *Mein Kampf*, Munich 1943, pp. 59ff.

democratic ideals, but incensed by the Jewish phenomenon were swept from a refusal to respect human dignity in the Jew to a denial of the very idea of human rights based on the conception of human equality. Nothing betokened this shift more strikingly than the brochure *The Jews and Music* which Richard Wagner published in 1850, only two years after the composer's fight on the barricades of Dresden at the side of the arch-revolutionary and anarchist Michael Bakunin.

"There will never be true liberty for humanity so long as there are still oppressed men left anywhere in the world, however few and far between they happen to be," the young Wagner wrote. In his discourse on *The Jews and Music*[2] so soon after, Wagner (made to feel uncomfortable by the Jewish composer Meyerbeer) dwells on the contradiction between reason that teaches men to view the Jews as human beings like all other humans—in this case like all other Germans—and the stubborn fact that the actual Jews whom he saw around him were in his eyes still German-speaking Orientals, despite the 2,000 years they had been living in Germany. This led the composer to cogitate on what was more real: the abstract idea, pure reason, postulating the unity of mankind, or the concrete fact of group peculiarity? the unity of the human species, or racial uniqueness? What should be, or what is? Humanism was teaching men to treat the Jews in a spirit of tolerance and respect for the human personality, for all men were created in the image of God, but a primeval and spontaneous instinct made them hated and shunned. When was a man truest to himself, when engaging in ratiocination or when obeying the voice of blood? Which had a higher claim to be the truth—the logical syllogism or the intuitive response?

The implication of these questions, once posed, reached out far beyond the subject of the Jews. The very nerve centre of rationalism and indeed Christianity itself was attacked here. The very concept of a universal natural law came under fire. The individual as a creature of a reason common to all men was no longer the primary element and most important fact, as he had been for millennia. The collective group of the

[1] Richard Wagner: *Das Judentum in der Musik, Gesammelte Schriften*, Leipzig 1869.

race became the primary and fundamental fact, and the *causa causarum* of everything. Language and art were invoked by Wagner and his followers as the conclusive proof, because they always bore the unmistakable and indelible imprint of race upon them. These were not contrived by reason deliberating, they sprang from dark forces welling up from hidden sources.

The two pamphlets by Karl Marx on the Jewish question and its connection with capitalist liberalism,[1] published just a few years before Wagner's pamphlet, reveal an attitude not entirely dissimilar to that represented by Wagner himself. Liberal-capitalist society appeared to Marx founded upon fraud. It had declared itself in favour of equal legal and political rights for all, irrespective of social origins and economic status. In other words, inequalities of wealth were proclaimed irrelevant, and hence beyond the limits of governmental intervention. The fraud, according to Marx, consisted in the fact that with the abolition of all other privileges—racial origin, family status, religious association—the privilege of wealth had become the most decisive social datum. In law, differences in wealth and property no longer existed, but in actual fact it was they that shaped society. In theory, the parties in a State struggled over abstract principles. But in fact, hidden and "unacknowledged" interests, one may say illegitimate interests, were turning the wheels of history. In the old society based on status, everyone knew his place and seldom dared to reach out beyond it. The new society, in which differences of class had been legally abolished, was seized by a fever of insatiable greed which distorted all values and profaned all ideals. Nothing now had any value, but everything had a price. That unacknowledged and illegitimate force which had become omnipotent was embodied in and symbolised by Judaism. The liberal constitution accorded full rights to the Jews on the ground that their religious affiliation was irrelevant, and in so doing did away as it were with Judaism. But instead of doing away with Judaism, it enthroned it, giving it free rein, liberating it from all restraint, in just the same way as it had declared

[1] Karl Marx and Friedrich Engels: *Werke*, Berlin 1958, Vol. I, pp. 347-77.

status and wealth irrelevant, while in fact giving supreme power to money to dominate society. For "money" read "Jews". The liberation of mankind therefore meant the liberation of mankind from Judaism. "Following the liberation of society from Judaism will come the social liberation of the Jews themselves" Marx wrote in the concluding section of his second pamphlet. The annihilation of Judaism would bring with it the liberation of the Jews. "There is only one possible way of redeeming the Jews from the terrible curse that hangs over them—annihilation"—Wagner wrote in the concluding passage of his essay on *The Jews and Music*.

Despite the things that we have quoted from Marx's writings, it would be a distortion of the truth to label him or the Socialist movement of Europe as anti-semitic. It is quite easy to collect many anti-semitic quotations from the writings of the early Socialists such as Fourier and his pupil Toussenel, the author of the book *The Jews, the Rulers of the Age*,[1] and from the voluminous writings of Proudhon. At the close of the nineteenth century a French Left-wing Socialist could still proclaim "the social question is the Jewish question", adding that there would never be any justice in the world until Rothschild had been sent to the gallows. But anti-semitism could never become an essential prop to hold up the doctrine of socialism. The primacy of the class war on a world scale runs counter to the belief in race as a factor of decisive importance. And the vision of a universal classless society is inspired by the idea of the unity of the human species. In the Messianic visions of the Socialist pioneers the international proletariat was destined to become humanity itself. Anti-semitic opinions, which lesser Socialists voiced as empirical statements, would inevitably be integrated by the great systematiser, Marx, into a cohesive *Weltanschauung*.

If responsibility for anti-semitism cannot be laid at the door of the Socialist movement, socialism should no more be looked upon as the sworn and consistent defender of the Jews against anti-semitism, certainly not before the end of the nineteenth century. Socialism emerged as a shield only when

[1] Alphonse Toussenel: *Les Juifs, rois de l'epoque; Histoire de la Féodalité financière*, Paris 1845.

the modern mass movements of the nationalist Right began to steal the Socialist clientèle by directing social wrath into channels of Jew hatred, and diverting it from the idea of class war. That process began about the year 1880, with the emergence of anti-parliamentary mass movements.

IV

The attack on parliamentary government was launched in the years when European liberalism had reached its apex. In the seventies of the last century constitutional régimes were celebrating their triumph in all countries of Europe except Russia. And even Russia itself had taken the road of reform in the 1860's. Alexander II, the Czar, was about to grant a constitution when he was struck down by terrorists. It was also the golden age of liberal capitalism. The principle of free trade was acknowledged as the very token of the harmony of interests between nations. Every country was overflowing with enterprise and furious economic activity. On the morrow of the war of 1870 Germany was swept by a frenzy of joint stock activity. The new companies vied with each other in daring ventures. France became intoxicated by a passion for quick profits and changed from an agricultural country in which the peasants hid their money under the mattress into a nation that served as a banker on a worldwide scale, financing railway building in Russia, the Suez and Panama canals, loans of huge sums of money to emperors and sultans in distant lands. In both France and Germany it was not long before wild speculation was overtaken by Nemesis. Small folk who had started with such high expectations found themselves grievously disappointed and cheated.

It was the contradiction between the triumph of parliamentarism on the one hand, and the disasters wrought by the workings of capitalism on the other, that gave birth to the anti-parliamentarian mass movements of modern times. The masses had been led to believe in representative government and elected bodies as a panacea for all ills and all deficiencies that beset society. Representative government was seen as the omnipotent sovereign, and the people had after all the power to elect or dismiss its representatives at will. And it was a time when people still believed that every problem had a ready-made solution and every difficulty was capable of being overcome. And so it was natural that the belief should spread that the failure of representative institutions in the fulfilment of their prime duty—the assurance of social-economic stability—was proof of some deep-seated illness. In people's minds the affairs of high finance and the workings of the stock exchanges appeared as black magic. And when crises were accompanied by scandals involving politicians and statesmen, the cry went up that the people's representatives were the servants and the agents of the men at the stock exchange who pulled the strings in a plot against the innocent masses. As European society became more democratic, the parliamentary régime became progressively more threatened. In the first half of the nineteenth century when the franchise was limited and the right to stand for election even more restricted, there were also strong limits to the scope of parliamentary legislation in that age of *laissez-faire*. When as late as 1864 Palmerston was asked what reference should be made in the Queen's speech to "domestic affairs and legislation", he answered, rubbing his hands with an air of comfortable satisfaction: "Oh, there is really nothing to be done. We cannot go on adding to the Statute Book *ad infinitum*."[1] And in so far as parliaments began to turn their attention from such matters of high import as foreign policy, imperial affairs and general legislation to economic questions, their members, nearly all of them landowners or big businessmen, could advocate their own particular economic interests without any inhibition or sense of guilt. For the noble and the wealthy did not at that stage feel guilty about being rich. On the contrary, they shared the naïve belief that "what is good for General Motors is good for America" in all sincerity. People still spoke of the rights of birth, wealth and talent as though these things were self-evident truths, and a judge would reprove workers who were on strike for their ingratitude towards their employer who gave them their daily bread. It was a

[1] Sir Llewellyn Woodward: *The Age of Reform, 1815-1870*, Oxford 1962, p. 169.

time when success was the sure proof of ability, and large profits were regarded as the reward for exertion.

Similar attitudes were also prevalent among Jews. The Prague correspondent of *The Jewish Chronicle* reported with considerable pride to his paper in London about 1850 that according to statistics the number of Jewish students in the ancient university of the capital of Bohemia was considerably in excess of the proportionate size of the Jewish population of the Hapsburg Empire. The correspondent goes on to point out other indications showing that the standard of living of the Jewish population was far higher than that of the Gentiles around them. They enjoyed higher incomes and managed to climb the social ladder faster. One has only to recall Disraeli's boast about the "pure and chosen race" to which he was proud to belong. It would one day conquer the world, he was happy to think. The Press was entirely in Jewish hands. In the national economy they were everywhere the dominant group, and they were now making inroads into the fields of science and the arts as well. Soon the whole world would be at their feet, Disraeli forecast.[1] Not so long afterwards, Jewish authors were turning themselves inside out to prove just the opposite. They realised in the meantime that in the eyes of many Gentiles the meteoric success of the newly emancipated Jews was not a reassuring confirmation of the principle of *carrière ouverte aux talents*, but a spectacle of a pariah growing too big for his boots.

Capitalist expansion and growing urbanisation called for control and direction. The fate of thousands of shareholders and the stability of the whole national economy were dependent upon the success or failure of this or that investment, and the investors needed permits, Government loans and State guarantees. In a democratic society every private interest is cloaked in the guise of a national interest. Every group of private interests discovers that it has to conduct a propaganda campaign in order to convince public opinion and persuade legislators, to use, in short, pressure upon those in authority. At the same time the members of legislatures are no longer those well-born and well-supplied gentlemen

[1] Cecil Roth: *Benjamin Disraeli*, New York 1952.

who could afford the luxury of independent judgement. The new men are dependent on changes in public mood, they have to cater to the needs of electors, and they take their cue from the party machine and orders from the Whips. The spectre of a *chûte dans le néant* is always before their eyes. Tempters appear on all sides, and where there are tempters many are likely to be tempted, when subject to very diverse and contradictory pressures and enticements.

It would be foolish to deny that the Jews played an active and extremely important part in the development of capitalism. Europe could not help noticing the fact that a Jewish banker—Bleichröder—represented Germany in the negotiations over war reparations, while France was represented by a Rothschild. Emancipation set free volcanic forces that had been lying dormant for hundreds of years. The emancipated Jew was not to feel that he had attained respite and reached a haven. He had cut himself off from Jewish tradition, but he had not been accepted by the society in which he lived, and many doors remained closed to him. He wanted to escape from his misery by intense activity in a field to which he had free access, and to win self-assurance and a recognised status by amassing capital and power, and often to show off, or indeed, by espousing the cause of the messianic Revolution, and in many cases by total dedication to learning.

The social mobility of the Jews exceeded that of any other group. The father could have been a beadle in the synagogue of some distant village, while his son could rule a whole empire of capitalist enterprises. There was nothing to keep the rootless Jew in his village or small town, but everything attracted him to the city. Every anti-semitic writer stressed the alarming flow of Jews into the big cities and capitals. Jews thronged to these centres which were the most sensitive arteries of any country, illuminated by the glaring lights of publicity and public attention.

Since there were only poor prospects open to Jews if they wanted to take up a university career, many of those gifted young Jews of keen curiosity and quick pen went into journalism. Jewish influence in the Press became a commonplace, not only among anti-semites. For hundreds of years Jews had to fight for their rights, the right to live, to breathe and move freely, with no weapons but persuasion and occasionally a bribe. It is not surprising that their descendants appeared to display a special aptitude in the field that has become known as public relations—an umbrella term used to denote various kinds of activities and endeavours.

The Jewish names involved in the public scandals, which shook a country from the days of the Panama *affaire* to Goldfine (Sherman Adams) and Gruenwald, attracted all the attention, for their sound was more arresting than the sound of such names as Dupont, Smith or Schmidt, and the Jew was always seen in the Western world as the heir of Judas Iscariot.

When the names of Baron Reinach (born in Frankfurt), Dr. Cornelius Hertz (an American citizen) and Artom (an Italian Jew) became tainted during the Panama scandal in France, the cry for a strong and pure man to sweep the parliamentary stables and expel the corrupt representatives just as Jesus threw the money-lenders out of the Temple, was mingled with cries of "Death to the Jews".

The principal victims of these crises and scandals that afflicted society were the lower middle classes rather than the proletariat which had little or nothing to lose, let alone invest. The petty bourgeoisie grew impoverished while lacking any real sense of identity or cohesion as a class. For they had no organisational equivalent of the workers' trades unions and Socialist parties. At the same time they dreaded more than anything else the spectre of sinking into the ranks of the proletariat and being absorbed by it. Nationalism, which was capable of giving them a feeling of belonging to the national brotherhood on the same footing as the upper classes, appeared as an anchor of salvation and a compass in a world shaken by upheavals. Lower middle-class chauvinism found in anti-semitism one of its main props. It was so gratifying to a Christian shopkeeper or artisan to feel superior to a Jewish intellectual or magnate, especially when menaced by the two "Jewish conspiracies"—international finance and international communism, both allegedly intent upon disrupting national unity. Nationalism was everywhere in ascendance.

In those early years after the 1870 war, Germany was drunk with victory. The France of Louis XIV, of the Revolution and of Napoleon, which for generations had been the arbiter of Germany's fate, had overnight been decisively crushed. In one stroke Germany achieved unity and the position of the greatest power in Europe, perhaps in the world, while France was wallowing in blood and shame, and seething with the desire for revenge. The collapse on the battle-field was followed by a bloody civil war. Under the very eyes of the occupying German forces the Paris Commune rose in arms and was suppressed in rivers of blood. The victorious bourgeoisie stigmatised the Reds as cannibals and national traitors, whereas the Jacobins among the Communards accused the bourgeoisie of cowardice. The latter preferred an abject surrender to a heroic *levée en masse* and made an alliance with the national foe against its own working class.

The implacable hatred which from 1870 divided the two greatest and most advanced nations in Europe put a decisive brake upon revolutionary Socialist internationalism. In 1914 the patriotic sentiments of the workers and their leaders were proved to be incomparably stronger than international working-class solidarity. Anti-parliamentarism with its social and anti-semitic flavour converged in France with the *revanche* mystique. The politicians, clamoured the revanchists, were selling France and her honour for a mess of pottage. France could never stand up to Germany as long as the country was run by egoistic profiteers. The masses of Frenchmen who cheered General Boulanger saw in him not merely a saviour who would rescue France from corruption, parliamentary *crétinisme* and Jewish finance, but also a hero who would avenge France's defeat by Germany and bring about France's national resurrection.

The conditions in the Austro-Hungarian Empire during its twilight period exerted the most direct and decisive influence on the shape of modern German nazism. In *Mein Kampf* Hitler admits that all his political and social ideas were born under the impact of the political realities he was able to observe in Vienna, specially the two pan-German anti-semitic movements; one founded by Schoenerer, and the other the Social Christian movement led by the popular Mayor of Vienna, Lueger.

The basic problem of the Austro-Hungarian Empire, as Hitler saw it, was the bitter struggle of the German-speaking part of the population to remain the masters of the country's destiny, despite the fact that other races—and in particular Slavonic peoples—formed the majority of the country's inhabitants. A parliamentary régime based on numerical majorities, and the principle of "one man one vote" threatened the special status of the Germans in the Empire. Two alternatives presented themselves therefore: either to dismantle the Empire and annex the German-speaking areas to Germany to form a Greater Germany, or to reject democratic parliamentary government in favour of the principle of a governing *élite*. In which case the party system would have to make way for government by an inspired leader. Viewed from this angle, the Social-Democrats and the Jews were the most dangerous enemies. The German-speaking Socialist in Austria who contended that the Czech worker was closer to him than the German bourgeois was undermining the unity of the German race. Austrian Socialists found themselves reluctantly defending the unity of the Empire, while demanding wide autonomy for its component peoples, because the break-up of the Empire was calculated to be interpreted as a victory for isolationist nationalism at the expense of international unity. The only racial group in the Austro-Hungarian Empire that was fully committed to the Hapsburg ideal of a multi-racial kingdom was its Jewish population. The Jews were convinced that any change in the existing order would be to their disadvantage. They were conveniently placed in the multi-racial, supra-national empire, where groups and entities of all kinds were assured the right of self-expression. Moreover, the principal leaders of the Social-Democratic party in Austria were Jews. So the conclusion could easily be drawn that there was a Jewish-capitalist-Socialist-democratic plot to destroy the German race in Austria. The equality of all the citizens of the country, the principle of the sovereignty of the numerical majority, the parliamentary régime with its political parties, were merely a smoke-screen laid by the Jews for their cunning schemes to liquidate racial *élites*. The destruction of the *élite* enthrones grey mediocrity, and the consequent weakening of the nerve of a nation was an opportunity for the Jews to exercise their destructive tyranny without hindrance. In *Mein Kampf* Hitler singles out the Soviet Union and France as proof of the correctness of his doctrine.

Hitler's criticism of the two anti-semitic movements of the Austro-Hungarian Empire deserves attention. He praised the pan-German movement for its adherence to the principle of race, but criticised it for its lack of social orientation and its remoteness from the masses. The chief virtue of the Social Christian movement on the other hand was its closeness to the masses and its understanding of the techniques of mobilising the masses. But Hitler found it wanting in that it did not have a doctrine of race and had its loyalties divided between Germany and the Roman Catholic church. Without a racial doctrine, Hitler thought, anti-semitism was bound to remain a tepid affair. It is no accident that a high proportion of Nazi leaders were from multiracial areas, where the Germans had played the part of a master race: Alfred Rosenberg came from the Baltic; Rudolf Hess was born in Cairo; Darré originated from the Argentine; quite a few, like Hitler himself, from Austria-Hungary, and especially the Sudeten.

Hitler learnt the lesson that the secret of political success was to concentrate on one enemy and to avoid a struggle on several fronts simultaneously. For a campaign on more than one front not only weakened one's forces, it might also arouse doubts in the minds of the masses: only we are in the right, and all other parties are in the wrong—how can one be sure? Political expediency demanded the selection of one principal enemy who could be shown to embody the characteristics of all the other enemies, while arousing fiercer revulsion and hatred than all the rest of them. If in this way the principal enemy could be isolated, it would then be a comparatively easy matter to identify other rivals with him and hold them up to contempt and ridicule, or even to deny their separate existence. The Jews presented an ideal target. Crudely understood Darwinist biologism, when juxtaposed with the inter-racial struggles of the peoples of the old Hapsburg Empire, created the vision of an inter-racial war of destruction. The words *Ausrottung, Vernichtung* ("destruction", "annihilation") crop up countless times in Hitler's writings, and not just as picturesque expression or a vivid metaphor. Since the conflict between races was a life and death struggle, there could be no laws to regulate it other than the law of the stronger. Such a war demanded masses of soldiers who would fight relentlessly, and still more a quasi-religious ideology— a *Weltanschauung* to stir men and fire them to action by rousing their fanaticism (another word that Hitler never tired of using). That faith must be based upon a set of ideas as few and simple as possible. The creed should not be confused by complicated questions, side issues, and unresolved problems such as religion or economic policies, for the main thing was to seize power. If there was no power to act, there was no point in putting forward political programmes; and once power was won, everything would come in its wake. In essence, the fight was not concerned with who was more right—we or they—but which one of us was it going to be? We personify the new faith of the master race. Our enemies are the forces of Satan.

The Movement initiated by the German Court preacher, Adolf Stöcker in the 1880's[1] offers us an insight into the transformation of anti-semitism from traditional hatred of the Jews into the demoniacal racial mass movements of our age. German conservatives of the old school were at first attracted by the crusade that Stöcker, himself a commoner, was waging against the Progressist-Socialist heresy which denied God, the Kaiser and the Fatherland. The campaign for the saving of souls was welcome to them, and incitement against the Jews did not particularly upset German Junkerdom: they were rather pleased by the discomfiture of the Jews. Kaiser Wilhelm I himself expressed his satisfaction with the

[1] Adolf Stöcker: *Christlich-Sozial. Reden und Aufsätze*, Bielefeld and Leipzig 1885, Part II, pp. 143-274.

preacher's efforts to put the Jews into their right place, for he thought they had become far too impertinent. However, the Kaiser hastened to add, although it was true that the Jews had been granted too many opportunities, this was a *fait accompli* and these rights had been incorporated into the statute book of Germany, and he (the Kaiser) had sworn to uphold the constitution. Similar opinions were voiced in the Reichstag when a petition with a quarter of a million signatures was introduced demanding an end to Jewish emancipation in Germany. "Put your house in order, otherwise . . ."—the conservative deputies advised their Jewish co-citizens.[1]

In his youth Bismarck used to say that he would never be able to serve under a Jew or to obey a Jew, and in the debate on the German defence budget of 1879—a date of prime importance in the history of Germany and the whole world— the Chancellor did not shrink from hitting his Jewish rivals Lasker and Bamberger of the Liberal party below the belt by dropping hints about those who "neither spin nor sow, yet reap rewards".[2] He was almost echoing Drumont's jibe when he asked how it was possible that the Rothschilds, who had invented no new technological inventions, unearthed no new natural resources, had been able to amass so many millions. Bismarck had no liking for the preacher "with the big mouth", but nevertheless he advised his son, who was an election candidate for a Berlin constituency, to make use of Stöcker in the common struggle against the Social-Democrats and the Progressive Party (which was generally regarded as a Jewish political group). As for mass agitation engaged in by Stöcker, and in particular his appeal to the *petit bourgeoisie*, Bismarck declared himself indifferent as to whether or not the priest incited people against the Jews as such. The trouble, as Bismarck saw it, was that he also attacked the rich Jews, including such men as his private banker, Bleichröder, and it was only a step from such preaching to Socialist propaganda against all private property, with its demagogic

---

[1] Walter Frank: *Hofprediger Adolf Stöcker und die christlich-soziale Bewegung*, Berlin 1928, p. 118ff.
[2] Erich Eyck: *Bismarck and the German Empire*, London 1960, p. 256.

promise of mountains of gold for the poor at the expense of the rich.

But Stöcker came to grief during one of his propaganda missions to England. His enemies disrupted a public meeting that he was due to address in the heart of London. The incident smelt of mob and scandal to the court in Berlin, for it was unthinkable for a preacher of the Kaiser to be mixed up in an ugly incident with the rabble of a foreign capital. And when in addition Stöcker became involved in a court case and convicted on a charge of perjury, Bleichröder's influence with the Kaiser and the Chancellor was enough to shut Stöcker's "big mouth" for good.

One may warrant the generalisation that the victory of extreme anti-semitic mass movements becomes possible only after the traditional Right has been completely demoralised. This is borne out by the history of Germany between the two wars and the Boulangist episode 50 years earlier in the French Third Republic.

It would not be an exaggeration to say that Boulangism was a curtain raiser for the fascist movements of the twentieth century, and Boulanger a prototype of the Fascist leaders of our time. The only difference was that the *beau général* was in fact a poor devil, had no ideas and was not even anxious to seize power. Publicity, to be talked about, that was all he wanted. A group of political adventurers belonging to various political parties came together to "build him up" in a conscious and systematic fashion, using all the propaganda resources that were available at that time. Among the supporters of the General, two Jews were prominent—Alfred Naquet, an atheist, anarchist and courageous fighter against all forms of anti-semitism who was the brains of the movement, and Meyer, a royalist, a convert to Christianity, who was an habitué of the aristocratic salons and a genius at raising funds. Boulanger started his career as the darling of the radical Left-wing and an ally of the young Clemenceau. When the Republicans took alarm at his popularity and decided to dispense with such an uncomfortable ally, the General became the hope of the Royalists who had despaired of restoring the French monarchy by parliamentary means and had turned their attention to the idol of the masses. He was badly in need of money, and might, they thought, be capable of fulfilling the role of a General Monk. The saviour proved a bitter disappointment. He came to the very threshold of dictatorial power, after a by-election in one of the districts of Paris which was given the character of a referendum and in which Boulanger scored a resounding victory over the representative of the united republican parties. While crowds were imploring him to march on the President's palace (where bags were being hastily packed), Boulanger collapsed. A little while after he fled from France in disguise, and later committed suicide at the graveside of his mistress in Brussels. The "handsome general" must be credited with consistency in at least one respect: throughout the affair he staunchly refused to conduct an anti-semitic campaign, although this idea was suggested to him by many of his supporters, especially in the last phase, as an anchor. There was too much of the French revolutionary tradition in the man, in spite of all.

On the eve of Hitler's rise to power in Germany, Right-wing politicians such as von Papen, Hugenberg and some Rhineland industrialists toyed with the idea of championing the "Bohemian *Feldwebel*" (as Hindenburg called him) and using him as a puppet. Paradoxically and ironically, Hindenburg was persuaded to appoint Hitler as the only way of restoring the parliamentary constitution. A coalition of Nazis and conservative nationalists would be able, he was assured, to command a parliamentary majority, and thus put Germany back upon the road of constitutional legitimacy which had been so badly battered by the governments of Brüning, Papen and Schleicher. These, for lack of majority support, were compelled to rule by Presidential decrees designed for situations of national emergency. The Nazis were in fact a minority in the first Government set up on January 31, 1933. It was humanity's disaster that Hitler was made of very different stuff from General Boulanger and that he was swept forward on the tide of an extremely cohesive movement based on a *Weltanschauung*, instead of, like Boulanger, being carried into prominence by a mob with

141

no identity, impelled by vague discontent, steeped in contemptuous bitterness and ready to protest in whatever contradictory and nebulous a way they could.

Hatred of the Jews by the traditional Right was rather a peripheral and empirical matter than a central point in a definite ideological system. We could even term it "defensive anti-semitism". The traditional Right recoiled from contact with Jews and wanted to set a limit to their influence. But the rights accorded to Jews were, as we saw, considered by them as part and parcel of the law of the land. The State was duty-bound to protect the life, property and safety of its citizens, and incitement that insulted a citizen's self-respect was considered vulgar and uncouth. Stöcker himself declared that though in principle he deplored the fact that "the Jews can vote and be elected, serve as civil servants and occupy commanding posts, sit on local councils and even in Parliamentary bodies, and are permitted to teach in our schools", he could not avert his eyes from the fact that "emancipation is a fact of life that cannot be ignored. There is not a Government or a Parliament that would consider abolishing it." He went on to say that if a conservative government were one day to put an end to Jewish emancipation, their action would be undone as soon as a more liberal régime were returned to power at a later date. "We are a nation based on the rule of law," Stöcker declared, "and we wish to stay that way." When elected Burgomaster of Vienna, Lueger dismissed Jewish officials from his municipal administration, but he took the trouble to find alternative employment for every Jew who had been deprived of his job: the world was no jungle, and people cannot be deprived of means to exist.

Treitschke may be looked upon as a watershed between the traditional hatred of Jews and modern theoretical anti-semitism. He adopted the popular cry that "the Jews are our great misfortune".[1] His immense prestige as national historian and prophet of the Second Reich lent respectability to the slogan. It was the mocking approach of Jewish writers to the sacred values of the Teuton race and the Prussian tradition

[1] Heinrich von Treitschke: *Ein Wort über unser Judentum*, Berlin 1881.

that aroused the ire of that poet of Prussianism. Börne and Heine represented in his view an alien influence, since they tried to nourish the Germans with Western ideas borrowed from the liberal tradition and revolutionary France. To Treitschke, as to German conservatives of all hues and the various radical Christian mass movements, "*Manchestertum*" (in the sense of liberal *laissez-faire*) was interchangeable with "*Judentum*". Both connoted to them selfish materialism, unconcerned with social welfare or national glory. Treitschke was shocked by a slip of the pen committed by Heinrich Graetz. Graetz had written—presumably in a fit of absent-mindedness—that Gabriel Riesser, the German-Jewish politician, was *by chance* born on German soil. So, the enraged Treitschke commented, the place of birth of a Jew is merely a matter of chance! The unfortunate Graetz had also said that although Jews had been accorded recognition in Germany, Judaism as such had not been similarly recognised. In what capacity does Judaism seek recognition?—Treitschke asks in his polemic with Graetz. In its capacity as a nation within a nation? If that is so, the answer is a categorical "never"—"*Nie*". If the Jews consider themselves to be a people, let them pack their bags and emigrate to the Land of Israel.

But Treitschke was not so extreme as to draw the conclusion that all Jews were foreigners and would never be able to form part of the German nation. On the contrary, he blamed the Jews for their stubborn refusal to assimilate. Yet it was only a short step from this opinion to the conclusion that the Jews would never be able to be absorbed by other peoples, and should therefore be denied the opportunity of mixing with the pure Germans. In order to arrive at so extreme a conclusion it was necessary to abandon certain restraints which neither conservatives nor anti-semites of the type of Stöcker could easily break. It was necessary to question the fundamental assumptions of Christianity in respect of the unity of mankind, the brotherhood of men, each created in the image of God. The whole of the Judaeo-Christian tradition had to be thrown overboard. There was indeed no escape from a denial of Christianity as such. Many of Stöcker's allies, such as Marr (who invented the term "anti-semitism"), Dühring, Henrici and others were bold enough to take this final leap.

V

Richard Wagner inspired Houston Stewart Chamberlain, and Chamberlain became the oracle of Adolf Hitler and Alfred Rosenberg. Chamberlain, son of a British admiral, who fell in love with the Teuton race, was the son-in-law of Richard Wagner, and the high priest of the cult of Wagnerism. In 1923 just before the death of Chamberlain, Hitler came to pay homage to the racist philosopher. After the meeting Chamberlain wrote: "My faith in the German people has never been shaken, yet I must confess that my hopes had sunk to a low ebb (in the last few years). But your visit has wrought a complete change in my mood." That was in 1923. Rosenberg's book *The Myth of the Twentieth Century* takes up the thread of Chamberlain's work *The Foundations of the Nineteenth Century*.

Alfred Bäumler, who was one of the first Nazi theoreticians in the Faculty of Philosophy at Berlin University, proclaimed that "When we shout 'Heil Hitler' to German youth, we are also hailing Friedrich Nietzsche";[1] he opined also that "the theory of race was the Copernican revolution of modern times".[2]

The theory of race is a compound of many and diverse elements: Ernest Renan's theory on the essential differences between Semitic and Arian languages, revealing basic differences in the spirit and mentality of the two racial groups; the studies of Count Gobineau purporting to prove the inequality of the respective roles of different races on the stage of world history; the philosophy of history propounded by Chamberlain, to which we shall revert later; biological evolutionism as taught by Darwin which substitutes the principle of the struggle for existence for the older vision of a universe of natural harmony; Nietzsche's glorification of the strong natural man, impelled irresistibly by elemental

[1] Alfred Bäumler: *Studien zur Deutschen Geistesgeschichte*, Berlin 1937, p. 284.
[2] *Idem: Bildung und Gemeinschaft*, Berlin 1942, p. 81.

forces, unhampered by hesitation or uncertainty, cunning or calculation, pity or the whisper of conscience; cruel and noble at the same time; Wagner's Gothic pagan Valhalla, the home of heroes larger than life.[1]

Yet it seems questionable whether these diverse elements would ever have combined to produce such a destructive and demoniacal gospel, were it not for the fact that there were Jews in Europe whose presence made it possible to demonstrate what the word "Aryan" meant. As for the other non-Aryan races, they were far away. Negroes were out of sight and presented no problem, let alone a threat. At the end of the last century Germany had not yet come into contact with the world of the Chinese and the Japanese. As for the Arabs, no one gave them a thought. The racial theory made possible the systematization of disparate anti-Jewish notions and anti-semitic sentiments into a coherent pattern. It raised the status of anti-semitism to the dignity of a comprehensive *Weltanschauung*, based on the findings of science, providing a key to the understanding of history and offering a political programme, armed with a ready-made guide to the art of political techniques. With the help of the theory of race, traditional dislike of the Jews on the part of those who wanted to preserve their historic national identity undiluted, and were concerned with nothing outside their own existence and purity, was transformed from a defensive reaction into a universal mission. The Jews were said to be a menace to all the peoples of the Aryan race, and the Teuton peoples, who personified the noble virtues of the Aryan and Nordic races at their finest, were called upon to act as a spearhead in the struggle against the force which threatened to destroy the Aryan brotherhood.

Both branches of Western civilisation, the Christian and the rationalist, despite other important differences, share the common premise of a direct relationship between man as an individual and humanity as a species. Differences of race,

[1] *The Third Reich*, published by Weidenfeld & Nicolson, London, under the auspices of the International Council for Philosophy and Humanistic Studies and UNESCO, 1955, Chapters 3-5, 20, 23, 26-27 contain very valuable contributions on the subject as well as on the Nazi philosophy in general.

origin, language and religion are of secondary importance in comparison with the primary fact of man's humanity. The Western tradition has always drawn a clear distinction between the human species, whose distinguishing attributes are soul and reason, and all other manifestations of creation. The destiny of man, in this view, is in the never ceasing endeavour to gain clear knowledge of reality and achieve a social order based on harmony. Man's path to clear thinking and ethical choices is clogged by all those obstacles which impede the recognition of the truth that is one, obstacles such as the senses, passions, lusts, the peculiarities of local or tribal traditions, which restrict or distort vision and pervert the will.

The doctrine of race negates the reality of man as man, as well as the conception of humanity as such. The oneness of humanity is regarded by the racial theory as an abstraction, an idea that is the product of mechanical modes of thought, which add up and put together data as if they were stones in a heap of stones. Such an artificial abstraction has no real life. Life, that is to say reality, is possessed only by organic entities, in other words races. This, the adherents of the race theory claimed, was true of animals and was also true of human beings. There was no unity in the animal realm between fishes and birds. And the same was true of the various human races in the world. To mate animals of differing species would be to breed monsters or mongrels. In the same way mixed marriages between members of different human races violated the laws of nature, which take their vengeance by giving birth to defective offspring.

For all its seemingly scientific basis the doctrine of race gives rise to a kind of mysticism which expands into boundlessness. Blood becomes the real primary cause that determines the whole personality of its bearer. It is held to predetermine the character, the mentality, indeed the values and preferences, dispositions and modes of thought of everyone who has a share of that blood. The blood is made to speak in the work of writers and artists, to urge on the protagonists in the political arena. The individual becomes nothing but a splinter of that great rock, the race. Thinking

146

is speaking with one's blood: man does not fashion his individual character out of his free-will, with the help of his autonomous power of decision and clear reason. His place, role, actions are determined for him by the great organism of which he is part.

The universe appears in the race theory as the fullness of life, the totality of power in it. The destiny of man is not to learn and to know for its own sake, but to live, to fight, like all other creatures, for his share of that fullness of life and power—the universe. The fact of struggle is the highest reality, and the word *Kampf* is a key-word in the vocabulary of Hitler and the Nazi party. The predetermined way in which every race struggles to express, assert and realise itself, and the requirements of that strategy at the given hour and in the given circumstances, are seen as forming together the supreme and sole laws of the race. It follows therefore that it is foolish to confront any race with an objective test of eternal validity, applicable to all mankind, and to judge it accordingly, praise or condemn. Laws, ethics, justice, customs and manners, as well as science, philosophy and art, are only part of the armoury in the war for existence, in the struggle for power, and these very instruments are forged in and by the struggle, without men knowing clearly what they are doing.

In this vision men do not come together to discuss and decide what to do and how to do it. They are impelled by primeval impulses without knowing whence and whither. The history of the Order of Teutonic Knights in the Middle Ages was the favourite myth of both Rosenberg and Oswald Spengler, whose essay *Prussianism and Socialism*[1] deserves no less attention than *The Decline of the West*. Polish princes invited the Order of the Teutonic Knights in the thirteenth century to form a garrison outpost against and a mission to the pagan Prussians on the Baltic seaboard. It was one of those suicidal acts with which Polish history is punctuated. Treitschke revered the Order as a supreme expression of the Teuton spirit and evidence of those irresistible dynamic forces which drive a people, or the finest flower of a people,

[1] Oswald Spengler: *Politische Schriften*, Munich 1933, pp. 31ff.

o fulfil the destiny of the race. A member of the Order had no life of his own. His life was service to the totality, with no expectation of personal gain or enjoyment. Obedience was an absolute duty, yet every knight-monk relied on himself. Religious missionary idealism, great military prowess and the constructive abilities of empire-builders and legislators were all to be found in the history of the Order. When the knights first set out to conquer the vicinity of Danzig, they never dreamt that in so doing they were laying the foundations of the modern state of Prussia and thus to the colossal might of united Germany centuries after. History was the overlord who called the Teutonic Knights into action, and they unconsciously fulfilled his command. Knights from many different European countries flocked to join the ranks of the Order, so that in serving the German people the Order became a magnet for all Europeans enamoured of the knightly-missionary ideal. In the same way the best Nordic types of all Europe were to gang up at a later date and form the new nobility of the Nazi S.S. order with whose aid Himmler planned to rule not only Germany, but the whole world. Himmler sought to revive thereby also the tradition of the German kaisers of the House of Hohenstaufen, of Friedrich Barbarossa, and of Frederick II (Stupor Mundi) who considered themselves not only kings of Germany but heirs of the Holy Roman Empire and God-appointed leaders of Christian Europe.

The racists proudly compared the Teuton myth to France's national myth—the capture of the Bastille by the Parisian mob seeking equality by means of anarchy, or the British national myth of an evolutionary constitutional struggle by a nation of shopkeepers, each of them seeking only his own benefit and building a fence around his home-castle. This egalitarian or utilitarian individualism was, according to them, brought to Germany by the Jews who wanted to break up the organic unity of the German people—a people whose existence was devoted to the service of impersonal ideals—so that they, the Jews, who had so strenuously guarded their own tribal unity, could rule over the human dust that remained of the German nation after it had fallen prey to disintegration.[1] What gave the Jews such effectiveness in the eyes of their enemies? The theory of the blood. When pure and undiluted, the power of the blood would never fail; its instinct would never err. Any lapse or failure, any weakening of will, loss of bearings or confusion, was a consequence of the adulteration of the good blood, of poison injected into it by the Jews around.

In its cosmic struggle the race must be permanently on the alert, mobilised and fit for battle. Viewed from this angle, reason was not a quality that could be singled out and judged separately from, let alone put above, other faculties. When isolated, on its own, it was bound to become sterile, for exaggerated analytical intellectualism weakened the will and lessened the individual's instinctive self-assurance. Intellectualism was a sure sign of the weakening of the voice of the blood and man's elemental impulses. Not with ideas will the leader come to the masses—taught Hitler—nor to teach them to consider dispassionately the pros and cons of any issue. He comes to excite their wrath, inspire them with aggressive self-confidence: the qualities of fighters. The intellect was a mere technician, a kind of book-keeper in the service of those mobilised and concentrated forces which reason had neither produced nor set in motion. Mobilisation for a break-through demanded the co-ordination of all those faculties that influenced the fighting ability. The different areas of life and endeavour could not therefore be allowed to retain their autonomy, a thing impossible anyway in the light of the all-determining quality of the race. The different efforts had to be guided by one single and exclusive principle so as to respond to the common impulse with the same thrill

[1] To Charles Maurras the decomposition of the French spirit was the result of the combined influences of Jewish monotheism, German protestantism and German Romanticism (because of its subjectivism, its enmity to the classical Latin tradition of light, order and style, and its yearning for the infinite). German Jews brought revolutionary socialism into France. "The barbarian from hell, the barbarian from the East, our Demos flanked by its two friends, the German and the Jew. The Fathers of the Revolution are to be found in Geneva (Calvin and Rousseau), in Wittenberg (Luther), and earlier still in Jerusalem . . . Jewish spirit . . . in the oriental desert and in the German forest. The Jew, monotheist and child of the prophets, has become the agent of Revolution."—Quoted in Ernst Nolte: *Der Faschismus in seiner Epoche; die Action Française, der italienische Faschismus, der Nationalsozialismus*, Munich 1963, pp. 168-70.

and rhythm. Totalitarianism is the companion and function of the permanent war-readiness of the race in its struggle for power. It is at the same time the logical outcome of the idea of organic determinism.

In according supreme significance to race, nature invested in the race the right to use its strength to the full. There was no room therefore for any respect for each other's rights, for relations based on equality or mutual consent or numerical majority between races. And the same was true within the framework of the race. Dominion and government were not matters to be decided by elections and negotiations. The leader would grasp power because his qualities, his vital powers, and sense of destiny egged him on with irresistible force. For he was the supreme personification of the race. Being the most perfect creation of the evolutionary process, overflowing with love for his race, he was endowed with the special powers of the visionary and prophet so that he was able to perceive the deeper meaning of his age, to hear the steps of the race's destiny, still hidden in a nebulous future. The leader's intuition was thus hailed as the highest law; the will of the supreme commander of the race in its life-and-death struggle was proclaimed the categorical imperative. An unbridgeable abyss separates the Wagnerian hero from the bespectacled Jewish intellectual, the clan of the Nordic Vikings from the cerebral or conspiratorial manipulations of Jewish conclaves.

It is difficult to establish whether it was hatred for the Jews that led to this denial of Christianity, or whether the rejection of Christianity removed all limitations from hatred for the Jews.

Christians may have disliked Jews, hated and persecuted them, may have treated them with contempt, held them responsible for all manner of misdeeds. Yet, they could not but stand in awe and fear before the mother-religion and the bearer of a divine mystery, the central figure in an enormously significant part of God's scheme of history. Furthermore, the Jewish element served to emphasize the universal side of Europe's history and culture: the unity of all believers in a church universal and the equality of all believers in the eyes of their Creator, race being wholly irrelevant.

Anti-semites such as Bruno Bauer (with whom Marx broke a lance in his articles on Judaism), Chamberlain, Julius Langbehn and de Lagarde, joined forces in destroying the Christian image of Judaism and denied to it its historic role. They cursed the hosts of Israel and blackened the name of Judah far more effectively than all the legions of anti-Jewish scribes within the Church in the course of many generations.

Did the Jewish race possess a religious genius and had it been its destiny to propagate the faith in a single God and bring Christianity to the world? Chamberlain claimed that there was no people with fewer religious gifts, less capable of genuine religious experience than the Jews. The Jewish religion was not the fruit of a Faustian wrestling with the mystery of existence and the great enigmas such as determinism and freedom, but merely a contract between a tribe and its tribal deity. The God of Israel had rescued the Jews from the land of Egypt, and promised to settle the Jews in towns that they had not built, in houses that were not theirs, and on vineyards that they had not planted, while the Jews undertook in return to observe His laws and to obey only Him. This religion based on historical facts lacked any metaphysical dimension or universal appeal. It was wholly anchored in historical events. The giving of the Law on Mount Sinai after the Exodus from Egypt, the covenant in the days of King Josiah, and the works of Ezra and Nehemiah were stations upon one and the same journey, new versions of the original covenant, invented by men consciously engaged in plotting and intrigue.[1]

Before Chamberlain had ever put pen to paper, Bruno Bauer advanced the claim that, besides not being an active factor in advancing the course of European history, the Jews were on the contrary an anti-historical force. Conscious of their uniqueness and desperately determined to preserve their identity, the Jews were led to segregate themselves completely, thus abandoning the main road of history. They did not want to progress, but rather to preserve and conserve.

[1] Houston Stewart Chamberlain: *Die Grundlagen des neunzehnten Jahrhunderts*, 2 vols., 2nd edn., Munich 1900, pp. 391-459.

They did not seek to co-operate with humanity, but on the contrary built a wall around themselves to keep it out. This self-centredness allowed only for the development of one quality—the will. The Jews lost in the process all innocence and all spontaneity, which are the very condition of spiritual and artistic creativeness. They found thus no interest in science, philosophy, art or politics. Their whole lives were restricted to the fulfilment of the 613 commandments, study of the Talmud and money-making. Their religion was based on a lie. Most of the commandments could only be fulfilled in the land of Israel within a fully-fledged Jewish society. Since the Jews were unable to fulfil the commandments of their religion properly in the diaspora, they had to resort to endless cunning in order to outwit God Almighty by the use of childish tricks. The Jewish Messianic hope was not a vision of the unity of the human race, but rather an expectation that the day would dawn when it will be given to them to dominate all other peoples and reap vengeance upon them.[1]

Bauer did not try to deny that Christianity had developed out of Judaism and had been born in the land of Israel within a Jewish society. But Chamberlain was convinced that Jesus did not belong to the same race as Abraham. He was sure that Jesus had fair hair and blue eyes, and the fact that He was the embodiment of all that is good was further proof that He could not have been Jewish. The philosopher also laid great stress on the fact that Jesus was born in Galilee where a considerable section of the population was Greek. The most important of Chamberlain's arguments was the claim that Jesus and Christianity were born among Jews in order to show up the tremendous difference between the irreligion of the Jews and real religion. Christianity came into being as a reaction to the caricature of religion that had its roots in materialistic Jewish racialism.

Chamberlain propounded his own theory of history in place of the traditionally held views. It seems to echo Nietzsche's famous distinction between the Nordic-Greek myth of Prometheus, the chained hero who tried to bring fire and redemption to humanity but was condemned to

---

[1] Bruno Bauer: *Die Judenfrage*, Braunschweig 1843, pp. 24-45, 75-9.

everlasting torture, and the semitic myth of Eve and the serpent, soaked in lust and laden with deception and fraud. Chamberlain did not accept as stages in the process of history the Greek-Roman starting-point, Judaism, mediaeval Christianity, the Renaissance, the Reformation and the French Revolution. The centuries from the break-up of the Roman Empire up to the year 1200 were, in his view, characterised by a confusion of races. The mixture of races accounted for the cultural sterility of the period and was the opportunity for Jewish ingredients to become dominant. Among these elements were scholastic hair-splitting, dogmatism, ritualism, intolerance, and priestly domination, which killed all spiritual spontaneity, and distorted the whole cultural heritage of the era. The turning-point came about the year 1200, when the Germans made their entry on the stage of European history. Since then every cultural achievement of worth had been the fruit of the Aryan genius and every creative artist had been of Germanic origin, including Dante and Michelangelo. The Renaissance had no significance either as a turning-point in history or a milestone, while the Reformation marked the triumph of the Nordic elements of Christianity over its Jewish elements. The entry of the Jews into European society in the nineteenth century threatened the peoples of the world with a return to that confusion of races that had marred the face of Europe between the fall of the Roman Empire and the year 1200. Peoples of the Aryan race, Chamberlain believed, should unite and close their ranks to fight the plague that was threatening them, with all their strength. The Jews, having been once more accepted in the ranks of society, were incomparably more dangerous than they had been when they were cut off from the rest of society in closed ghettos.

Bruno Bauer had in a later pamphlet likened the Jews, in a terrible comparison, to the proverbial Russian woman who only felt sure of her husband's love when he beat her. Jews only felt really at ease and at peace with their Maker when persecuted. When the whip was withdrawn, they felt miserable. They were alienated from their true nature and tradition, but they were unable to assimilate to the ways of the peoples who surrounded them and to live a full, organic life. Jews become then, in fact, an anti-race. They had always lacked the conditions for an organic existence—a soil and a political organisation, but the Law served as a sort of ethereal motherland for them. Having lost their religious cohesion, the Jews became a kind of human dust with no base on the ground, living in the pores of other organisms, and the experiences which held them together were feelings of bitterness, emptiness and rootlessness. These emotions were loosed by the Jews upon society, in the form of movements of protest and revolt. From antiquity up to the present day, the Jews had always acted as a solvent, a virus of disintegration and fomenter of social troubles, for the Jewish soul responds with a thrill to upheaval and destruction. Empty of genuine experiences and lacking organic forms of existence, the Jews had no creative originality. This is why they were so clever in satire, sarcasm, caricature, in imitation and distortion. Modern Jewish universalism in the form of international capitalism or international Marxism, was the same thing using two differing disguises, for both aimed at weakening the organic unity of the race and national solidarity. Many Gentiles were also anaesthetised by the Jewish drug of cosmopolitan pacifism. In brief, two forces were pitted against each other: the nations torn by class war, debilitated by the admixture of Jewish blood, their unerring primary instincts undermined and confused by the corroding influence of the Jewish spirit; and closely knit, highly integrated world Jewry, with its lust for power and revenge.[1]

The "stab in the back" explanation of Germany's defeat in 1918 was seized upon with the greatest avidity as conclusive proof of the correctness of the racial theory. The bankrupt nationalist Right found it easy to fasten upon international Jewry its old obsession with encirclement plots by envious neighbours, especially so as in the mounting wave of the international Revolution, Jewish devotees of universal political Messianism played so prominent a part. It could be said that it was upon the corpse of the assassinated Jewish intellectual, Kurt Eisner, the ephemeral and ineffectual

[1] Bruno Bauer: *Das Judentum in der Fremde*, Berlin 1863.

dictator of the Revolutionary Republic in Munich, that Adolf Hitler began his climb in the Bavarian capital to supreme power. Jewish international finance was in turn made to bear the odium of the ravages of inflation. The Jew thus became the target of the two most powerful resentments, nationalist rage and social protest. Instead of being at odds as they had previously been, the two passions were now fused to form an infinitely more dangerous dynamite than the anti-semitic movements a generation earlier in France, Germany or Austria-Hungary.[1]

"The decline of civilisations is the most horrifying and most mysterious spectacle in history"—with these words Count de Gobineau opens his *Essay on the Inequality of the Human Races*. Oswald Spengler's influential book was entitled *The Decline of the West*. Drumont, author of *La France juive*, wrote in a similar vein: "There is nothing more instructive than the examination of the first signs of those diseases which slowly but relentlessly weaken, pervert and finally destroy the body of ... society."[2] Extreme Right-wing French authors whose writings are full of poisonous hatred and wild bloodthirsty incitement, such as Maurice Barrès and Charles Maurras,

---

[1] Alfred Rosenberg: *Die internationale Hochfinanz als Herrin der Arbeiter-bewegung in allen Ländern*, Munich 1924. Ernst Nolte *op. cit.*, has recently unearthed a forgotten pamphlet by Dietrich Eckart of 1924 containing a dialogue between Hitler and himself. Eckart was a poet dabbling in meta-physics and mysticism, problems of sin and redemption, and a quack economist who wrote copiously on the slavery imposed by (Jewish) usury dictatorship, "*Zinsknechtschaft*", that is to say finance capitalism, in contra-distinction to productive (Aryan) industrial capitalism. In the pamphlet, *Der Bolschewismus von Moses bis Lenin. Zwiegespräch zwischen Adolf Hitler und mir*, the whole of history is portrayed as the sustained effect of the evil doings of the three great Jewish Bolsheviks, Moses, Jesus and Lenin, the three fomenters of the rebellion of the lowly, the inferior and the envious mob against the *élite* which upholds civilisation. To Eckart's suggestion to burn down all synagogues Hitler replies "hopelessly": "Burning them down will help us damn little. ... Even if not a single synagogue and not a single Jewish school is left, and (even) had there been no Old Testament, the Jewish spirit would still be there and fully active. It is there since the beginning of time; and there is not a Jew, not a single one, who does not embody it." "The substance of flesh and blood" has to be an-nihilated, concludes Hitler (*ibid.*, p. 407) re-echoing an earlier statement by his mentor Eckart that "no nation in the world, be it even the race of assassins of Attila, would leave him (the Jew) alive, once he saw through him, realised what he *is* and what he *aims at*; screaming with horror (*Grauen*), he would strangle him the minute after" (*ibid.*, p. 403).

[2] Edouard Drumont: *La Fin d'un Monde*, Paris 1889, Introduction pp. ii-iii. *Idem: La France Juive*, 2 vols., Paris 1886. J. A. Gobineau: *Essai sur l'Inégalité des Races Humaines*, 2 vols., Paris 1933.

reach the heights of genuine lyricism in the description of the sadness of cemeteries, death of civilisations, twilight melancholy, the disintegration of traditional and stable forms of life in towns and villages, under the impact of the industrial revolution.

The writers' dread of some approaching end, the sense of decline and degeneration are accompanied by a morbid fear of infection. As if a single contact with the cancerous virus, a single drop of blood carrying within it the germ of, one may say, venereal disease, was enough to bring doom eternal. In the same way Chamberlain remarked that one could be infected without coming into physical contact with the Jews. It sufficed to read newspapers to which Jews contributed, or books they wrote, for their poisonous influence to penetrate the human mind, and there was no defence in the face of this creeping death. One has only to recall the notorious passage in Hitler's *Mein Kampf* describing a dark-haired Jew with crooked legs prowling surreptitiously after a blonde Aryan girl "to desecrate her most treasured possession"—her Nordic blood. One of the chapters of the book ends with the awful prophecy: Our planet still revolves around the sun, but it is shrouded in impenetrable darkness, for life and all human activity have come to an end on earth as a result of Jewish domination.

At the same time the writings, pamphlets and papers of the Nazis and various other groups of Fascists are teeming with expressions such as "assault", "charge", "break-out", "break-through", and "thrust". It is strange to note that baffling contradiction between the dread of Jews, and the fierce desire to demonstrate strength and to assert superiority.

VI

The frightful deeds of the Nazis and the awful acts committed by the henchmen of Stalin cannot be accounted for in the usual categories employed by the historian, such as economic change, class conflict, party struggles or constitutional deadlocks. One is driven back to theological terms. For indeed, an evil spirit is abroad, and a profound malaise has been gnawing at the springs of societies for some generations. "God is dead and buried", Nietzsche proclaimed. There is no more far-reaching revolution in human history than the loss of faith in a Providence hovering over men and societies, leading to some rational and salvationist dénouement, a power to whom one may turn in supplication. How many seemingly religious men still retain this confidence in all its former liveliness? Men wished to grow up and stand on their own feet and be self-sufficient, and they rejected the doctrine of original sin, the rule of priests, and all the illusions of the weak who need external props. But with liberation from the chains of dogma and the fear of hell, the longing for certainty became more pronounced and with it the yearning for happiness on earth. Independence is won at the price of loneliness, and every rebellion leaves a residue of a sense of guilt. There are those men of damaged souls, whose need for affection and dream of love can never be stilled, and therefore strive in vain after them. The concrete here and now appears to them as no more than a shadow or caricature of the real thing, only to make their hunger more desperate. In its yearning for certainty and craving for happiness, humanity is swaying and swinging from one message of salvation to another, throwing itself into the arms of now one saviour now another. And when the intoxication has worn off, the hangover makes men feel sicker than ever. From whence cometh my help? They long for certainty, happiness and love, but they cannot have it, for the sense of guilt prevents the enjoyment thereof. Man is weighed down by the feeling that he does not deserve those bounties, they are not due to him. He is, in fact, out to spoil the enjoyment for himself, indeed to punish himself for reaching out for something to which he has no right.

The disintegration of traditional and stable forms of life under the impact of the industrial revolution and massive urbanisation deprived man of the instinctive self-assurance of a creature of routine. Too many choices are placed before him, and he is called upon to decide between widely varying possibilities, but he has no longer that instinctive certainty to sustain and guide him. Yet, the multiplicity of choices in the modern world is only apparent. For although every man is free to choose his own way of life and to indulge in any experiment of living that he wishes, the majority of humanity are no more than cogs in a vast machine. It is not for them to decide or to assume responsibility in most cases. The enhanced sense of human dignity feeds new desires, and evokes longings which cannot be stilled. The loss of traditional stability makes man increasingly uncertain of his real identity and true wishes, when placed before seemingly infinite alternatives. With forces so intertwined and interlocked, the life of each person is interlaced with the lives of countless other men, and made dependent upon unsurveyable impersonal forces. Modern society bristles with impediments that thwart and frustrate us. The unsatisfied desires and frustrated hopes engender dumb and bitter resentment. The citizen is today in theory sovereign all over the world. The kind of régime that is based on universal suffrage is accepted today in almost every country of the world (whether the elections are really free is another question). But there never was such a feeling of impotence and frustration as man feels today when confronted with the terrible problems brought about by the development of technology—the fruit of man's genius, and the glorious vindication of his mastery over nature; and in face of the great world conflict, conducted by governments chosen by the common man.

Reason has not succeeded in preventing or curing the neurosis of the modern world, and many believe that intellectualism is the essence of that neurosis. Reason has not been able to achieve the position of the final arbiter. In comparison with other faculties, it showed itself to be the weaker force. There was no single clear voice of reason, and experience has taught us that the sword of reason has been employed to defend every possible cause, and no evil action has ever lacked intellectuals to offer a rational justification for it. We seem to be falling back upon David Hume's view that reason is after all the handmaid of passions, and we seem to hear de Maistre cursing that mean, perverted sophist.

Influential trends in science and thought arose to shatter the self-confidence of the intellect. From the age of the romantics up to the time of Freud and Jung, clever men took great pains to lay bare, with the help of magnifying glasses, the irrational impulses that lay behind every idea and every decision. Philosophers, economists and historians would not rest in their earnest endeavour to prove that ethical concepts as well as political and social ideas were just a function of historical processes and a rationalisation of interests. Sociologists such as Pareto taught that men do not treat things at all on their own merits and for their own sake, but are impelled by the need to repeat, almost automatically, certain semi-instinctive actions and go through certain motions. It was not the object that was desired, the action was compulsive. Frightening vistas, or should one say abysses, have been opened by the teachings of Jung on the collective unconscious and the dependence of the individual upon the slumbering instincts of his remote, early ancestors. Man appears to wish not to know, but to be alive and have experiences. He wants to break out of the confines by which he is hemmed in, to tear up the net in which he is caught, and to float upon the crest of the wave. Nietzsche, Bergson, Sorel, Spengler contributed most to the cult of the *élan vital*, and the glorification of the myth that stirs to deeds, no matter how the myth stands to the truth. They wanted to replace the intellect, analytical and irresolute, fearful of error and unsure of results, by unerring intuition that grasps the living totality and the situation in its uniqueness.

The mass movements of Messianic totalitarianism came into being as an expression of and response to the neurosis that has held humanity in its grip throughout the modern age. In *Mein Kampf* Hitler describes the impression made on him by the outbreak of war in 1914 in these words: "For me those hours came as liberation from the oppression that weighed me down so heavily in my youth. I am not ashamed of admitting it, I was overcome by the enthusiasm of the moment. I fell on my knees and thanked the Maker of heaven and earth from the depths of my heart for his abundant kindness in giving me a chance to live in such a time."

Was the declaration of war justified or not? Did Germany have a chance of winning or not? What kind of war would it be? These questions and others were not asked. The vagabond who had neither home nor profession but ambitions and desires that encompassed the whole world, however nebulous they were, the outcast who was lonely not just because he had no friends, but because isolation kept him encrusted in himself, and made him incapable of having true *rapport* with others, had at least found an anchorage: war. From now on he would be able to sink his personality into the big collective totality and swim with the current, without having to decide for himself, choose between alternatives and make up his own mind. The man who was so eager to sink his identity, to find an escape from his personal predicament, would eventually emerge as a leader, in the towering loneliness of absolute power. At the root of both the lonely outcast and the sole supreme leader was the inability to have an ordinary give and take relationship.

It has been pointed out many times that the secret of Hitler's extraordinary success as a mob orator lay in his uncanny ability to strike the most sensitive chords in the hearts of the masses. He knew how to release the most hidden passions in the masses, to liberate them from all feelings of malaise and frustration, and enable them to take part in an ecstasy of anger, hatred and fanatical enthusiasm. There was a hypnotic effect in the permanent repetition of the same themes, while the demonstrations of strength and acts of violence were intended to create the impression that here was a force that could not be resisted, that fate had already decided, and history had already pronounced and carried out its verdict. The masses were only too happy to be raped. Ironically, in the late stage of the war Goebbels would implore and urge the Germans not to weaken, for they all shared the common responsibility, and the "Jews will never forgive us what we have done unto them and will never make any distinction between one German and another". Man needs to hate Satan more than he wishes to love God. Man loads Satan with all the evil that he finds in himself. In denouncing the Evil One he punishes himself. The student is often struck by the fact that so many of the charges heaped by anti-semites upon Jews are indeed true of the anti-semites themselves.

And yet, and yet; after one has sorted out all the data, followed up every line of thought of a perverted mind, explored every nook and crevice of a twisted soul, one is still left with the unanswered question: how could it all have happened? That systematic planning in cold blood, in well-heated offices by clean-shaven civil servants, walking upon thick and soft carpets; that scheme of tracking down every Jewish child and baby hidden in a cellar, or left to the tender mercies of Aryan Christians; that mobilisation of man-power and transport for the mass-murder of defenceless and anguished men, women and children, when a total war-effort was crying out for every pair of hands, and every vehicle; those mass executions upon prepared open graves, that smashing of heads of babies.

The Nazis had a preference for the *Jude* in the singular rather than for *Juden* in the plural, when speaking of the Jewish people. They refused to recognise differences, to discern individual faces or acknowledge different characteristics. One can detect in this the culmination of a long trend, whose dangerous potentialities were for the first time revealed in the French Revolution—the frame of mind that thinks of collective entities upon which history has pronounced a verdict of death. They are to be eliminated not for any crime committed by each of them or all of the members of the group together at that hour and in that place, but for the crime of having been born into that collective entity, be it aristocracy, the bourgeoisie, Kulaks, the Jews.

The individual, his guilt or innocence, are irrelevant. The individuals are "they", specimens of a force which has to be destroyed, eliminated, annihilated.

This pernicious frame of mind was strongly enforced by those biological teachings which tend to abolish the barrier between human beings and the world of animals and plants. Formerly the bearer of an immortal soul, raised above all creation and creatures by his soul, reason and consciousness, man has now been as it were integrated into the universal evolutionary process, and the fullness of life universal. As one of the protagonists, along with others in the struggle for existence, the human species, itself allegedly divided into

F

struggling races, loses its uniqueness, and human life forfeits the sanctity that hallowed every individual soul for so long. Races emerge and races perish, and are wiped out from the surface of the earth. There are fine races and harmful species. The absolute sanctification of the totality of Life on earth in the spirit of universal pantheism, as upheld for instance in India, is really conducive to an attitude of indifference to the life and dignity of man. In India a flea must not be killed, but in the streets of Calcutta people lie down to die, and no one pays attention. And the shadow of an untouchable defiles the member of a high caste more than contact with a dog. For the difference between man and any other living creature has been blurred. Both are part of Life universal, and the body of a man is only a temporary receptacle for that tiny fraction of Life.

There is little doubt that the instinctive revulsion from taking away a human life had been greatly weakened in our day in comparison with the climate that has prevailed for some two centuries after the end of the wars of religion. If that be so, apocalyptic fears of an imminent Day of Judgement should not be lightly dismissed. The power of exhortation in making men actually do things is small indeed. The most important, the most effective safeguard against the deluge of lawlessness has always been the deep-seated horror, the unreflecting and spontaneous revulsion against evil and injustice. When the death of millions produces so little shock, there is the appalling danger that the new technological means and modern perverted idealism may in combination be enough to put an end to mankind. At the time of the French Revolution every victim of the Terror (with the exception of the *noyades*, mass sinking of boats with counter-revolutionaries on board) had to be guillotined singly. When some 18,000 people had been put away in that manner, a saturation point was reached, and the executioners themselves had had enough.

It is possible today to put to death millions in a split second, and those responsible for the mass murder will never see the victims in their agony. And indeed the neo-Nazis have been proclaiming that the gas chambers were really no more than a twentieth-century version of the French guillotine.

A little while ago there appeared among the spate of books on strategy in the age of atomic warfare a very bulky treatise by Herman Kahn. The author cogitates, sorts out his material and makes calculations: if the American preparations are adequate, the United States may be expected to lose some 20,000,000 dead; if the preparations have not been completed—a figure of about 80,000,000 dead has to be reckoned with. The figure of 20,000,000 dead Americans should be regarded as a "tolerable situation", for "objective research", the book goes on to say, teaches us that "although the sum total of suffering will increase very considerably in the wake of the [nuclear] war, that increase will not prevent a normal and happy existence for the majority of survivors".[1] The number of victims in the country of the enemy is of no interest. These calculations are made as if the subject was the import and export of some wares. The "unthinkable" has indeed become "thinkable", almost plausible and acceptable.

Small as the power of ideas may be to move men to do good, their power to offer rationalisation for all manner of cruel and sadistic urges is boundless. One of the most frightening documents submitted to the Jerusalem Court was a speech made by one of the arch-hangmen at a conference of the planners of mass murder. The speaker grew lyrical about the wonderful qualities of his men. They walk in Jewish blood up to their knees, Jewish corpses are piled up before their eyes till they reach the clouds, the cries of Jewish babies pierce their ears, and they, without faltering for a second, proceed with their work. They, indeed, deserve a monument. It seems that nazism achieved considerable success in stifling in many of its adherents the sense of the unity of the human species. Ideology, combined with aggressive sadism, seems to have taken away from them any sense of obligation towards the Jew or the Negro as a human being. The image of the Jew had not merely been

[1] Herman Kahn: *On Thermonuclear War*, Princeton 1961. *Idem: Thinking about the Unthinkable*, New York 1963.

dehumanised, he had become Satan incarnate or an evil subhuman breed. The imagination and feelings of the butchers were no longer affected by signs of pain and sorrow manifested by the Jew.

There are prophets of gloom and doom who claim that racism, far from having disappeared with Hitler, has become the greatest peril to humanity owing to the emergence of the coloured races on the one hand, and the spread of nuclear weapons on the other. The population explosion in the world, the blunting of the sense of the absolute sanctity of human life, finally the weapons at the disposal of the combatants combine to create the conditions for an apocalyptic war of racial annihilation. No one can say for certain whether the murdered Jews are the first, the pioneers, the guinea pigs, rather than the only and the last race to be annihilated.

5

Right and Force

EVERYONE TALKS of rights but everywhere violence triumphs. Rights are won by force alone, and every act of violence is committed in the name of rights. There was a time when rights were thought of as the prayer of the downtrodden. More recently it has come to seem that rights are the slogan of aggressors. There was a time when right was described as the shield against might. Now we hear of the rights of power, and the right to employ violence has been given the dignity of a dogma.

I

For some 200 years the right of oppressed peoples to independence and self-determination has been recognised. Yet in the Thirteen Colonies as in Kenya, in Ireland as in Indonesia and Algeria, liberty was not freely granted but was conquered. Sometimes the rising nation won its freedom by its own exertions. Sometimes a foreign power extended help to the subjects of a vanquished empire to rid themselves of their oppressors whose power had waned.

We have seen in our time revolutionary leaders who only yesterday were exiled, imprisoned, even sentenced to death, received next day with honour, even with flattery, by the rulers who had so recently vowed never to negotiate with terrorists and never to submit to force. Now these same men are described as far-sighted and responsible statesmen with whom it is an honour to discuss freedom and plan progress.

Even the right of every nation to be united in one State has for the most part only been realised by force. This was the case not only of nineteenth-century Germany or Italy;

American unity too had to pass through the ordeal of the Civil War, and even the British Dominions did not become continental federations without their periods of convulsion. To claim that non-violence triumphed in India is surely to over-simplify: passive resistance undertaken by tens of millions is a more efficient mode of coercion than plastic bombs planted by a handful of men. And the massacres and the uprooting of millions which accompanied the emancipation of India and Pakistan are still vivid in one's memory. Reference is often made to independence granted voluntarily to the colonial peoples, but who would deny that even here, although the trigger was not pulled, the gun was loaded and pointed at its target?

Generations have laboured to build a network of laws and institutions which could ensure the rights of all, balance right against right, check the anarchy inherent in the claim that "possession is to the strong". Yet again and again claimants resort to "direct action", like those French farmers who erected road blocks, roused Monsieur Jean Gabin from his sleep and literally forced him to yield to their threats. Millions of American Negroes may soon be swept into fearful "direct action". In many countries established Labour Unions are rocked by wild-cat strikes; in others co-operatives, originally set up to ensure mutual aid and prevent unrestrained exploitation by profiteers, have degenerated into a conspiracy against the public, like any selfish pressure group which can hold society to ransom.

Men have dreamed of a society so secure in the reciprocal recognition of each other's rights that no man need ever fear the law-breaker, of a society in brief without crime, because all its members have been freed from the fear of want and injury: much idealism has gone into the fight for the rights of the under-privileged. Yet the era of affluence has proved to be the age of violence for its own sake, seemingly an end in itself. Every night the young and the old are inflamed by the screen, every day by newspapers and books which specialise in horror and violence, murder, sadism and rape. The purveyor knows his customers and he merely satisfies the demand. One may legitimately ask how much of this cult of and addiction to violence is due to the glorification of the right to full self-expression.

Is there anything really new in all this, apart from the fact that man's aggressive cravings and claims to enjoyment can be gratified so much more easily and fully today than ever before? The powerful and those with strong appetites have ruled since the beginning of time, since Cain and Abel. "A man hath no pre-eminence above a beast." After all, until quite recently hardly anybody questioned the right of a conqueror to impose his will, and enjoy the booty of war. Only at the end of World War II was it suddenly decided to initiate (retroactive) legislation against the deliberate instigation of war and to punish those who had planned aggression. Those conquering invaders throughout the ages, like the Assyrians and Babylonians, the Mongolian bar-barians sweeping down from innermost Asia, the German tribes who destroyed the Roman Empire, the Europeans who spread out across the two Americas subduing or even exter-minating the native populations as they advanced—they hardly ever paused to consider by what right they trampled upon the rights of others. A few Spanish priests and a few extreme Puritans among the British colonists had the courage to speak out for the rights of the natives and to question the doings of the conquerors, but their voices were not powerful enough to halt the strong-arm methods of men who were riding on the crest of the wave of elemental self-assurance and the joy of conquest. The cynics have wondered whether the pangs of conscience suffered by the colonial powers in the twentieth century were anything more than confirmation of Nietzsche's view that the whisperings of conscience were tokens of decay and attempts to justify feebleness.

Surely, the whole of history is the story of force, oppression, rapine. Slavery, the rule of exclusive privileged classes, feudalism in all its variations; that entire framework which divided mankind between those born to serve and those born to be served, between those who laboured for others and those privileged to live off the lowly; every authoritarian State against which the slaughter of their masters was the only resort of subjects—all these were based not on mutual agreement and trust but on force, fear of force, subjection to and acquiescence in a law born of violence, but sanctified by time and usage, and made effective by human docility.

Of concern to us here is not violence as such, but the motives that drive men to resort to violence and the ways in which they justify, especially to themselves, such action. It may be, of course, that the question itself is wrongly formulated. For it is possible that drives and motives inspiring violence are purely instinctive. The hardened criminal who resorts to violence may well never question his own right to do so except *post factum* when he stands accused in a court of law or before the forum of public opinion. We are not concerned here, however, with violence as an irresistible elemental urge. We are interested in that type of violence which flows from an abundance of self-righteousness, above all in that particular modern phenomenon of violence resulting from perverse idealism. We wish to probe into the ways in which a claim to a right evolves into a claim to the right to use violence to gain it and eventually to the apotheosis of violence as such.

A right is not an elemental craving or a subjective claim. The latter becomes a right only when acknowledged, if not by society as a whole, then at least by many, including those against whom the claim is pressed, if not fully and directly, at least by inference and implication. Thus, a right involves a measure of reciprocity and is not compatible with all-encompassing exclusiveness. The paradox of modern times is the incompatibility between the boundlessness of the claim to rights and the sacred postulate of equality.

In earlier times, it was an ingrained assumption of man that he was born to service. He had his duty to serve the Creator, to suffer and toil in order to atone for his sins, to fulfil his obligations. To this very day, members of the ultra-orthodox Jewish group, Agudat Israel, use the word "free" as a term of abuse. They hardly distinguish between liberty and licence. As we have said before, the claims of man in the modern era are, in a sense, boundless. There can be no limit to demands such as that for a higher standard of living. When in earlier centuries people spoke of rights, they meant the rights of each man according to his station in life, *suum*

cuique. Man came into the fullness of his rights as abstract
man only when he stood before his Creator in the next world.
On earth there were only the rights of the lord and the serf,
of the priest and the townsman, of the Jew and the Gentile.
These fundamentally unequal rights were equal only in that
all alike were inviolable. Even in the most catastrophic social
rebellions the demand for totally new and equal rights was
never formally raised (at least, not in so many words). The
rebels fought for the good ancient rights which had been
taken from them or trampled underfoot, but not for the
equality of peasants with lords; not for the total destruction of
patrician rights, but against the abuse of them. Fringe sects,
which inscribed the equality of men on their banners,
claimed that they merely wanted to return to ancient ways,
to the Garden of Eden before God had driven out Adam, to
the state of nature before man had plucked the fruit from
the Tree of Knowledge and become the victim of cruel
temptations, to the days when Adam delved and Eve span,
to the days before the Norman Conquest or the invasion of
Gaul by the Goths.

Past ages have witnessed rebellions without end, but only
modern times talk of revolutions. In the past, the hungry and
the angry would unleash bloody devastation, but they had no
plan to change the structure of society, no alternative
programme. The property-owners and the privileged feared
slaughter and arson but not revolution. In the modern era,
an alternative social plan was born, and since then every
disturbance has been heard as the tocsin tolling the oncoming
revolution. In the past when the discontented demanded only
the restoration of their good old rights, the rights of other
classes were, in theory at least, not under attack and, as a
result, there was some basis for reciprocity. In more recent
times, the claim to equality entailed the right to revolution,
and there was no longer room for reciprocity. The powers-
that-be of course defended their rights as an ancient heritage,
but these rights would be utterly repudiated by the revolutionaries in the name of the exclusive rights of equality.
Equality had thus to be imposed by sheer force. Its maintenance again implied the use of force, since anything that

tended to disturb it had to be held down. But even if mechanical levelling was not intended, but only equality of opportunity, what was really implied was equal opportunity to display inequalities of all kinds by exerting one's whole strength and force, in competition with others.

II

The necessity for violence and the justice of coercion came to be voiced as the vision of the rights of man, of the equality of all men, and the unity of mankind was entering upon its first tests. Political theorists preached the ideal of social harmony, but politicians, who foresaw or learned from experience that the established and powerful would not yield voluntarily, concluded that there was no alternative to violence. Sixty years before the Communist Manifesto Babeuf developed his idea of revolutionary dictatorship as an essential stage in every revolution. He had been preceded by Robespierre who, originally a passionate advocate of the abolition of the death penalty, soon came to distinguish between normal democratic government, the sole *raison d'être* of which was the defence of liberty, and a revolutionary government which was in duty bound to employ all forms of coercion in order to enthrone freedom. This is what he meant by *"La tyrannie de la liberté"*. Indeed earlier still, before the first shot had been fired, Sieyès had understood that only force could decide between those clinging to the *status quo* and those committed to its destruction. A class could hardly be expected—any more than an individual—to surrender its rights and privileges voluntarily, and there would therefore be no choice but to amputate such a class as a limb harmful to the body social.

Once this discovery had been made it was endowed with all the significance of a truth no less universal or eternal than the doctrine of the rights of man itself. The whole of history came to be seen as the struggle between classes till Friedrich Engels could talk of violence as the midwife of every great social change, and Lenin could proclaim that "a dictatorship of the proletariat is a scientific term which defines . . . a mandate grounded not on legality nor on election but

directly on the armed might of one section of the population".
Rights in general were hardly spoken of any more as attention concentrated on the right to employ force and on the
best methods of doing so. Machiavellian standards were now
applied to the social conflict in the same way as a few
generations earlier they had been invoked in reference to
international relations.

Wherein lay the originality of the Florentine scholar and
diplomat? Relations between states had always been determined by considerations of power, by victory on the battle-
field or by threat of war. During the Middle Ages, however,
men were ashamed to admit that this was in fact the real
relationship between the nations of Christendom or, rather,
they were ready to recognise the bitter truth, but they
condemned it as sinful or as just a piece of the old Adam.
Machiavelli not only taught that things had always been like
this, but actually announced in a defiant tone that this was
the norm, the way of the world, and that the great man was
therefore the strong man whose power overshadowed that of
his fellows, the fox who outwitted the other foxes, the man of
cunning who excelled in deceit and in the treacherous use of
violence. In a ruler these characteristics were virtues, because
affairs of State were not ordered with the help of the Heavenly
Father. So, every weakness, hesitation or humanitarian
inhibition could only play into the hands of the enemy who
was free from such debilitating sentiments. The power of the
State, which really meant the well-being of the citizens, was
the one asset of the ruler and it was an asset that he had no
right to betray. To Napoleon too the strong was the good.

In contrast to early revolutionary romanticism which had
eyes only for the downtrodden and the suffering throwing
off their chains and the masses awakening from their
slumber, the prophets of revolution never ceased to remind
their disciples that a revolution meant guns and rifles, blood
and fire, mass arrests and numerous executions, in brief,
stern dictatorship. And, indeed, however paradoxical it may
sound, a revolutionary régime has more need to wield
coercive power than an old-fashioned despotism. A long-
established régime, however despotic, does not depend solely

on naked and brutal coercion. It profits from inertia and apathy; overawes with its majesty; rests secure in its centuries of legitimacy, and acts as a rallying point for the habits and interests of the common run of people. Moreover, an old régime is never an efficient instrument of terror, for age undermines its strength, while multifarious entrenched interests for which it serves as a cover, frequently conflict and hinder every attempt to take vigorous action. A victorious revolutionary government bounds forth with all the vigour of youth, propelled by fiery enthusiasm, or as Edmund Burke said, "It is struck out at a heat." On the other hand, unlike an *ancien régime*, it cannot rely on inertia, habit or custom. The more thorough-going its programme, the more it threatens established interests, prejudices and customs, the more it is bound to use force. A maximal programme demands a maximum of violence. A revolutionary régime can never rest until all possible opposition has been suppressed; it can afford to grant freedom only when it need no longer fear effective opposition.

At first glance, the term right is associated with the image of weakness. The man who seeks rights is, as already said, somebody who is under-privileged and is clamouring for redress of a grievance, compensation for injustice done to him. If, however, the view is taken that rights and property are not transferred on a reciprocal basis out of obedience to objective rules of justice and morality, but are rather seized and held by force and conceded to force, then it follows that ultimately it is only power that bestows rights. The Germans maintained, for example, that the Polish nation, having permitted the destruction of its own independence, had thereby shown that it was not fit to enjoy political sovereignty and thus forfeited the right to exist as an autonomous political entity. If political and social history is a succession of rising and declining powers, then that power which is ripe at a particular moment must triumph and nothing can stand in its way. And when its strength has wasted away because it has grown old and decrepit, then its hour has passed and fall it must. Particles of power, that is of vitality and achievement, divide off from each other like the elements of chemistry, clash, swallow each other up and form new compounds. Friedrich Engels carried this line of thought so far that he did not even regard the barbarian invasions in the period of Roman decline as a destructive elemental blow of nature. If they succeeded, then it was a sign that history had assigned them a creative role and that they had come to infuse a new vitality into European society. The invasions could have been regarded as mere ephemeral outbursts of violence only if they had culminated in the rapid disappearance of the barbarians themselves.

Does this mean that right is might, that no tests can decide what is moral and what immoral, that there can only be a crude Darwinist naturalism? The answer usually given to this is that a refusal to accept the judgement of nature is in itself a sin, a moral betrayal. After the rise of Hitler to power, the supporters of appeasement argued that the policy of the Versailles signatories was not merely stupid, but also a blasphemous sin. This accusation rested on the argument not that the men of Versailles had grievously wronged the German people but that they had blindly believed in the possibility of strangling a nation sixty to seventy million strong, a nation possessed of such enormous human, cultural, technological and industrial potentialities. An attempt of this kind to muzzle power, to strangle a potential, was bound sooner or later to rebound against those who made it. So, too, the boycott of Russia between the wars, and the isolationism of the United States, were acts of repression, which by being inevitably ineffectual carried a double Nemesis with them. And the result was that the European statesmen, particularly those of France and England, had to play hide-and-seek, to conduct a policy not in accordance with realities but with shadows, to deceive themselves and others alike, and then be overwhelmed by the explosion of elemental forces.

Neither the French nor the Russian revolutions were followed by any successful spontaneous revolutions beyond their own frontiers. The revolutions were carried to other countries by the bayonets of the French and Russian armies. One is thus justified in asking whether the triumphs of revolutionary ideologies across the globe were due to the power of truth and justice or to the fact that its champions were great and rising world powers. Would the revolutionary ideology at the end of the eighteenth century have been able to transform the face of Europe, if the revolution had occurred in Portugal and if, as a result, it had not had at its command a nation with an intense sense of mission, with the most effective army and the largest population on the Continent? And would communism have won its victories, if the Bolshevik revolution had broken out not in Russia but in Bulgaria?

We thus seem to be driven to give up the idea of abstract rights. Noble sentiments and humanitarian theories appear to have only emotive significance. A right becomes a reality only and when it is embodied in a force ripe for triumph. In the days of Stalin's greatness I asked a Communist during an argument what he thought were the rights of the workers and what he meant by progress. Without a moment's hesitation he replied: the strength of the Soviet Union. I was reminded of how, in the 1830's, Buonarroti, the friend of Babeuf and historian of the latter's Communist egalitarian conspiracy, had defined freedom as the power of the State to take over and redistribute all property according to egalitarian principles and to instil into its citizens the faith and the sentiments required for the triumphant reign of equality, and to stifle the instincts opposed to it.

If the Communists had concluded that there was no chance of spontaneous Communist revolution outside Russia, that the initiative had therefore to come from the one great power already successful in building socialism (and it seemed only natural that the historical force of the future—rising, vital, progressive—should have consolidated itself in the greatest and strongest country) then they were entirely consistent when they identified the rights of the world proletariat with the might of Stalin.

To a Communist all talk of an absolute morality, the eternal rights of man and the purity of judicial processes, was simply bourgeois hypocrisy, even if not all the bourgeois spokesmen were fully aware of the fact. It was the property owners' vital interest in the sanctity of private property as an inviolable and eternal right that gave rise to the doctrine of the citizen's inalienable rights and the individual's holy freedoms: to serve as a fig leaf and cushion for the rights of property. The rights of man were put by liberal bourgeois writers outside the orbit of State interference, even of the State based on a majority vote. For they knew that although the property owners individually, and even more collectively, were extremely powerful, they were nevertheless only a minority, and if the question were put to the vote they might lose their wealth. They therefore proclaimed the rights of man (property) as eternal, immutable and inviolable, quite independent of the changes in the processes of production, class structure, and of historic circumstances.

Proletarian morality was based in its entirety on collective solidarity, which was itself the product of a particular historical situation and a stage in the unceasing struggle for liberation. So long as the individual proletarian was isolated, he was hopelessly weak and the doctrine of the rights of man, far from giving him support, could only act as an opiate. The proletarians could become a force to be reckoned with only when they worked together. They had no rights to preserve, and their rights had still to be gained through victory over the capitalist world. To the proletariat all moral values were encompassed in the vision of liberation, while the régime of capitalist exploitation embodied every kind of immorality. Proletarian morality was manifested in the battle against oppression. This morality was not immutable but, on the contrary, was subject to dialectical development and changed its form in accordance with the strategy and tactics of the class war. In other words, proletarian morality was a function of the struggle for victory and had to be defined afresh each time by the leaders of the world-wide campaign, from whom the combatants were to receive their battle orders.

III

It was in France that the idea of revolutionary ethics was first elaborated, and it was France which first showed the way how Right could go left, thereby forcing the Left to shift its ground.

Reeling from pain and shame, the French people gave itself up after 1871, as it did after 1940, to a grand inquest on the deeper causes of its disaster. The Right pointed an accusing finger at the whole of the French revolutionary tradition which, it claimed, had poisoned the life of the nation. The heirs to the Revolution had rejected the authority of age-old values and traditions, be it religion or the hierarchical principle, the family or respect for ancient custom. They had unleashed an anarchic and nihilistic individualism and had made the uncouth and brutal *hoi polloi* led by upstart demagogues or fanatical doctrinaires the supreme arbiters of the nation's fate. Addiction to abstract universal principles, and a missionary zeal to propagate them combined to sap the vital forces of the nation, to estrange France from herself, from her past, her true personality, and her true destiny. France was called upon to recover her own true identity.

As against this abstract call to return to a true self there stood out the fact that for generations France saw her title to pride, and based her claim to uniqueness and greatness on her universal mission. All the symbols and legends of the nation's history were imbued with this universalism. Such prophets of a pure and organic French nationalism as Charles Maurras saw in their moments of clarity the tragic irony of promoting French nationalism through a call to isolationism. Highly revealing indeed is the fact that the word "nationalism", was given its first benediction by Maurice Barrès in an article of literary criticism in which he attacked the imitators of foreign fashions who bowed down before the works of Tolstoy, Ibsen or Maeterlinck. The French, whose pride had been so wounded in the political sphere, were the more sensitive to the loss of that exclusive cultural hegemony which their writers and thinkers had enjoyed for so long.

It was Barrès who argued that truth was not the exact reflection of objective facts but the function of the angle of the viewer. It was the French point of view which determined

what the truth was for the French. That truth was forged by
the traditions, customs, needs and aspirations of the French
people, in other words, it was a compound of the responses,
modes of self-adaptation and self-defence which had been
developed over the centuries, by a people living in the same
climate, observing the same landscape, sharing the same
historical experiences and destiny. "What is the truth?" asks
Barrès. "It is not a question of factual knowledge but of
finding a particular and unique viewpoint from which we
can see the facts in their correct proportions ... I have to halt
at that particular point which best suits my own vision. My
vision has been created over a period of many generations.
And I take my stand at that point from which everything
that radiates outwards is in a sense French. Truth and
justice for the French, the French intelligence, is this unity
between the limited man, the Frenchman on the one hand,
and exact, precise relationships that have their own existence,
on the other. Nationalism in its pure form is simply awareness
of the fact that this viewpoint exists, a willingness to seek this
viewpoint and a determination, once it has been discovered,
to remain loyal to it in order that from it we can draw our
beliefs, our politics and our actions."[1]

A philosophy of this type clearly implied that aliens, such
as Jews, Protestants, outsiders of any kind were simply not
eligible to partake of this French truth. After all, they did not
constitute an integral part of that unique organism which for
generations had fought for its survival and self-expression.
The aliens were sapping and emasculating the instinctive
confidence, and poisoning the creative vitality of the French.
Unfortunately, continues Barrès, as if in a cry of anguish,
while the English and Germans were pure races carried
forward on the wave of their national pride and national
mission, the French were no longer a race.

They could hardly have their cake and eat it—insist on
the purity of French blood and at the same time demand
that Alsace-Lorraine, inhabited by German-speaking members of the Teutonic race, be returned to France in accordance with the right of men to choose their national allegiance

[1] Maurice Barrès: *Scènes et Doctrines du Nationalisme,* Paris 1902.

regardless of the deterministic criteria of language and race. Racialism of the Nazi type could hardly become the creed of a nation which was made up of racial elements so diverse as Provençals and Bretons, Normans and Basques, and which owed its very unity to the fact that political voluntarism had triumphed over geographical and racial determinism.

According to Barrès, France was suffering from an infirmity of will, from a loss of direction, from the anarchy of contradictory impulses, conflicting interests, heterogeneous ideas—all personified by the parliamentary system which was contrived by sophists or copied from the Anglo-Saxons and was unsuited to the French. "What cripples us", explained Barrès, "is the fact that we are divided against ourselves by a thousand private desires, by a thousand idiosyncratic modes of thought. We are isolated one from the other. We are not aware of an end to be shared nor of means to be employed in common nor of a single purpose in life. Happy are those nations in which all movements are linked, in which all undertakings fuse as if they had been directed from above by a single plan. Nationalism means that every question must be solved in relation to France. But how can we do this if we do not share a common definition and idea of France? . . . Unity cannot be forged on the basis of ideas so long as they remain mere exercises in logic. They have to be reinforced by emotion. At the root of everything lie the emotions. Men labour in vain who attempt to base truth on logic alone, for the mind can always find grounds to question every statement. How minor a role is played in our actions by reason! Fundamentally, we are creatures of the passions." There arose in these circumstances the craving for a leader to give a lead, stir the emotions, sweep men on to determined action, by embodying in himself all the *énergie nationale*.

At the end of the nineteenth century there were many factors at work in France which could have led to the triumph of a Fascist type of régime. That the danger was averted was largely due to the *Affaire*, the case of the Jewish officer, Dreyfus. This episode also marked a turning-point in the history of the Socialist movement in Europe. This is a neglected aspect which calls for a closer analysis, if only because a study of it can throw a good deal of light on the analogous developments in post-1918 Germany.

To the devotees of "the moral order", the traditional French Right, the army was a supreme value, a kind of totem. The monarchy was dead, the hierarchical principle whether based on lineage or wealth could never hope to regain acceptance; anti-clericalism and the alliance between altar and throne had combined to discredit the Church. Only the army was above reproach, at once the incarnation of authoritarian discipline, the magnet drawing to itself mass fervour, and a popular symbol for moral purity by being the guardian of the code of honour. As against the multiple partial interests the army embodied the Nation in its indivisible unity.

At first, almost everybody was convinced that Dreyfus was guilty and the case seemed to justify those theories of integral nationalism which ascribed a poisonous effect on the French body politic to all alien elements, and above all the Jews. The publication of Emile Zola's famous article dealt a crushing blow to the symbol on which were centred all the values and hopes of the Right. The army stood condemned for corruption and conscious deception. This was so unbearable to the nationalist Right that when Colonel Henri committed suicide and left a letter actually confessing to the forgery, certain Right-wing writers surpassed themselves in a despairing effort to exalt the theory of "the holy lie".

From a movement upholding the "moral order" and condemning moral anarchy and licence, the Right was transformed into a movement which incited to mass violence, glorified irrational emotionalism, and replaced universal moral absolutes by antinomian moral relativism. Black was called white and white black, for justice was now seen as a function of the war for survival, as a means in the struggle for self-preservation and power. Barrès' thesis that truth was the French point of view was put to the test by the Dreyfus case to result in the verdict that regardless of facts, a Jew could never be right in a dispute with the General Staff, with the glorious French military tradition, with the Catholic

Church, with the values that had "made" France and which were essential to France if she were to be strong and true to herself. And those who fought for him, who justified him, had, in so doing, cut themselves off from the French organism, from the body of the nation.

IV

Until the imprisoned rebels of the Paris Commune were amnestied, and indeed for years after, the revolutionary Left in France regarded themselves as outcasts, who could have no common language and no common interests with the bourgeois world. Only the sword could decide between them. From this point of view, those who were not for them were against them. There could be no grounds for distinguishing between a noble and a bourgeois, between a royalist and a republican bourgeois, a Catholic and a free thinking bourgeois, because all those who did not labour, who did not share the sufferings and hopes of the proletarians were unclean, untouchable and enemies, for history had proved that when it came to a real show-down they would all unite in a single anti-proletarian front. There were the Blanquists who, like the Bolsheviks of later years, held that a compact band of professional revolutionaries, trained in the underground, should seize the centre of governmental power and impose the revolutionary régime by force. A successful coup was sure to have the effect of an electrifying and cleansing shock upon the whole of France. There were those, Syndicalists and Anarchists, who rejected every type of centralised national government and dreamed of direct action which, in the form of violent political strikes, acts of sabotage and rebellion would lead to expropriation and nationalisation, at first on a local, but eventually on a national scale. There were those, like the Marxist Guesde, who maintained that unceasing class war would eventually grow into a vast revolutionary upheaval. At all events, the necessity to resort to violence in the struggle against forces which held the workers down by coercive violence was accepted by all, and with it the proletarian morality of a class at war.

As the Dreyfus affair unfolded, many of the more clear-sighted among the Socialists became uncomfortably aware of the similarities between their own proletarian Socialist conception of morality and the doctrine of "the French truth" expounded by the anti-Dreyfus Right-wing. Of course the Socialists appealed to a class truth, the Right to a national or racial truth, but the former now frequently saw themselves reflected in the latter as if in a distorting mirror. Inevitably, many Socialists began to look with new eyes at themselves and their own creed. Did the entire non-Socialist world really represent an undifferentiated, homogeneous entity, an indivisible kingdom of darkness? Were the Socialists really right in insisting that they had no place and no interest in the preservation of the (bourgeois) Republic and that their sole concern was to destroy it by force, root and branch?

Even Guesde, the tight-lipped and morose doctrinaire, had to admit that the article, "J'Accuse", by the bourgeois writer, Zola, was "the most revolutionary testament of the nineteenth century", for, acting in complete isolation, the novelist had dared to attack immensely powerful and entrenched forces. If the proletariat, continued Guesde, was waging war on behalf of all the downtrodden, and if Dreyfus had been terribly wronged, it followed that Dreyfus himself had been transformed into a fully-fledged proletarian. If moral nihilism was permitted to spread utterly unchecked, then in our hour of triumph will we not, he asked, find ourselves left with a material so decayed and so rotten that it will be useless to us in our attempt to build a just and pure society? Will the victory then have been worth while? Can we really stand aside while the bourgeoisie decays? Should we not step in to save that bourgeoisie from the total corruption threatening it?

From here it was only a short step to Jaurès' distinction not merely between the various segments of the non-Socialist, non-proletarian world, but also between those strands in the traditional moral and legal code which were indeed a rationalisation of bourgeois egoism and those which were unsoiled, pure and immutable, which formed the heritage of mankind as such and which, during the French Revolution of 1789, had received sanctification in the Declaration of the Rights of Man and Citizen. The Socialists could hardly reject the laws and ethics of bourgeois society and state, and at the same time invoke those very laws and ethics against the police and the army who were putting down strikes and demonstrations by force. If anti-semitic propaganda and violence culminating in the destruction of Jewish lives and shops were so repellent, then it might be time to have another look at violence committed by the workers. Furthermore, the Socialists began to fear that anti-Dreyfus propaganda might well rob them of many of their clientèle. Democratic Caesarism—the word "fascism" still lay in the future—with its appeal to patriotism, the defence of the honour of the army and its heroes, with its mass hysteria and street fighting, was a variation on the theme of "direct action" upheld by the revolutionaries on the Left.

It so happened that while the workers were seething with resentment against the police and the army for suppressing a series of strikes, which had no connection with the *Affaire*, the honour of the Republic was one day brutally insulted by an enraged reactionary aristocrat who raised his stick against the President of the Republic, known to favour a revision of the Dreyfus trial. When a mass demonstration held by Republicans and Socialists to protest against the outrage was ruthlessly handled by the police, the Socialist leaders concluded that the Republic and the proletariat alike were threatened. The police and the army were determined to deny the workers their right to strike, to dragoon them into docile auxiliaries, in brief to deprive them of even those meagre rights which they enjoyed under the bourgeois parliamentary régime. When the Third Republic then found itself faced with one of the most severe and prolonged governmental crises in its history and a Right-wing military coup was expected any day, Waldeck-Rousseau, the radical Republican, turned to the Socialist leader, Millerand, with the request to enter his coalition government in order to help save the Republic.

The Socialist camp in France was thus put to its most severe test. The doctrine of the class war "to a finish" rejected out of hand the very idea of coalition with any bourgeois party and regarded Socialist participation in national elections as justified only as a periodic opportunity to mount propaganda campaigns and to rally the proletarian forces. But this vision of a single revolutionary camp pitted against one capitalist world (which included also clericalism, militarism, and the remnants of the feudal classes) had not reckoned with those new forces which were not a mere off-shoot of the old Right or capitalist bourgeoisie, but represented new demoniacal and defiantly perverse forces to which the old categories could not be applied. The Socialists had to make an agonising choice. They could argue that the worse things became, the better; that the Socialists should welcome those divisions in the bourgeoisie which threatened havoc or even a military dictatorship, for these would act as the prelude to the final revolutionary spasm. Or the Socialists could rally to the support of the Republic and enter a coalition with the radical and progressive segments of the bourgeoisie. In the years 1918-33 the Independent Social Democratic Party (U.S.P.D.) and the Spartakists (the Communists) faced a similar dilemma in Germany. Today we are all too familiar with the path they chose and with the consequences that stemmed from the refusal of the extreme Left in Germany to ally itself with the Social Democrats and the liberal elements in order to buttress the Weimar régime.

Those who were opposed to participation in coalition governments argued cogently that the principles of collective responsibility and Cabinet secrecy would inevitably contradict the theory, upheld by the moderates, that Socialist ministers would participate in a coalition government simply as the emissaries and agents of labour and collaborate with the non-Socialist Cabinet only on matters of national interest, but would refuse their support for policies designed to foster bourgeois class interests. Would such ministers oppose the suppression of a strike if a majority of the Government decided in favour of it on alleged grounds of national defence or interest? The moderates argued that Socialist ministers should resign if the Government took any action in a labour dispute detrimental to the workers. But was not the very idea of an alliance with bourgeois parties a negation of the fundamental thesis that a bourgeois government could be nothing else but the agent of capitalistic exploitation, the strong arm stretched out to hold down the workers? Moreover, if a Millerand was justified in France, the orthodox Socialists argued, why should not the Italian, the English and the German Socialist leaders emulate his example? What would happen then to proletarian solidarity, and the unity of the workers of all nations?

Eduard Bernstein, together with the other Revisionists in Germany and the Fabians in England, developed socio-economic theories designed to justify turning away from revolutionary chiliasm towards a conception of socialism as a higher evolutionary phase in the continuous and unbroken history of European society. It was Jaurès who provided this transformation with its ethical philosophical justification. He described socialism militant and triumphant not as the negation of all the evil past, but as a ceaseless process of purification. In a highly thought-provoking passage, he argued that since the Renaissance every man had become an individual in his own right, and could not therefore be coerced. The goal was not the defeat of one class by another, but the opening of the gates of the city to every man, and particularly to those who had lagged behind. Socialism, therefore, was to be considered as a later, a more mature and a healthier variety of democratic liberalism. It is possible that the Dreyfus affair and the consequent reorientation of the Socialist Left made a decisive contribution to the French war effort in the 1914-18 War and to her ability to hold firm as one nation in her hour of supreme crisis.

V

Without actually surrendering the principle of class war or disavowing the vision of the revolutionary day of judgement, the Socialist parties gradually evolved into parliamentary and reformist parties bound by the rules of the parliamentary game, and deferring the revolutionary Apocalypse indefinitely. It was not only that Marx's prophecy of progressive proletarianisation had not been fulfilled and that the workers had entered on the road of *embourgeoisement* and felt no urge to risk the fleshpots for the sake of heroic gestures. It was now seen that the prophets of revolution had vastly exaggerated in their picture of the devilish cunning and utter ruthlessness of the liberal-capitalist régime, and in condemning all its laws and institutions as one gigantic malevolent conspiracy. The bourgeois enemy now appeared much weaker and more hampered by scruples, not so sure of himself, and not quite as purposeful as the prophets of revolution claimed. He was open to pressure and ready to withdraw in the face of threats and to waver under the impact of an appeal to reason and humanity. He also had a genuine horror of lawlessness and violence. In moments of clear-sighted objectivity, Marx himself was ready to acknowledge that in the course of its struggle against the arbitrariness of monarchic absolutism and feudal nobility, the bourgeoisie had evolved precious values—precision and fairness in the relations between man and man, a sense of responsibility as the condition and the by-product of constructive effort, respect for the due process of law, all flowing from a sense of self-respect, peculiar to the self-reliant individual. Only since then, according to Marx, the bourgeoisie had become alienated from its own values, from itself by becoming the slave of Moloch, of acquisitiveness without limit. The very nature of capitalist production was such that it could never be halted and was spurring those engaged in it relentlessly forward, to fight or perish. The workers themselves had absorbed many of the bourgeois values and attitudes, and, as a result, the revolution in the West, in contrast to Russia, lacked determination, as it was hampered by too many bourgeois inhibitions. The vision of a sudden redemption from Egyptian bondage, of a rapid passage from total darkness to the blaze of noon grew pale. Instinctive confidence that revolutionary coercion, despite the violence and the Machiavellian methods, embodied absolute justice, was shaken, especially in Germany, when every new election was returning larger and larger numbers of Social Democrats to the Reichstag, in spite of the attempts of Bismarck to stem the flood by half-hearted repression.

The Socialist ideology failed to send its believers to the

barricades. While its revolutionary drive was halted by the absorption of liberal ideas and the yielding attitude of the bourgeoisie, the doctrinal impact of socialism was strong enough to imbue the workers with a conviction that property was illegitimate, wage labour was an evil, and the employer, whatever his subjective qualities, was an enemy. With the weakening of the revolutionary ideology, which had thought in terms of universal working-class solidarity, this conviction lost its noble quality. Instead of a stimulus to heroic struggle, it easily evolved into a narrow or even selfish claim upon society, which when no longer visualised as on the way to a redemptive transformation, came more and more to represent the collective employer. Class solidarity assumed the character more of an expedient than of a deep experience and a vision of brotherhood.

The revolutionary *élan* faded, but the actual bargaining power of the workers increased beyond measure. The trends towards industrial concentration and the growing division of labour did not lead to the fulfilment of Marx's prophecy that monopolistic capitalism would result in the destruction of the handful of owner-managers and their replacement by the representatives of the workers. But they gradually culminated in a situation where the strike of a few workers in an essential industry or service—electricity, sanitation, the docks, the post offices—could bring an entire country to a standstill. A broken bolt, however minute, can halt an enormous machine and a grain of sand in the eye of a giant can render him helpless.

With the steady growth of the power of the labour unions, the line between defence and attack, between the assertion of rights and a policy of extortion, became blurred. A gulf opened up between theory and practice. Although feared alike by statesmen and industrialists, and quite prepared to enter bargains, the labour leaders still continued to feel and talk as if they were weak, downtrodden outlaws, struggling for their rights against an enemy both powerful and ruthless, as if they were the champions of pure ideals face to face with a world of evil.

It was Charles Péguy who said that it was the fate of every

idea to start as *mystique* and to degenerate into *politique*. Waiting for the revolutionary apocalypse was a *mystique*; the struggle for the amelioration of living conditions by the exploitation of opportunities became a *politique*. The Luddites in their fury had smashed machinery. The early revolutionary trade unions had advocated a mammoth general strike, "the grand holiday", had dreamed of worker co-operatives that would absorb or choke the capitalist economy. But as the wave of militancy ebbed, the workers, above all in England, came to realise that sporadic outbursts of violence, convulsive demonstrations of force, and self-isolation were less effective than an unceasing, modulated struggle based on the opportunist exploitation of situations as they arose. Concentration on limited advantages and a narrowing of vision and consequently of the sense of solidarity could go well together with a shrewd understanding that in the long run it was in the interest of the workers to work on a broad front. "Direct action" taken on the spot only by those immediately concerned gave way gradually, almost absent-mindedly, to far-flung organisations, complete with secretariats and permanent professional officials. But new difficulties arose. Those in command of the federations would be guided not by the immediate and sectional interests of one individual union or another, but by a general strategy, by a concern for the trade union movement as such. They would have to establish an order of priorities, even to abandon one position now in order to advance on another front or at another time. Moreover, if the battle was for advantages that could be won without the total overthrow of the existing social structure, then it became increasingly difficult to dissociate the interests of the union or the class from those of the community as a whole. This proved particularly true when the State ceased to be an outsider looking on as the employers and employees fought their battle to a finish, or concluded their bargains, but was compelled by the national interest to step in. In one way or another trade union leaders inevitably came to share actively in responsibility for and planning of national economic policies, and were drawn into the intricacies of the political parliamentary game. The stronger the trade unions grew, the more aware the workers became of the doctrine of Rousseau, who, thinking in terms of the city state, with its direct democracy in the style of ancient city republics, insisted that to elect a representative was to give oneself a master. It was inevitable that tension should develop between the represented and their representatives, between the members of the local branch, totally immersed in their own affairs, and their representatives caught up in a bureaucracy with its distinctive mentality, its broader horizons, its own methods of warfare, its particular power ethos. Both the sense of collective identity and of personal responsibility weakened. Many countries also became familiar with tension between the trade unions and the political representatives of the labour movement. The "intellectual" politicians would often be accused either of a doctrinaire leftism alien to the needs and the spirit of the workers fighting their daily battle for tangible improvements, or of exploiting the workers' cause for the sake of interests which, even when not actually egoistical, were utterly remote from the problems and needs of the ordinary worker. It was in France again that such tension grew most acute, because of the strong anti-parliamentary tradition there and because the pessimistic prophecies of the opponents of collaboration with the bourgeois governments have so often been proved right. So many a former Leftist combatant ended as a strike-breaking Prime Minister: Millerand, Viviani, Briand, Laval, and many other renegades who failed to get to the top. It was against this erosion of Socialist militancy that the Syndicalists of the type of Georges Sorel proclaimed their gospel of good honest violence and direct action.

VI

"Against noisy, garrulous and lying socialism, which is exploited by ambitious people of every description, which amuses a few buffoons and which is admired by decadents, revolutionary syndicalism takes its stand. Syndicalism, for its part, leaves nothing in a state of indecision. Its ideas are honestly expressed. It does not indulge in trickery but is absolutely frank. Its doctrines are not diluted by a stream of confused commentaries. Syndicalism strives to express itself in ways that illuminate phenomena, that assign those phenomena to their natural place and do justice to the various conflicting forces. Conflict should not be blurred over but accentuated. . . . Every effort should be made to stress the distinctiveness, the compactness of each of the groups now locked in battle. In short, the revolutionary movements of the masses must be described in a way that will make a deep and permanent impression on the soul of the revolutionaries.

"Such results cannot be attained by the use of ordinary language. A series of images must be exploited in order to produce an immediate instinctive effect, before there has been time for intellectual analysis, in order to arouse at one stroke all those jumbled emotions that are associated with the various aspects of the Socialist war against modern society. This aim is fully attained by the Syndicalists when they channel the whole of socialism into the drama of the general strike. Here there is no longer room for professorial equivocations. Everything is clear-cut and socialism cannot have more than one meaning. This method enjoys all the advantages that, according to the doctrines of Bergson, distinguish 'integral' knowledge from analysis. . . .

"Predictions take the form of myths. Within these myths are enclosed the most powerful urges of the people, the party, the class. With all the force of instinct, these urges constantly reveal themselves anew. They lend an aspect of reality to those hopes of immediate action . . . that guide the desires, passions and thought of men.

"The myth must be judged as a means of acting on the present. It is senseless to discuss how far it can be considered as a literal prediction of the future. The myth is important as an indivisible unity. Its component parts are significant only insofar as they give expression to the basic idea. No useful purpose, therefore, can be served by arguing about particular incidents which may occur during a social revolution or about those decisive trials of strength that may give victory to the proletariat. The picture of the general strike, painted by the revolutionaries, could prove a total illusion and yet, if it has included within itself all the aspirations of socialism, if it has given a unique precision and temper to the entire corpus of revolutionary thought, then it will still have acted as a great source of strength in preparing for the revolution. . . . It matters little whether the general strike is only in part a reality or even a mere product of the popular imagination. All that we have to know is whether the general strike embraces everything that Socialist doctrine expects of the revolutionary proletariat."[1]

This was the message of Georges Sorel, prophet of syndicalism, who saw no inconsistency in claiming both Lenin and Mussolini as disciples, and was emphatically claimed as teacher by the future Duce. Sorel voiced his condemnation of the Socialists of his day for degenerating from selfless and daring fighters for a holy cause into spineless philistines (a word of abuse beloved by Marx and Engels) and flabby sophists. His was a call for a clean fight between the two sides, for a direct trial of strength between giants in which the best man should win. Like Lenin, Sorel did not wish employers to be humane, susceptible to compromise and ready to see the other's point of view. On the contrary, it was preferable that Pharaoh should harden his heart, not only because an ardent thirst for battle was the sign of a worthy enemy, but also because employers who were callous and cruel were sure to instil a proper fighting spirit into the workers.

Every local or trade syndicate was seen by the Syndicalists as a combat unit engaged in direct action and thus free from the servitude that comes from surrendering the power of decision, the freedom to choose one's own weapons, to a distant bureaucracy. The syndicate spurned every attempt at joint action or offer of a bargain with employers or even with State authorities, such as elected assemblies, that claimed a spurious neutrality. Direct action meant mass strikes, aggressive acts of provocation and sabotage, the unleashing of a chain of strikes that would eventually extend into a general strike, into the great revolutionary spasm; but violence could also mean a show of such overwhelming

---

[1] Georges Sorel: *Réflexions sur la Violence*, 2nd edn., Paris 1910, pp. 159-60, 167-8.

strength and unflinching resolve that the enemy reeled and gave up.

The goal was the destruction of the established capitalist system by constant resort to direct action, by a relentless succession of offensives launched against the fortress from all sides. Following the total destruction of the State in its existing form, all centralisation—even those temporary and flexible forms seemingly demanded by the exigencies of revolution and civil war—must be shunned, because bureaucratic centralisation always entailed slavery, the betrayal of high ideals and deep-seated aspirations. On the ruins of the State would rise a loose-knit grouping of Syndicalist units, each of which would embrace all the producers and consumers living in one small district. Only loose federal ties would connect the separate units. Syndicalism preached the right to use violence against all forces of impersonal coercion (the State, capitalism, the entire structure of centralisation even if erected by the workers), in order to attain true, direct, immediate freedom (that of the Syndicalist units).

The general strike was to serve as the ultimate weapon to meet the most deadly weapon of the capitalist State—the army—and the proletarian myth of the general strike was to be pitted against the myth of the bourgeoisie—the national war. Since barricades had been shown to be completely ineffectual in the face of modern weapons, an army could be defeated only by a strike that would bring industry and transport to a halt. The workers were unable to prevent capitalist conspiracies from leading to imperialist wars, but they could, when a war had actually broken out, sit with folded arms, confident that the trains meant to carry troops and weapons would not run, that the soldiers would go unfed. And if the Government incited the soldiers against the treasonous strikers, it would simply unleash a civil war, and bring nearer the hour of revolution. In a period of general conscription, the young workers and peasants would respond far more readily to the myth of the general strike of the Socialist apocalypse, than to that of a trench war waged on behalf of capitalist interests.

However, as we have seen, Georges Sorel was not primarily

interested in the goal. He refused to go into details, to weigh
the chances of success, to discuss the ultimate destination.
With a kind of exaltation he dwelt on the history of such
Messianic movements as early Christianity and the Reformation which showed how widely results diverged from
expectations. Essential to him was the *élan vital*, the display of
heroic energy, the very act of self-sacrifice; not the end, but
the vision; not the destination, but the movement.

It is as a disillusioned and furiously contemptuous reaction
against the smugness, the hypocrisy, the conventional lies,
the mean pettiness of the bourgeoisie that we have to view
the wave of anti-liberalism and anti-intellectualism that
began to gather momentum in the last decades of the
nineteenth century and was represented by such diverse
thinkers and movements as Nietzsche, imperialistic racialism
which in the late nineteenth century sang hymns of praise to
the mission of the Teutonic race destined to inherit the
degenerate Latins, Georges Sorel with his doctrine of
Syndicalist violence, social Darwinism in various forms,
Bolshevism, Ibsen, Tolstoy, Max Nordau and Sigmund
Freud. From being a class of self-made captains of industry
and dedicated pioneers, the bourgeoisie—so ran the indictment—had sunk into smug complacency and mean cowardice. Its corruption had infected even the proletariat.

Hence the longing for primary impulses, elemental energy,
fresh, immediate and strong emotions. The intellectual's
sophisticated casuistry was condemned by the prophets of
wrath as token of infirmity of will and uncertainty of purpose.
Reasoned compromise was branded as mean cowardice when
compared with the passion for power, the urge for self-
expression, for domination, indeed for destruction. A
morality based on compromise, on turning the cheek, on
consideration for others was merely a rationalisation of
impotence. Psychologists and sociologists made a very effective contribution towards undermining respect for man as an
autonomous personality possessed of reason and guided by
an absolute moral code. The cohesive personality with strong
contours disintegrated and in its place was revealed a criss-
cross picture of dark desires, ugly lusts, aggressive egoism,

unconscious fears, dumb obtuseness, irrational impulses and aversions. Could the subjection of such a creature to a more cohesive personality and more determined will really be considered the violation of the autonomy of a rational personality capable of making moral choices? For what was the art of government and the secret of the great constructive achievements in history—it was being asked—if not that those who were able to do so never hesitated to use power, to coerce, to simplify complex problems by reducing them to the simplest choices. It was no accident that Pareto, who was one of the writers to undermine the self-confidence of European liberalism and individualism, should also have been responsible—together with his fellow countryman Mosca—for the theory of *élites* destined to rule, and to have openly commended physical violence against politicians well before the advent of Fascism to power, that régime which made him a Senator. The Italian by choice, Robert Michels, set out to unmask all political parties and trade unions as nothing but selfish and self-perpetuating oligarchies. "Democratic freedom is not only dead, but the stench is already rising from the corpse," declared Mussolini. The exclusive totalitarian party of Right or Left is the *élitist* theory incarnate.

World War I made a decisive contribution to the triumph of violence during the inter-war years. Insanity stared mankind in the face. A generation earlier, the spiritual stability of society had already found itself threatened by numerous dangers. But these were marginal symptoms or mere omens —scattered clouds on the distant horizon. Man knew (or was confident that he knew) what to expect. He knew the correct relationship between investment and profit, effort and result, plan and product, goods and price, ends and means. In this sense, it can be said that he knew his place in the world and was in command of himself and of his environment. This certainty was destroyed during the years from 1914 to 1918 and by the upheavals that followed in the wake of the war. At the outbreak of the war both sides were convinced not merely that they would be victorious but also that it would be all over by Christmas. Yet the war surpassed the most fiendish nightmares in its dimensions and horrors, its destruction of life and property, its impact on the human spirit. Its cost was out of all proportion to anything that could possibly be gained even by total victory. It was the curtain-raiser to the impasse that was to be reached a generation later with the invention of the atomic bomb and nuclear missiles. What end, what reparation, could make the use of such means worth while?

And so total war gave rise to totalitarian ideologies. Extreme suffering could be justified only by absolute ends, while expectation of total salvation in turn justified most extreme measures. The war and the feelings of shame and revulsion that it aroused have been movingly described by Remarque, Arnold Zweig, Barbusse and Hašek in books which received much publicity. But there were other writers such as Ernst Jünger and Gabriele D'Annunzio who exercised enormous influence in Germany and Italy and who, with the terrible pride of despair, gloried in the intoxication of reckless bravery, in the lust for killing and blood, in the song of those doomed to die supremely contemptuous of the flabby cowardice of the good-natured bourgeois with his fireside slippers.

Trench warfare developed forms of comradeship and types of organisation which later proved to be of major significance and wrought their destructive influence during the span of an entire generation. In their army unit, soldiers of different origins and character discovered a new companionship, not that of the trade union, the political party or the recreational club, but that of life, danger, destiny shared. Despite hierarchical structure and military discipline, there developed a fraternal spirit among soldiers when the squalid conditions and the danger of death made them all equal. From these men, particularly from among the many officers who rose from the ranks—and it has to be remembered that the professional officer class, which at least in Germany came mainly from the nobility, had been virtually exterminated during the first months of the war—were drawn the *Freikorps*, the storm troop officers of Mussolini and Hitler, and perhaps (we cannot know) the Soviet secret police. Many of these junior officers could not or would not return to civilian life. Frequently they had no home to which to return. And the time was soon to come when once again they could indulge the habits they had acquired, be it in command, be it in the ranks, when once again they could attain self-expression by murder and cruelty, and satisfy their need to belong to a band of men who shared an entire way of life.

The para-military formations of the post-1918 period developed a much more effective style of violent, terrorist action than that of the occasionally assembled amorphous proletarian mob, seized by hysteria and easily given to panic, or of the organised groups of rowdies of the *Action Française*, specialising in breaking up meetings of opponents and the lectures of Republican professors. Theirs was terror sustained and well-regulated; to the victims infinitely more deadly, to sympathisers "clean" and orderly.

VII

At the close of World War I, in Russia and Italy, organised violence was first made into a system of government. Why were these countries the first? And why did Bolshevism conquer in the one, Fascism in the other? This latter question receives its peculiar significance from the fact (to which we return below) that in the immediate post-war years, it was Italy which, after Russia, seemed to be the country ripest for a Communist revolution, the Italian Socialist party having early joined the Third International. Bakunin had expended much energy in Italy and he left behind him a school of anarchist and Syndicalist radicalism. Benito Mussolini, until he chose a different road, had been an extreme Left-wing Socialist. By origin he was a pure proletarian and in his youth he had immersed himself in the works of Marx and Engels. He had studied Bergson and Sorel, and sat at the feet of the "grandmother" of the Socialist revolutionaries, Angelica Balabanova. It should be noted that Mussolini was the first example of a trend that requires analysis—conversion of out-and-out Left-wing Socialists, including Communists, to Fascism: Oswald Mosley, Marcel Déat, Jacques Doriot, in a certain sense Hendrik de Man, Joseph Pilsudski, a number of the Vichy leaders and many more. (In Germany however, such examples are not to be found, and this in itself is a fact that still has to be explained.) It is in this connection legitimate to ask what is the justification for the view which selects totalitarian violence as the common denominator of the two vast political movements which between the two wars seized the initiative and threatened (one of them is still threatening) to drive out the liberal-democratic tradition. And if the two movements can be brought under this common denominator, why did one country turn to the Right and the other to the Left? And should we not regard Fascism as a violent reaction to Socialism on the part of men who passed through Socialism but found it wanting, instead of treating Fascism as the direct heir of old-fashioned conservative reaction?[1]

[1] Paradoxically as it will sound at first, this curious development may to a large extent be traced back to the after-effects of Eduard Bernstein's revisionism. Bernstein admittedly preached a parliamentary-democratic form of Socialism. Yet quite different conclusions were likely to be drawn and indeed were drawn from his theory. Bernstein denied the historic inevitability of Socialism. He described that notion as cant and coined the beautiful phrase "from cant to Kant". He meant to imply that far from having to be given up, Socialism should become a categorical ethical imperative, a good which will not drop into the lap of men in God's own time but should be brought about by human resolve. This gave rise to Kantian Socialism of the Marburg school of philosophy on the one hand, and lent support to the idea of a great active élite dedicated to a mission and to strenuous effort on the other hand. It still needs investigation to what extent Bernstein's revisionism provoked Lenin's firm decision that the Revolution was a matter for a closely-knit, disciplined confraternity of professional revolutionaries and his fear that Socialism left to workers' spontaneity would degenerate into mere trade-unionism. The case of Georges Sorel is quite clear. Under the impact of Bernstein's work he writes La Décomposition du Marxisme, and this is followed by Les Illusions du Progrès and still more significantly the Réflexions sur la Violence. But the confusion engendered also a movement in the opposite direction. Bernstein refuted the idea of an international Revolution as a predetermined universal catastrophe. He placed strong emphasis on local conditions, national characteristics and historic tradition, and came close to giving his blessing to nationalism, while some of his German followers went so far as to adopt a friendly attitude towards German imperialist ambitions, at first on the ground that denial of colonies to Germany amounted to support for British monopolistic imperialism. Strenuous socialist activism of an élite could—once the idea of universal revolution was given up—easily coalesce with that type of nationalism which proclaims nationalism to be socialism confined to a single nation, as Enrico Corradini put it as early as 1911. There was also the urge for planning, administering, in brief getting things done which, once the idea of world Revolution was relegated into the far background as unreal, was bound to fasten upon the nation state as the natural field of action, challenge and objective. It is no accident that some of the closest collaborators of Georges Sorel, notably Georges Valois

Lenin's attitude to revolutionary coercion was the classical one of revolutionaries of the type of Blanqui. Czarism for him typified a régime based upon arbitrary violence and so its laws were not laws, its courts not the guardians of justice. Essentially, this had been the argument of Blanqui in 1832 when, appealing to the chivalry of his French judges, he demanded that he be treated as a prisoner of war. Lenin felt no need to plead or justify the principle of revolutionary coercion. That was beyond discussion. For him the problem of how to make the revolution was a question of technique, although the technical decisions themselves were, of course, dependent upon fundamental assumptions and portentous historical evaluations. In his opinion, a mass party with a democratic structure— elections, decentralisation, an accountable leadership— could not be established in a state like Czarist Russia which was based on oppressive laws and the secret police, which choked all free expression, and prevented every attempt at

and Edouard Berth, struck up—with Sorel's blessing—on the eve of 1914 an alliance with the extreme nationalists of the *Action Française*—an episode seen by some writers as the hour of birth of Fascism. This proto-Fascist *élitism* found its expression in such ominously entitled books as the wholly Nietzschean *L'Homme qui vient* of Georges Valois and *Les Méfaits des Intellectuels* of Edouard Berth. The flirtation between the Sorelian syndicalists and the French ultra-nationalist Royalists had its parallel in Italy, where Sorel was indeed better known and more influential than in his own country, contributing to various Italian journals and maintaining a regular correspondence with Croce, Pareto, Michels and other important figures. The child of the liaison between the Italian syndicalists such as Paolo Orano and Angelo Oliviero Olivetti, and the nationalist prophet Enrico Corradini in the years 1909-12 was according to Gaudens Megaro the totalitarian Fascism of Italy in 1925 (Gaudens Megaro: *Mussolini in the Making*, London 1938, p. 235). Still more interesting of course is the case of Benito Mussolini. At a certain moment of his development the ardent young Marxist falls under the spell of Nietzsche. And a seed of far-reaching developments is then sown. The war of 1914 was the decisive moment in his life. To the extreme revolutionary and preacher of "direct action", a policy of neutrality towards a world conflict which was bound to change the destinies of mankind and—as Mussolini at first feared—bring the triumph of reactionary Prussian militarism and Junkerdom, appeared as the very negation of Socialism, with its vision of some total break-through. The dismal collapse of Socialist internationalism and then the experience of war drove home to the reviler of patriotism and fatherland, who only yesterday was calling the national flag "a rag upon a dunghill", the intense, all-pervasive reality of the national sentiment and the primacy of the national interest. The young revolutionary Socialist found it easy to transfer his early ardent contempt for parliamentarism in all its forms, his cult of violence, his glorification of the role of *élites*, and his passionate craving for action and history-making to the service of a national "*socialism*". (See Ernst Nolte: *Marx und Nietzsche im Sozialismus des jungen Mussolini, Historische Zeitschrift*, Vol. 191, 1960.

independent organisation. There was no realistic alternative to the narrow, tight-knit, highly disciplined organisation of professional revolutionary commandos who day and night had to be on the alert and ready for battle.

The Mensheviks and other critics of Lenin's doctrine claimed that it entailed a *putsch* along Jacobin or Blanquist lines and that it ignored Marx's concept of the bourgeois revolution as an essential stage between feudal absolutism—Czarism—and the Socialist revolution. There could be no Socialist revolution before the objective conditions had matured, before industrialisation had so far advanced that the means of production had become concentrated in the hands of a few, and the industrial workers could be numbered in millions. By such standards, Russia of all the important countries of Europe was of course the least prepared for a Socialist revolution.

In reply it was argued that the Russian economy was not really so backward, that prior to 1914 Russian industry had advanced at a far greater speed, with far greater energy, than had its British counterpart during the long drawn-out industrial revolution, and that essentially industry in Russia was the creation and the preserve of foreign monopolistic capital. Moreover, nobody imagined that the revolution would remain confined to Russia nor, indeed, that it could survive there unless it spread to other countries and so was able to frustrate the efforts of the capitalist powers to uproot the Socialist revolution. (That such attempts would inevitably be made was an axiom among the faithful.) Thus, it was possible to describe Russia as the weak link in the world capitalist chain and the Bolshevik revolution as a thrust at the universal enemy, as the opening campaign of a global struggle rather than as an isolated upheaval in one country.

Considered at another level, Lenin's view was much more acute, more suited to Russian reality, than that of his critics who argued that it was essential to go through a period of constitutional freedom and bourgeois liberal government. The critics urged that the proletariat needed such a period of freedom of speech, of association and of cultural self-expression in order to equip itself for its historical role. Lenin,

however, had followed the development of Western Europe
and he was well aware of the elements of absurdity and, in a
sense, of Machiavellian chicanery, that were contained in
the Socialist plan first to make an alliance with the bourgeoisie—or perhaps merely with the *petit bourgeoisie*—and then
all in good time to destroy it. Moreover, he had learnt that a
proletariat which had tasted the bourgeois freedoms and
grown accustomed to the rule of law, to impartial justice, to
the inviolability of the individual's personality, would no
longer act as an efficient instrument of violent and bloody
revolution. If the revolution was the primary goal—and this
was not in question—then elemental violence in the tradition
of Stenka Razin and Pugachev, the leaders of peasant and
Cossack risings, would be an infinitely more effective vehicle
of historical advance than parties which had accustomed
themselves to parliamentary ways.

To those critics who accused him of preaching *putschism*,
without paying heed to the objective situation, without
waiting for the masses to be ready for action, and for the
balance of power to be tipped, Lenin could answer that he too
was opposed to the capture of the governmental machine by a
mere handful of men representing only themselves who would,
as it were, make the revolution by announcing that they had
made it. Although the Leninist revolutionary vanguard was
to seize the initiative and engineer the uprising, it was sure of
support from those countless peasant masses who in Russia
were always ready to unleash havoc. The decisive role in
spreading the revolution throughout the length and breadth
of the vast empire would thus be played by the peasantry,
but the revolutionary Socialists who had ignited the fuse
would not have to fear it as a rival for power. The peasants
were never eager for political power, for they had eyes only
for the land of their noble and rich neighbours. Once the
peasants had seized the land they coveted, they would return
to their homes to enjoy the booty. And thus the revolutionary
vanguard, the Communist party, the organisation of the
dedicated revolutionaries, would be able to remain at the
helm. The strategy outlined by Marx in his speech of 1850
to the Communist League would now at last be executed,

with this one modification. Marx had envisaged a permanent revolution, a continuous transition from the anti-feudal bourgeois revolution to the Socialist revolution, and this revolution in permanence required that the proletariat should first ally itself with, and then betray, the *petit bourgeoisie*; in Lenin's doctrine the peasants were the allies to be destroyed eventually in the same way as the *petit bourgeoisie*. Initially the peasants would be incited to appropriate the land of the nobles and the gentry, but eventually it would of course be taken away from them by force.

It is highly instructive to compare the attitude of the liberal West with that of the Bolshevik East. Ramsay MacDonald wrote in bitter despair shortly after the outbreak of hostilities in 1914 that although he was convinced that the war was totally evil, a moral disaster, he could not bring himself to say this in public while the youth of the nation was dying in the trenches of Flanders.[1] He felt that it would be a great wrong to those youngsters if they were told that they were dying in vain, giving their lives for the sake of a frightful evil. Lenin did not hesitate for a moment to call upon the soldiers to drop their rifles and flee to their homes. When he appealed to the peasants with the slogan "Plunder the Plunderers!", he was showing his scorn for the fine scruples of the other Socialist parties which during 1917 tried to halt the mounting anarchy in the countryside and which insisted that only the Constituent Assembly, acting according to the full legal formalities, could decide whether or not to expropriate and redistribute the land. Otherwise, they argued, Russia would rapidly return to the law of the jungle.[2] (When in 1962 a group of British anti-Fascists raided a Nazi summer camp situated in private grounds, the Socialist,

[1] Ralph Miliband: *Parliamentary Socialism*, London 1961, p. 44.

[2] As E. H. Carr remarks, Lenin was genuinely unable to understand the legal scruples and liberal-democratic convictions of Western Social-democracy. He was at a loss to explain the shock which Western workers felt at the unceremonious dissolution of the Russian Constituent Assembly by the Bolsheviks. When an anarchist representative pointed out in a debate in 1918 that, whereas the Russian proletariat was not "state-minded", the Western proletariat "feels itself as the bearer of a fragment of power and as a part of this same which it is at present defending", all that Lenin could say in reply was that the view expressed was "so stupid that I do not know how it could be more so". E. H. Carr: *The Bolshevik Revolution*, London 1953, Vol. III, p. 180.

and anti-Fascist, *New Statesman* criticised the incident as an act of violence incompatible with the rules of democracy.)

Violence spawns violence. The Bolsheviks had breached the dykes and they could halt the waters only by constant and ever more frequent resort to violence and terror. Communists point out that the achievements of the revolution were constantly threatened by enemies who ranged from the White armies on the right to Socialist revolutionaries and Anarchists on the left. Yet it must not be forgotten that if a movement bases itself on an ideology that defines the elect as an exclusive group, it thereby places very large sections of the population, if not everyone, beyond the pale and is bound to treat them with suspicion and hostility. It will try to suppress or intimidate them and in so doing will turn them into potential or active enemies. The same will happen in the sphere of foreign relations. It is true that the Soviet Union was encircled by hostility, but is this surprising when one remembers that day and night its rulers kept proclaiming themselves the assault group, the vanguard, of the armed revolutions that were destined to break out in every land? The enmity of the Soviet Union for the capitalist states was characterised by an unwavering determination that was in marked contrast to the vacillating and inconsistent policies of England, France and the U.S.A. And, in the last resort, the Western powers declared war not, as the Bolsheviks had prophesied, against the Soviet Union but against Nazi Germany, which had then just concluded its pact with Russia.

If the October Revolution had been followed by a Communist revolution in Europe, it is quite possible that a relaxation would have taken place in the Bolshevik rule forty years earlier. Once the European revolution had failed to mature, once it had been decided to build socialism in one country (and there was no apparent alternative), then it followed that defence requirements had to be given top priority and that heavy industry took precedence over consumer goods. Such a decision, bound up as it was with the collectivisation of the land—to foot the bill of industrialisation, and not merely for the sake of doctrinal consistency—

necessitated maximal centralisation, the mailed fist, coercion and terror. An exclusive Messianic ideology demands coercion, and coercion develops according to its own inexorable logic.

VIII

The tragedy of the Italian Socialist movement (and, indeed, of Italy as a whole) was that, although the post-war years were ripe for revolution, the Socialists could not find the courage to choose between the alternatives open to them and to embark upon a clear-cut policy—violent revolution in the Russian style or whole-hearted co-operation with liberal parliamentary democracy which, as G. D. H. Cole has pointed out, would probably have laid the foundations of a modern welfare state.[1] Such hesitations at such a moment played into the hands of a new force, the Fascist Right, which in its readiness to use violence was handicapped by no scruples or inhibitions.

Geography and history alike had prescribed that Italy be a unified state. The peninsula was marked off from the outside world by mountains and sea. Its population spoke one language, professed one religion, shared the glories of the common cultural tradition. Yet there was a flaw which for hundreds of years delayed unification, and after the unification hampered the development of an effective parliamentary régime. Loyalty to province or to sectional interest had proved stronger than the more abstract allegiance to the national interest. Coastal cities looked outward in pursuit of trading empires rather than to their hinterland, and with industrialisation the gulf between the flourishing North and the backward feudal South grew wider and wider.

In Italy there was even more justification than in France for the accusation of Oswald Spengler that to engage in parliamentary politics was simply to conduct private business by other means. The Italian city states had maintained for many centuries the tradition of the ancient city states with their close identification of parties with particular classes,

---

[1] G. D. H. Cole: *History of Socialist Thought. Communism and Social Democracy, 1914-1931*, London 1958, Part I, pp. 392-3.

trades, professions or guilds, and no ideological pretence to clothe class or sectional interest. When, in medieval or Renaissance Italy, internecine political warfare of this kind threatened utterly to destroy a city state, order had to be restored by a local tyrant or else the people would call in an outsider to act as Podestà, as a supreme arbiter to whom they would yield almost unlimited powers for the sake of peace and security. In *The Prince* of Machiavelli can be heard the despair of an Italian patriot, and Hobbes could well point to the lessons of Italy.

At the close of World War I, Italy was a profoundly disturbed and restless country nursing a grievance. In 1915, on the strength of the innumerable promises given her, she had deserted her allies, Germany and Austria-Hungary. Among other things she had been promised an empire in Asia Minor. (Later, the Caucasian mountains were suggested instead.) Italy suffered a number of humiliating defeats at the hands of the Austrians and was only saved from disaster by effective Allied help. As a result of the miserable contribution she made to the Allied war effort, the victors showed greater sympathy for the Serbs who had fought with such great valour, and who were the first victim of the Central Powers. The cavalier manner in which Italy was treated at Versailles was regarded as an insult to the nation, and the Italian delegation walked out of the conference after Wilson had asked Orlando if he was also seeking to unite the two million Italians in New York with the Italian kingdom.

Moreover, in these years Italy was subjected not only to pangs of conscience and to national humiliation, but also to a series of weak governments which were driven hither and thither by events. Every few weeks one government would be replaced by the next, but the composition of the ministries hardly changed. Always there were the same parties, the same men, and consequently Government prestige declined disastrously. The rage aroused by a government that did not know how to defend the interests and honour of the nation, provoked the poet D'Annunzio and his armed disciples to seize Fiume by force and to convert it into an independent, and somewhat operatic, state. The Italian Government could not find the courage either to expel these modern Condottieri or, in face of forceful opposition from the Powers, to annex Fiume. On the Left, the economic crisis, the inflation and the Bolshevik Revolution, which had an electrifying effect on Italian Socialists, all combined to unleash a series of strikes, accompanied by acts of sabotage and by Syndicalist demands for the nationalisation of industries and a workers' share in the management of factories, and many plants were actually seized by the workers. The Government looked on helplessly, sometimes yielding amid a flurry of promises, sometimes compelled to rely on the power of the police. It was constantly falling between two stools, whether because of its undoubted weakness or because of the simple dishonesty of cowardice. The prestige of the representative institutions was reduced still further by major scandals which involved party leaders and other exalted figures of the parliamentary world. The latters' inability to solve the national and social problems confronting the State shook all faith in the parliamentary régime as a viable instrument of government.

"Direct action" by the workers culminated in two general strikes, but the revolution failed to come off. When the Fascists reacted by resorting to "direct action" themselves, they succeeded in seizing power and establishing a dictatorial régime. Why were the revolutionaries on the Left unable to follow in the footsteps of the Bolsheviks in Russia? And why did their defeat lead to a Fascist victory?

The Fascists and the Communists alike claimed to speak in the name of the real interests of the nation. To the Communists, the working class constituted the nation, for all other sections of the population lacked real legitimacy, and were destined to disappear. The Fascists spoke in the name of a national state which was beyond and above classes, parties and sectional interests. Both Russia and Italy had suffered defeat in war. Yet, in contrast to Italy, Russia, for all its military disasters, was so conscious of its ultimate might that it remained relatively immune to sentiments of national shame. No appeal to national pride could stem the flood of social revolution in Russia once the dykes were breached. In

Italy, wounded patriotism proved stronger a passion than social wrath. The Italian Government was weak and its conduct was unedifying and ineffectual, but it was not as brutal by far as Czarist Russia had been, not therefore cruel enough to goad the workers and peasants into a *jacquerie*, and a leap in the dark. Russia had nothing to rival Italy's very long tradition of urban self-government and civil liberties, its proudly independent middle class, its Catholic Church strong in the faith of many millions, or, indeed, its conservative peasantry of the South. Thus, when it came to the test, the Italian Left lacked the strength and the daring to launch a real revolutionary offensive. Because of this lack of real determination, its sporadic sallies, its strikes and sabotage, could evoke neither respect nor resigned fear. They came to be regarded as a punch below the belt, as hooliganism threatening the very foundations of the national economy and the very survival of the State, to which foreign powers had denied justice. The exasperated bourgeoisie and Nationalists joined in a resolve "to put an end to all this anarchy". They were thus only too ready to welcome the Fascist "crusade" against all sectional interests (represented by Socialists, trade unions, parties, capitalists) which divided the nation against itself, sapped its strength and paralysed its progress. Their government was to act on behalf of the nation as a whole and restore national discipline. There is no doubt that financial interests supported Fascism and contributed to its success, but it is erroneous to see the Fascist movement as inspired by or merely a tool of the capitalists. Big business was quite ready to use Fascism as a shield against Communism, but it did not create it. Both in Italy and in Germany, the capitalists were to discover in due course that they had jumped on to a runaway train. In a famous speech, Mussolini, albeit speaking in a different context, coined the slogan that in Italy it was not one particular class but the entire people which was underprivileged. After World War I, he claimed, the problem was not class war, not the division between the downtrodden classes and the well-to-do, but the international schism between the hungry nations and the satiated nations, between Italy, Germany and Japan, on the one hand, and the Western powers, on the other. In such a situation, he claimed, a revolutionary explosion on a global scale was inevitable.

The emergence of Fascism and Bolshevism may from a certain point of view be regarded as the repudiation of politics as the traditional contest between competing interests, views and parties. Government, untrammelled by these, would serve one all-embracing and exclusive cause: of the nation or the working classes—the real nation. And who would govern? Not men chosen in competitive elections, for they would merely represent sectional interests, attitudes and parties, but the elect, the pure—the party of the proletarian vanguard in one case, the unadulterated national party in the other.

IX

Should society be modelled according to a blue-print, be directed towards a well-defined and all-inclusive goal? Or should it rather balance the multifarious factors and forces, give voluntary associations free play, permit tensions and even dangerous collisions, resort as little as possible to control and coercion? In short, is a monolithic preferable to a pluralistic society? The latter may produce anarchy, the former must culminate in totalitarian dictatorship. Inherent in pluralism is the danger that the strong will be able to lord it over society, that the weak and the unsuccessful will be exploited by the ruthless and the unscrupulous, that politics will become the instrument of sectional and selfish interests. The monolithic society gives free play to the despotism of rulers who do not have to account for their actions, become intoxicated and corrupted by power, and can be removed only by force.

The difference between the two schools of thought may be reduced to the fact that the one affirms the necessity of and the other denies the need for politics. From Plato until our own time there have always been thinkers straining to turn politics into an exact science or claiming that competent and honest administration can render politics superfluous. Even before Marx and Engels, Saint-Simon had held the theory that politics—the rule of man by man—would eventually be replaced by the administration of things. Lenin prophesied that the affairs of State would one day be so simple that even an ordinary cook would be able to administer them. And the Nazi-Fascist one-party system with its single electoral list reflects the same eagerness to eliminate politics in their traditional form.

The case against politics, particularly against the politics of parliaments and parties has been stated and restated again and again. To Plato and Saint-Simon, politics as they were belonged to the sphere of mere opinion and mere belief or even make-believe, whereas they should deal in an exact and scientific manner with facts that were open to precise assessment. Political life was guesswork, its perpetual debates were devoted to trivialities and it was characterised by the contradiction between words and deeds, by the mixture of sheer place-hunting and ideological self-inflation and never ending strain and humbug. At root it was an immoral game. Either the politicians did not know what they were talking about, and were simply deluding themselves and others at the same time, or else they knew full well and used their knowledge deliberately and wickedly to deceive. In short, politics were a screen for sectional interests, lust for power, and love of self-display.

Moreover, parliamentary government gave the stamp of legality to irresponsibility, incompetence and inactivity. A constant succession of new ministries was calculated to destroy continuity, to sap all sense of responsibility and to produce a government that was either anonymous or else demagogic. The political mediocrities, anxious above all to be re-elected and not to fall out with the voters or the party organisation, would cautiously refrain from the dangerous risk of taking up a determined stand, while the bold and the insolent, particularly when in opposition, would have no scruples in using any demagogic trick in order to attract attention. To be effective a government must be ready to adopt energetic measures, however unpopular, but it was just these measures that would never be pushed through by a parliamentary and multi-party régime. It could not act with the necessary vigour, for the conflicting interests, the rival parties and the warring pressure groups effectively cancelled each other out and the net result was paralysis. The coalition system itself was the victory of immorality. While each party boasted about its own unique ideology, parliamentary coalition demanded that every party constantly denies its avowed principles and agrees to one compromise after another.

Why should not economics and sociology define the needs of man and of society in precise statistical terms, set these needs against the available resources and so enable us to estimate exactly where we stand? Power should go to the technocrats, the administrators and the statisticians. If, as the Marxists maintained, the economic basis was the essential determinant, if the parties were motivated by economic interests and not by ideological convictions, then the destruction of the class society, and of the sectional interests that cloak themselves in ideas, would be enough to render parties superfluous. Trotsky carried this line of thought to extremes and argued during the years following the October Revolution for the abolition of the trade unions in the Soviet Union. Strictly defined, the trade unions were weapons for the defence of the working class against the capitalist order. Once a Socialist régime had been established, once the State and the means of production were in the possession of the workers, what justification could there be for the survival of the trade unions? Should they fight against their own government, the government of workers and peasants?

Italian Fascism boasted of its Hegelian heritage. Like Marx and Engels, Mussolini went back to Hegel's central and portentous distinction between Society and the State. While the Socialists drew conclusions diametrically opposed to those of Hegel, Mussolini claimed to have realised Hegel's original vision. Society embraced all the spontaneous and fundamentally selfish aspirations and interests of individuals and groups, much as egoism was tempered by the individual's belonging to one group or another, the family, the professional association or trade union, the class,

to which he surrendered a part of himself, from whom he
accepted a measure of moral restraint and discipline, and
to whom he felt a sense of obligation. Above Society was
poised the State, the embodiment of impersonal values,
indeed of the categorical imperative. The State was morality
incarnate because it laid down absolute norms without
promising any personal reward for obedience. It demanded
service but did not offer privileges in exchange. The State
was God because it was an end in itself. Its goals were
objective, neither representing any narrow sectional calculations, nor directed to the benefit of any particular segment
of the nation. Mussolini preached a form of State based on
corporations composed of the delegates of the workers, the
employers and the technocrats. These corporations, in some
ways reminiscent of the Syndicalist concepts, were to act
according to exact scientific methods for the co-ordination
and reconciliation of the diverse interests which they
represented—labour, industry and finance. The Fascist
Chamber of Deputies, on the other hand, was to represent
the State, the nation one and indivisible. It is worthy of note
that at first the electoral law guaranteed a majority of
parliamentary seats to the party receiving over twenty-five
per cent of the total vote and that only with the passage of
time were the other parties eliminated.

X

Indeed, the sphere of politics is the realm of guesswork, of
ambitious rivalry, at times of deliberate deception, and
political life is a web of base motives and unholy bargains.
Its jealousies and hatreds, the futility of political debate, and
the frustrations of parliamentary life drive many to despair.
Many a forceful and purposeful statesman conscious of his
powers, and convinced of the purity of his intentions has been
tempted to send home or imprison all these fatuous babblers,
all these evil-doers or fools, in order to free himself from the
constant badgering and interference of selfish or misguided
intriguers, and have room to do things smoothly, efficiently
and effectively. In truth, however, these snares and stum-
bling blocks which exasperate and sometimes even crush a

statesman of initiative and daring are also salutary safety valves. The irrational passions, bred by dark urges of aggression or revulsion, are an integral part of man's nature, and are ingredients in the compound structure which we call society. Plato dreamed of philosophers who had acquired real knowledge instead of mere opinion, who had freed themselves from those egoistical desires which cloud the mind, and were therefore fit to rule. He was not without fear lest the philosophers, once having escaped from the cave of his famous metaphor into the sunlight, would find themselves totally blinded when they first returned to the darkness which the majority of mankind had never left. But he ignored the truth that politics was doomed to remain for ever a dark cave and that it would therefore constitute an act of violence to attempt to impose the ways of the bright light on the world of shadows, the ideas of pure reason on men of flesh and blood sunk in eternal doubt, of pure will on a world of extremely mixed motives. Like all the Greek philosophers, Plato believed that to acquire truth was to act according to its dictates, oblivious as he was of the unbridgeable gulf between knowing and acting, which is the core of the human tragedy, sometimes called original sin. Max Weber caught a glimpse of the innermost recesses of the cave, when he wrote that "the world is governed by demons ... he who lets himself in for politics, that is for power and force as means, contracts with diabolic powers, and for his action it is not true that good can only follow from good and evil from evil, but that often the opposite is true. Anyone who fails to see this is, indeed, a political infant."

As has been amply proved in modern times, every attempt to impose the rule of certainty in politics brings to power not the philosophers with a clear knowledge of the truth but the most arrogant power seekers, the most insolent tyrants. Such attempts have not brought the ship safely into port, but on the contrary have set it helplessly adrift into the midst of stormy seas. For if legitimate government in both its traditional forms—that of the hereditary monarchy claiming divine right, and that of the representative régime based on popular sovereignty—is replaced by the principle of rule by an *élite*, then there can no longer be any objective and stable criteria. The leader will emerge, in other words, he will prove himself the leader. The proof is in the act. The *fait accompli* of usurpation through the elimination of all competitors and the suppression of opposition is the vindication of his rights. On the morrow of the night of long knives in 1934 good Western liberal journalists admiringly acknowledged that Hitler had shown himself a real leader. The master of violence has to recruit ever new members into his *corps d'élite*, his praetorian guard, to train them by means of progressive brutalisation for their task of maintaining ruthless discipline. He has to buy them by satisfying their lust for power and prestige, or else to corrupt them by surfeiting them with tawdry pleasures. Such recruits are usually not the truly brave, but men suffering from an inferiority complex and frustrations, men feverishly eager to prove their own potency and power by destroying others; not pure, incorruptible ascetics, but men seeking opportunities to gratify their own hungers.

As the *élite* designate themselves and rule by coercion, and as there is no legal way of removing them, they can only be brought down by violence. While the suppressed have every right to employ force, those threatened by this force are bound to rule by force. When an *élite* monopolises power and does not have to face an official opposition or to fear the results of the next election, and yet must live by prestige and stunts, it will be driven to ever greater violence at home and risky adventures abroad until it finally destroys itself utterly.

In our day, the demand for rights has reached an unprecedented level, and so too has the temptation to use the infinitely effective means to obtain them—force and violence. But these very instruments of force and violence have also become weapons of absolute destruction, indeed self-destruction. It means that there can be no right which would make it worth while to employ such terrible weapons. The age-old question of means and ends, of value and price, has lost its meaning. True, it is still possible to achieve the goal, to destroy the enemy, but only at the price of self-destruction. For generations man has dreamed of salvation and has developed technology in order to achieve it, or at least, to obtain total control over nature. But the paradox of our time is that, although man now enjoys unlimited power, he dare not and cannot use it. And under such circumstances, men are bound to ask themselves whether power is everything, whether power is really the only thing that matters. And is not a right, if extended too far, no longer a right but simply a way to suicide?

6

The Age of Revolution

HISTORIANS nowadays may roughly be classified as up-holders of the Leopold Ranke maxim that the historian's task is to describe *"wie es eigentlich gewesen"*, or as followers of Jacob Burckhardt's school whose view is that history is "the record of what one age finds worthy of note in another". There is not much love lost between the two camps. The former sulkily murmur that the others are journalists, and those among them who are addicted to strong language hint at charlatanism. The Burckhardtians shrug off their opponents more indulgently as antiquarians or stamp collectors, certainly useful wood-choppers, but dullards all the same.

Mr. E. H. Carr is certainly right in his Trevelyan Lectures on *What is History?* in having "no patience with the fashion set by J. B. Bury in his inaugural lecture of pretending that Mommsen's greatness rests not on his *History of Rome* [a thinly veiled tract on Mommsen's time and for his time] but on his corpus of inscriptions and his work on Roman constitutional law: this is to reduce history to the level of compilation. . . . Great history is written precisely when the historian's vision of the past is illuminated by insights into the problems of the present."[1]

The late Sir Lewis Namier put it neatly—"the historians imagine the past and remember the future". The key-word in this controversy is surely significance, but significance in a twofold sense. The historian is called upon to portray things in the order of importance they had for the people who

---

[1] E. H. Carr: *What is History?*, London 1962, p. 31.

lived at the time; to see through their eyes, trying his utmost to recapture the way this or that fact or event seemed significant to them. He is no less, however, concerned with what came of those events when looked upon from the vantage point of his own age. Consciously or unconsciously he is egged on by a quest for identity and the need for self-justification. He looks for situations in the past to help him to fix his bearings in his own world. More generally, he searches for samples of the human condition as a whole.

Events which excited one age as colossal appear to men a century after as episodes of no consequence, while things which hardly attracted any notice from most people at the time assume from the standpoint of future generations the character of beginnings of vast and world-shaking developments. The affairs of Spain and Portugal—to take examples from the period covered by the book under review[1]—exercised the minds of all politically interested around 1840. Those events received added spice from the shabby attempt of that sage and upright Protestant statesman, philosopher, and historian, Guizot, to force an impotent bridegroom upon the unfortunate Queen of Spain, Isabella II. As so often in Spanish history, "a civil war became internationalised" by inter-power conflict over intervention and non-intervention. Even a publicist of the Left like Louis Blanc devotes, in his *Histoire de dix ans*, endless pages to that crisis. A historian today would make himself ridiculous if he were to accord so much attention to those Iberian troubles and then, in keeping with what attracted the contemporaries' notice, was to dismiss as a marginal occurrence the opening of the five Chinese ports to European trade at the end of the Opium War. The goings and comings of the Czar of all the Russias, Nicholas I, the Emperor of Austria, the feeble-minded Ferdinand I, and the half-demented (and soon wholly insane) Friedrich Wilhelm IV of Prussia in the very centre of the world's stage in 1840 seem now almost irrelevant, in comparison with what was going on at that very time among the rough frontiersmen of North America, when Andrew Jackson became President; or when compared with the debates in the conventicles of the obscure

[1] E. J. Hobsbawm: *The Age of Revolution: Europe, 1789-1848*, London 1962.

radical exiles in Paris and Bruxelles, from whom the invitation went out to the youthful Dr. Karl Marx and Friedrich Engels to prepare the political statement of aims which came to be known as the *Communist Manifesto*.

All the same, no historian of integrity, however intense his preoccupation with distant consequences, could feel himself free from the obligation to bear in mind that things looked very differently to the people with whom he is dealing than they appear to him. One may say he should always experience a kind of sense of guilt towards our ancestors for treating them not as ends in themselves, in the spirit of Ranke's other dictum that all ages are born equal in the eyes God, but as intermediary stations and stepping stones to dénouements of decades or even centuries to come. This constant and gnawing reminder may act as a salutary antidote and hold the historian back from simply selecting samples from the past to fight an issue of his own time. The "present-minded" historian is supposedly in no danger of regarding any historical work as definitive, and no historical judgement can be to him final.

Dr. Eric Hobsbawm presents his credentials and formulates his intentions unambiguously in his preface: "The object of this book is not detailed narrative, but interpretation and what the French call *haute vulgarisation*. Its ideal reader is that theoretical construct, the intelligent and educated citizen, who is not merely curious about the past, but wishes to understand how and why the world has come to be what it is today and whither it is going."

The author defines his theme as "the transformation of the world between 1789 and 1848 in so far as it was due to what is called the 'dual revolution'—the French Revolution of 1789 and contemporaneous (British) Industrial Revolution", and calls it "the greatest transformation in human history since the remote times when men invented agriculture and metallurgy, writing, the city and the state." He intelligently draws our attention to the fact that so many of those words without which our language today could hardly be imagined like "industry", "factory", "middle class", "working class", "capitalism", "socialism", "aristocracy", "railway", "statistics", "sociology", "liberal", "conservative", "nationality", "scientist", "engineer", "proletariat", "economic", "crisis", "ideology", "journalism", "strike", and so on, were all coined in the period with which *The Age of Revolution* is concerned. That age cast the mould of our thinking and it produced the climate in which we still live. In other words the sixty years between 1789 and 1848 are contemporary history.

It is no accident that Dr. Hobsbawm called his book *The Age of Revolution*, in the singular. He appears to consider the series of revolutions from 1789 to 1848 in the various countries as incidents of one revolution. It is not out of place, considering the well-known political views of the author, to go further and enquire of him whether his title meant to imply that the revolution which had its take-off in the late eighteenth century was still on, had not yet run its course, and would not come to a halt till it had brought about a preordained universal dénouement. It is out of genuine respect for Eric Hobsbawm and his brilliant work that the reviewer feels prompted to use such a measuring yard as this. It would be no compliment to treat his book as just another useful handbook of *haute vulgarisation* setting out all the known facts in a well-constructed treatise written in a highly readable style.

Dr. Hobsbawm represents a remarkable combination. He has a keen interest in detail, often colourful and unusual detail (about, for instance, primitive rebels in outlandish places),[1] and is at the same time endowed with a speculative mind. And he has the taste and ability for generalisation. He writes vividly, with a knack for a cutting, ironical phrase, and with no trace of that wooden jargon of writers of his persuasion. His enviable assortment of languages is matched by the width of his interests (among which his expertise in jazz opens to him a source of life-enhancing enjoyment denied to so many other workers in his field). Finally he is an *"engagé"*, who is not inhibited by any considerations from identifying himself openly and organisationally with a camp

---

[1] *Idem: Primitive Rebels*, London 1959.

set apart from the common run. He is a person of such integrity that his virtue becomes his vice; too loyal to quit, he is too independent to conform; he thus comes to earn the unspeakable name of "revisionist".

The most significant thing about *The Age of Revolution* is that it stops short of 1848. In the concluding chapter, "Towards 1848", Hobsbawm rightly says of the revolutionary wave of 1848 that "rarely has revolution been more universally predicted . . . an entire continent waited . . . for the revolution which broke out in the first months of 1848 was not a social revolution merely in the sense that it involved and mobilised all social classes. It was in the literal sense the rising of the labouring poor in the cities—especially the capital cities—of Western and Central Europe. . . . When the dust settled on their ruins, workers—in France actually Socialist workers—were seen to be standing on them, demanding not merely bread and employment, but a new state and society . . . their dream of a new and better world gave their desperation eyes and a purpose."

The evaluation of 1848 is vital for any attempt to answer the question: was the nineteenth century the age of revolution or the century of the *taming of the revolution* (at all events in the West) ? The author is not unconscious of the problem and he says: "Looking back on the 1840's it is easy to think that the Socialists who predicted the imminent final crisis of capitalism were dreamers confusing their hopes with realistic prospects. For in fact what followed was not the breakdown of capitalism but its most rapid and unchallenged period of expansion and triumph." In the final passage of his Introduction, Hobsbawm writes: "The 'spectre of Communism' already haunted Europe by 1848. It was exorcised in 1848. For long thereafter it was to remain as powerless as spectres in fact are, especially in the Western world immediately transformed by the dual revolution. But if we look round the world in the 1960's we shall not be tempted to under-estimate the historic force of the revolutionary Socialist and Communist ideology born out of reaction against the dual revolution, and which had by 1848 found its classic formulation."

Indeed, no one would. But anyone is bound to raise the question upon a higher plane and to employ more emphatic terms by querying whether the victory of the revolution in the East should be treated as the delayed action of the revolutionary spirit which seized the West 125 years ago. If in the West the revolution had been tamed for good by 1848, the revolution (or revolutions) which overtook the East in the next century may well be a phenomenon springing from a context of its own, notwithstanding all the efforts to hitch it on to pre-1848 Western patterns of thought. In this case the Communist movement in the contemporary West may appear as a response to a myth which took on flesh only in the East, a wash-back rather than an autonomous growth.

These questions can hardly be answered without a prior definition of the concept of revolution. Do we mean a series of revolutionary changes in the social-economic structure which lead to the remodelling of the institutions and laws of a country and the replacement of certain ruling groups by others? Or do we mean the all-pervading conviction that history is moving to a revolutionary dénouement on a global scale, to a break-through towards some final social order embodying total justice and reason? That the authors of the *Communist Manifesto* and then Lenin and Trotsky unshakeably held such a belief there can be no doubt; as presumably Mao Tse-tung still does. No reader, however, of the West's Socialist literature of sixty and seventy years ago—Kautsky or Jaurès, indeed even Engels in his declining years, not to speak of Eduard Bernstein or the Fabians—can be impervious to the difference in climate and tone between them and the young Marx or Lenin.

Whether one speaks of revolutionary changes or "Revolution" is decisive for the assessment of the nature of the crisis created by the coming of industrialism. If the latter view is held, one is bound to set out with the assumption that the Industrial Revolution brought with it a structural crisis in society, produced an apocalyptic situation which had never existed before and is inexorably driving to a world-wide and total revolutionary transformation. The historian who thinks in terms of evolutionary changes will portray an age overwhelmed by changes for which it was caught unprepared, and requiring time and experience to respond to the challenge. There appears then a straight road from the first Factory Act to Keynes, the health service, and the welfare state, the travellers upon which—some sluggishly, some selfishly—were prodded on by strong pressures and rebellious threats from below.

"The labour movement [writes Dr. Hobsbawm] provided an answer to the poor man's cry. It must not be confused with the more collective revulsion against intolerable hardship, which occurs throughout recorded history, or even with the practice of striking and other forms of militancy which have since become characteristic of labour. These also have a history which goes back beyond the industrial revolution. What was new in the labour movement of the early nineteenth century was class consciousness and class ambition. The 'poor' no longer faced the 'rich'. A specific *class*, the labouring class, workers, or proletariat, faced another, the employers and capitalists. The French Revolution gave this new class confidence, the industrial revolution impressed on it the need for permanent mobilisation. A decent livelihood could not be achieved merely by the occasional protest which served to restore the stable but temporarily disturbed balance of society. It required the eternal vigilance, organisation, and activity of the 'movement'—the trade union, the mutual or co-operative society, the working-class institute, newspaper, or agitation. But the very novelty and rapidity of the social change which engulfed them encouraged the labourers to think in terms of an entirely changed society, based on their experience and ideas as opposed to their oppressor. It would be co-operative and not competitive, collectivist and not individualist. It would be 'socialist'. And it would represent not the eternal dream of the free society, which poor men always have at the backs of their minds but think about only on the rare occasions of general social revolution, but a permanent, practicable alternative to the present system."

All this has been formulated more emphatically before

Dr. Hobsbawm, who seems often rather sparing and selective in acknowledgements. The essential difference is between social resentment and rebellious wrath (which for centuries expressed itself in sulky anger, occasional *jacquerie* and riot, or in paradisal dreams) on the one hand, and the birth of an alternative programme of a total, revolutionary, and, as it were, predestined transformation, on the other—but when, how, and why did it come about? The new attitude was not the outcome of the Industrial Revolution, however intensified it was by industrial growth. It was postulated by the philosophers on the eve of 1789 and became a living and articulate passion of the masses in the French Revolution, to be then applied to the experiences of the Industrial Revolution. Events, facts, data, happenings assume their significance from the way in which they are experienced. To be kicked about was for a slave in antiquity or for a Chinese coolie only yesterday a matter of course, but the birching of a schoolboy in our day is considered by most people in the West as something absolutely horrifying.

That the conditions created by the Industrial Revolution were bad is not to be doubted (although Dr. Hobsbawm himself recognises the very great uncertainty as to whether there has really been an all-round deterioration in the condition of workers, and he is even prepared to admit that the industrial workers were rather better off than before). They appeared all the more terrible because those who were formerly called "lower orders" had by then a totally different notion of what was due to them—men—than the wretched poor of the old days. The social system appeared absurd, wrong, and unjust, because there was a vision of a rational and just order which was frustrated only by deliberate selfish wickedness.

It is, of course, nonsense to portray history as the abstract story of interlocking disembodied ideas (are there still historians who do that?), but it is certainly lack of imagination and crude doctrinaire addiction that leads some historians of the French Revolution who belong to the Marxist persuasion to reduce "mighty longings and strivings" to riots over the rising price of bread, and to play down the "ideologues". Any one of them would be up in arms at the suggestion that the writings of Marx and the ideas of Lenin had nothing to do with the Bolshevik Revolution and the shape of the Soviet system, and were the result of nothing but the evils of the Czarist régime, its contradictions, deficits, and bad harvests. We live in a soberer age and use greyer prose than Michelet, Lamartine, or Carlyle, whose incantations and flamboyant tableaux make us wince today, and who could see only ideas and destinies personified in an epic struggle. But even a much more restrained writer like Alexis de Tocqueville (who certainly took great pains with administrative detail and constitutional practice) could do justice to the intense reality of creeds and passions, of men and masses, of faith moving mountains.

It is difficult to imagine a more effective clarion call to Revolution than Rousseau's *Discours sur l'inégalité* and *Contrat social*, when taken together. One is a paranoiac *cri de cœur* about the way all things have gone wrong; cupidity and avarice had destroyed original equality, and in order to draw a veil upon their selfish dominion gave to their *arcana imperii* the name of law and morality. The other formulates a sole and exclusive principle of political legitimacy: the "social contract" concluded between men who are both free and equal. The very essence of the contract is the postulate of unanimity, because liberty and equality can be reconciled only if and when we are all unanimous (in fact, or made to appear so); otherwise there is no escape from the dominion of men over men. The expectation of eventual unanimity and the condemnation of parties as vehicles of selfish partial interests at variance with the general will (and interest) add up pretty well to a vague and rudimentary vision of a classless society and one-party system. Pending the arrival of that state of things, or rather in order to hasten its coming, "all revolutionaries"—Dr. Hobsbawm rightly observes, when speaking of the plotters and rebels of the first half of the nineteenth century—"regarded themselves . . . as small *élites* of the emancipated and progressive operating among and for the eventual benefit of a vast and inert mass of the ignorant and misled common people which would no doubt welcome liberation when it came, but could not be expected to take much part in preparing it". Ultimate perfect democracy must be preceded by the dictatorship of the vanguard, which is called upon to carry out the break-through and then bring about the social-economic and spiritual conditions necessary for unanimity to come to fruition.

The fact that (as Dr. Hobsbawm says in an aside) Rousseau is mentioned only three times in the whole of the correspondence between Marx and Engels (in their writings the name appears more often) proves nothing. We all talk the Gospel and Kant, Marx and Freud, without mentioning them explicitly. They have become essential, and therefore unnoticed, ingredients of the atmosphere we breathe and the language we speak. Just as Lenin and Plekhanov, Trotsky and Stalin were steeped in Marx, and were under the almost obsessive compulsion to think what Marx said or would have said and done in each new situation, so were Robespierre and Marat, the early Sieyès and Saint-Just soaked in Rousseau, that "divine, sublime philosopher", and "friend of mankind", Tocqueville concludes the chapter "How, towards the middle of the eighteenth century, men of letters became the chief politicians of the country, and the effects resulting therefrom" in his *L'Ancien régime et la Révolution* with the words: "I have often been astonished in the course of my public life at the sight of men, who have scarcely read books of the eighteenth century or indeed of any other and have strongly expressed their contempt of authors, and yet retain so faithfully some of the worst faults created by the literary spirit before they were born."

No one would suggest that Rousseau's ideas (or should we rather employ Burkean vocabulary and speak of Rousseau's massive sentiments?) came into his brain from the thin air, and then sprang fully armed from the forehead of that lonely, exasperatingly contradictory madman from Geneva. Nor would one be so silly as to maintain that Rousseau "alone" made the French Revolution. It is not a question really of abstract, syllogistic reasoning at all, but of patterns of thought, feeling, and behaviour, of frames of mind and the climate of an age, of what is nowadays called the "collective traumatic experiences" of a generation when faced with concrete events and unexpected situations.

Man is in need of bread, but he is no less in need of a faith in the broadest sense of the word, of a system of values, a set of bearings.

A great vacuum was created by the decline of the religious sanction which was the concomitant of the utter weariness with religious quarrels and bloody, inconclusive wars of religion. It was filled by the secular religion of "political Messianism" or "totalitarian democracy". The rapid spread of the new creed was facilitated by the break-up of fixed forms and traditional ties resulting in both greater social mobility and spiritual uprootedness. When the revolutionary upheaval of 1789 broke out, men were already fashioned to face it, conditioned to read a certain meaning into the events, and to act in accordance with that reading. Of course there was no ready blue-print, and men improvised under the impact of unforeseen situations. But while improvising they could not help generalising their own particular experiences and reactions to them into lessons of universal validity for all times and all nations. These experiences and generalisations were taken by the devotees of the revolution to be no mere empirical precepts, but part of a colossal drama, and were woven into a myth with an almost unimaginable grip on the minds and hearts of believers.

There is nothing new, says Tocqueville, in powerful and rebellious spirits rising against this or that belief or custom. "What singles out the eighteenth century is that that audacious and reforming curiosity was experienced by a whole generation, and was directed at the same time to all beliefs in a way that the principles upon which the sciences, the arts, philosophy, politics rested until then, were attacked together by a sort of universal commotion." "To hear them talk"—writes Guizot—"one might think that they had the elements and ages at their command . . . and that these were the first days of creation or the last days of the world."

In the first place there was the traumatic feeling that the

French Revolution had not really come to an end, but was still in motion, although it had been temporarily over-powered. And it would not and could not come to a halt till it had run its full preordained course. Earlier people spoke of revolutions; now they talked of The Revolution. The discovery made in the revolution, indeed before it even started—by Sieyès in connection with the method of voting in the Estates General—that privileged classes do not give up willingly, that sweet persuasion was of no avail where massive interests were at stake, that force had to be used, was at once universalised into the doctrine of the eternity of the class struggle and the inevitability of revolutionary dictatorship and terror. War and famine, treason and corruption, acted of course as catalysts of terrorist dictator-ship. But it was the depth of fanatical devotion to the revolu-tionary cause that made opposition or resistance appear the more devilish, and therefore the more deserving implacable punishment and necessitating suppression. If the revolution-ary side raised the stakes to their utmost, things were bound to be driven to a pass where there was either total victory of the total revolution or total triumph of the most vindictive counter-revolution.

It was not that the Industrial Revolution by engendering new conditions gave rise to new ideas. The French Revolu-tion, its ideas and traumas, conditioned men to experience and interpret the Industrial Revolution in a way that would have been quite unthinkable had the technological and social-economic changes taken place earlier. And that is true even of the seemingly strictly economic lessons of the Industrial Revolution. Because there was a postulate of a rational social order, *laissez-faire* capitalism looked all the more anarchical, chaotic, and absurdly wasteful. Babeuf, and even more articulately the Saint-Simonists and Fourier, detected a dialectical economic inevitability driving towards collectivism, and worked out a rudimentary theory of the recurrent crises leading to an apocalyptic dénouement. The lessons of the scientific and technological revolution were harnessed as scientific proofs for the ethical-political postulate. The shape of things to come was no longer merely a pious wish or righteous dream, but a scientifically proved necessity. History similarly was harnessed in order to anchor the foretold great transformation to a vast chain of historical evolution, with the various necessary phases marked out from the beginning till the end of time. It was due to the ideas of the rights of man that the workers woke up to the fact that they were the producers of all wealth, a truth that somehow had escaped the notice of the countless generations of serfs and small folk up to that date.

After the right to happiness—"a new idea", according to Saint-Just—had been proclaimed, it was natural that the evils of the Industrial Revolution should be taken to be intolerable. When the idea of equality was faced with the fact of an unprecedented and seemingly limitless growth of productive capacity, men nurtured on the revolutionary faith would no longer submit to the old-fashioned teachings that the many must labour for the few because (God's bounties being limited) a sample of civilised life upheld by a small number of the privileged was preferable to general barbarism resulting from equal distribution.

In Dr. Hobsbawm's own submission the changes around 1840 were after all smaller than popularly imagined: "The bulk of the world inhabitants continued to be peasants as before ... the position of the landed aristocrats also changed less than might have been thought, the middle classes increased rapidly, but even so their numbers were not overwhelmingly large ... the working classes measured against the total population of the world was still ... numerically negligible. . . . Yet, its political importance was already immense and quite disproportionate to its achievements."

Why? Because men were sharing a traumatic experience, were on the look-out for signs and proofs, and their sensitiveness was conditioned to respond more powerfully to certain stimuli (which of course no one denies were real enough). French writers around 1840 made a very acute distinction between old type *pauvreté* and contemporary *misère*. The former was felt to be a punishment from heaven; the latter was experienced as man-made (and was also different in that it included the added malaise of the uprooted and the injured).

We find a striking corroboration of the "primacy of ideas" in Engels' short essay *On the History of the Communist League*. Speaking of the members of the League in the 1840's when he and Marx first came in contact with them, he writes: "I do not believe there was a single man in the whole League at that time who had ever read a book on political economy. But that mattered little; for the time being 'equality', 'brotherhood', and 'justice' helped them to surmount every theoretical obstacle."[1]

Hobsbawm speaks of "the gigantic paradox" that is France. "On paper no country should have advanced more rapidly (on the road towards Industrial Revolution). It possessed . . . institutions ideally suited to capitalist development. The ingenuity and inventiveness of its entrepreneurs was without parallel in Europe. . . . Yet in fact French economic development at the base was distinctly slower than that of other countries." In France "they [the revolutionary measures] established that impregnable citadel of small and middle-peasant proprietors, small craftsmen and shop-keepers, economically retrogressive but passionately devoted to Revolution and Republic." Dr. Hobsbawm fails to see the other aspects of the paradox, that notwithstanding this social-economic backwardness, France produced in the first half of the nineteenth century the most luxuriant crop of Socialist theories, myths of revolution, and programmes of direct revolutionary action. A traumatic experience was working itself out. The late Sir Lewis Namier has dwelt on the traumatic nature of the "gigantic paradox" from a different angle. For well over a century French political life was decisively bedevilled by spectres of perils which were as dead as cold mutton. The Right dreaded another 1793, and the Left lived in constant fear of the return of feudalism. This is why the parliamentary system could strike no roots in France. The essential condition for its success—mutual trust

[1] Karl Marx and Friedrich Engels: *Selected Works*, 2 vols., Moscow 1954, Vol. II, p. 344.

and a determination to observe the rules of the game—were lacking where protagonists looked upon each other as mortal enemies, instead of alternative trustees of a common weal.

Dr. Hobsbawm forgets another "gigantic paradox" and that is nineteenth-century England. It was the only country in which the Industrial Revolution had reached maturity by 1848, and in that very year Chartism, the greatest proletarian mass movement of the century, fizzled out on Kennington Common; and the evolutionary trend of English history was never again seriously threatened. Why? Because the French Revolution failed to touch England directly.

Dr. Hobsbawm has some relevant things to say about romanticism in the context of the Age of Revolution. In all its aspects that maddeningly elusive and heterogeneous movement had one root cause—the break in historic continuity. Owing to this, reality ceased to look self-evident. It was no longer simply taken for granted and unreflectingly lived. The sense of alienation, which was to play such a crucial part in Marx, drove some to social rebellion, made others turn inwards and cultivate the ideal of the anarchical "genius", evoked in some a craving for the bizarre, supernatural, and grandiose, caused many to worship the past and yearn for the warm groove of medieval Church and organic community; it inspired, finally, not a few to build vast systems of historic inevitability.

The author adds a rather Marxist slant when he points out that "the real problem was that of the artist cut off from a recognisable function, patron or public, left to cast his soul as a commodity upon a blind market, to be bought or not, or to work within a system of patronage which would generally have been economically untenable even if the French Revolution had not established its human indignity".

Dr. Hobsbawm fails to notice that in their reaction against "the liberal assumption that society was a mere aggregate or combination of individual atoms", the Socialists found themselves standing on the same ground as the Right. What he calls the return "to the oldest of all natural ideological traditions, the belief that man is naturally a communal being"—and "that society was not a necessary but regrettable diminution of man's unlimited natural right to do as he liked, but the setting of his life, happiness, and individuality" —was common to both the Left and the Right, and at a deeper level than suggested by the author. Both stumbled upon the idea that it is not men who create society by making a social contract, but society which creates man. The Left spoke of "modes of production"; the Right of race, soil, blood, immemorial tradition and custom, the power of the dead over the living. The cast of mind was the same. There are some fine sociological insights in that ultramontane scholastic, Bonald, who upheld the "*nous*" as against "*moi*", "*religion de société*" against individualistic atomism, in a way very reminiscent of Saint-Simonism. The dangers to liberty inherent in that kind of approach are obvious.

This leads us to a crucial problem to which Dr. Hobsbawm fails to do justice, partly because he stops before 1848. He notes the fissure, which was in 1848 to become a chasm, between what he calls "bourgeois constitutionalism" (with limited suffrage) and Jacobin radical revolution or a social and democratic republic. The present author found the very strong awareness of this fundamental difference between two types of democracy expressed around 1840 in the juxtaposition of two brands, Girondist and Jacobin, Voltairian and Rousseauist, American and "popular" (the word is actually used) democracy. Another vastly important dichotomy escapes Dr. Hobsbawm's attention: namely the rivalry between socialism and nationalism in the struggle for the soul of man. Admittedly so long as the various forces working for a liberating change considered themselves as one single camp pitted against a single enemy camp (that of old dynastic, counter-revolutionary Europe), men took it for granted that the struggle for constitutional, social, and national rights was indivisible. 1848 revealed that nationalism, far from being the natural ally of democracy and socialism, was the most dangerous obstacle in the way of a revolutionary universal confraternity—and that when the national interest is proclaimed an end in itself and the

supreme law, nationalism might well become an instrument
of the Right and exercise the most corroding effect on liberal
as well as Socialist values. In 1848 the historic nations—
Germany and Hungary—in full tide of the anti-dynastic
revolution were out to crush their national minorities, whereas the "unhistoric" awakening peasant Slav nationalities
swelled the ranks of the Hapsburg armies which destroyed
the revolution.

Dr. Hobsbawm does not even consider nationalism as one
of the causes of the 1848 wave of revolutions.

A rehearsal of the dialectical interplay between universalist
proselytising and nationalist pride was given by the French
Revolution itself. To Dr. Hobsbawm "the world of the 1840's
was out of balance" and the revolution was therefore
inevitable, only because of the contradiction between the
"unprecedented, irresistible . . . forces of economic, technical,
and social change", and the "as yet modest . . . institutional
consequences".

The Age of Revolution is the story of a tremendous traumatic shock experienced by one generation and then working itself out in the following generations. We have in this
century lived through a series of traumas which continued to
shape all our reactions and reflexes long after the actual
experience had seemingly come to an end: the traumatic
experience of World War I working itself out in the 1930's
and well into World War II; the shock of the Spanish civil
war and its effect on the European intellectuals of the Left;
the Great Depression ghost continuing to stalk; Nazism-
Fascism and appeasement irresistibly egging on Sir Anthony
Eden to Suez; the October Revolution and then Stalinism;
the murder of the Jews; Hiroshima. These experiences—
coupled with Freud and Jung and modern psychology in
general—lead one to think that the nineteenth-century
historian's preoccupation with conditions and his search for a
horizontal *Querschnitt* of reality caught at a certain moment
are no longer adequate. A more vertical approach seems
necessary, not indeed a return to the old-fashioned narrative
type of history, but a reorientation towards a kind of case

history method: not of individuals, but of groups, masses, nations, and (one almost fears to say it) mankind. It is to psychology that we have to look for a new fertilisation of historical thinking, just as historians in the eighteenth century sought guidance from the sciences, and their successors in the nineteenth had their sights sharpened by economics, sociology, and biology.

The Age of Revolution is an unfinished story, not merely because it stops on the eve of 1848, but also because, as said before, the waves set in motion then have not yet come to rest. But then no history is ever a finished story; true, and for this reason any historical statement is only a provisional one, and there can be no "definitive" histories. Periodic reviews and reappraisals are both inevitable and salutary. There is a marked air of indefiniteness and inconclusiveness about *The Age of Revolution*, in spite of the clear economic slant, when one considers the firm ideological commitment of the author. There is little in it that a progressive liberal or even enlightened conservative might not have said, if with more reservations and greater qualifications. The question arises whether that inconclusiveness is not another token of the fact that iron-cast certainties are in the process of loosening up and the dazzling mystique of Revolution has ceased to thrill or haunt.

7

The Irresistible Force and the
Immovable Wall[1]

"THE BALFOUR DECLARATION" by Mr. Leonard Stein,[2] every page of which bears the imprint of infinite toil and shining integrity, is the work of a lifelong believer who will have no truck with self-righteous cant or propagandist humbug. In this the book is almost an exercise in masochism. The author brings his voluminous study to an end not with concluding sentences, but with quotations.

In November 1919, two years after the issue of the Balfour Declaration, General Smuts, one of its architects, told a Jewish meeting in South Africa that "you will yet see an ever-increasing stream of emigration towards Palestine, in generations to come you will see a great Jewish State rising there once more". In a newspaper article published some three months before the 1920 San Remo decision to hand over the Palestine Mandate to Britain for the fulfilment of the Balfour Declaration, a British Cabinet Minister, Winston Churchill, spoke of "a Jewish state under the protection of a British Crown which might comprise three or four millions of Jews".

On April 28, 1920, General Bols, the Chief Administrator of Palestine, made a statement to a gathering of the Moslem, Christian and Jewish communities on what had happened at San Remo.

"The Supreme Council has decided upon the Mandate for

[1] I wish to acknowledge the copyright of Dr. James Parkes in the present title. I heard the phrase from his mouth many years ago.
[2] Leonard Stein: *The Balfour Declaration*, New York 1961.

Palestine and that Mr. Balfour's Declaration regarding a Jewish National Home in Palestine is to be included in the Turkish Peace Treaty.

"I will now read you Mr. Balfour's Declaration, the inclusion of which in the Treaty means that there will be no interference with religious customs or the Holy Places or any curtailment whatever of the religious liberty of the subject, but only the maintenance of public order and security. Immigrants will be allowed to enter only as required for the development of the country, and immigration will be controlled by the British Government of the country. . . . The British Government will govern and in no sense will a minority be allowed to control the majority of the population when the time arrives for any form of representative government. . . . The decision has at last been given and henceforward there must be an end to political strife and unrest. All true Palestinians must now strive with one another in healthy rivalry to the good of Palestine and the welfare of future generations. . . ."

There can hardly be a more striking example of right hand not knowing what left hand was doing than the difference between the unambiguous and strident promises, or should we say prophecies of the leading statesmen of the empire, and the studied vagueness, the minor key note and the abundance of negatives and reservations in the statement of the man on the spot, sent there to carry out Government policies, sanctioned by an international instrument. No wonder Jews were clamouring that no sooner was the Balfour Declaration issued than the British embarked upon a policy of its liquidation.

I

The Balfour Declaration of November 2, 1917, contained in a letter from the then Foreign Secretary, A. J. Balfour, to Lord Rothschild, is a maddeningly vague document, and to a common-sense reader the policies enunciated in it could well appear at odds with the general principles upheld publicly at the time by those who issued it. International law knew then no such term as "National Home". The Declaration speaks of "a national home for the Jewish people". There was no authoritative explanation of what was meant by that—a state, a cultural centre, local self-government or communal autonomy. Similarly ambiguous is the statement that the British Government "view with favour the establishment in Palestine of a national home for the Jewish people"—was the wording intended to underline the distinction between Palestine as a national home for the Jewish people, and a Jewish national home in Palestine?—". . . and will use their best endeavours to facilitate the achievement of this object." Granted that the Declaration does not pledge H.M. Government actually to establish the national home, what was meant by using "their best endeavours to facilitate the achievement" of the object? When the Declaration was published, Britain was a member of a Grand Alliance, and the fate of Palestine and of the Turkish Empire as a whole was still a matter to be determined at the end of the war by a peace conference of all the Allies. In theory, Balfour's pledge might have meant no more than that Britain would offer diplomatic aid to the Zionist cause before an international forum. This Britain did, she was then charged by the international authority with carrying out her own promise to facilitate the actual upbuilding of the National Home. But, of course, the hardest nut is the first half of the second part of the Declaration—"it being clearly understood that nothing shall be done which may prejudice the civil and religious rights of existing non-Jewish communities in Palestine". Whatever these rights may mean, they are not defined as national or political. If the Balfour Declaration contains no explicit promise of a Jewish state, it certainly carries no hint that the non-Jewish communities would ever be granted political sovereignty. Nothing is said about the eventual sovereignty over Palestine. All the same, "the civil and religious rights" having been left undefined, it became most difficult to say in what way and when these rights would or would not be prejudiced. The believers in the National Home would maintain that in spite of the use of the term "non-Jewish communities", or perhaps because of the avoidance of positively naming them as Arab or Moslem, nothing more was promised than respect for the status of the non-Jews as individuals. The trouble was that the idea of national self-determination was not merely in the air, it was solemnly proclaimed (though in practice sadly ignored) as the basis upon which the new world was going to be built. If it was thus excusable, perhaps even warranted, to interpret the national home as a promise of statehood, there was also sufficient inducement to stretch "the civil and religious rights" to signify national self-determination, or when the text itself failed, to appeal to the abstract right and the concrete fact that in 1917 the Arabs constituted the vast majority of the inhabitants of Palestine, and they had not been consulted.

To facilitate the establishment of a national home was a positive undertaking, to prevent civil and religious rights being prejudiced was a reservation. The former would certainly carry more weight than the latter. But could not the latter negate the former? An ocean of ink has been spilled on the interpretation of the few lines which constitute the Balfour Declaration, among others by Mr. Stein himself, not indeed in his book, but in his capacity as Political Secretary of the World Zionist Organisation from 1920 to 1929, and then as adviser to the Jewish Agency for Palestine, especially on the occasion of his most able presentation of the Jewish case before the Palestine Royal Commission in 1936.

Were the British statesmen so stupid, blind, irresponsible, as not to see all these pitfalls, or did they see them? What prompted them to give such an undertaking in the first place? What were their motives and what did they hope to get in return? How did the whole thing come about, considering that all the negotiations were carried on by individuals, and in the case of the Zionists, by individuals without recognised international status? Were the British statesmen beguiled happy-go-lucky optimists, or farseeing Machiavellians? As soon as the Balfour Declaration was issued, the British began to look upon it as a vexatious embarrassment and the Arabs proclaimed their implacable hostility. What enabled in the end the Jewish community in Palestine,

55,000 in all in 1917, to become a Jewish state in the larger part of Palestine by 1948? The ultimate solution was of course not the result of the victory of the more cogent interpretation of the Balfour Declaration. By 1948 the Balfour Declaration had already become for practical purposes irrelevant. Yet, without the Balfour Declaration there is no saying how or if ever a beginning could have been made on the road to independent Jewish statehood; which journey is the subject of the Weizmann memorial volume.[1]

The authors of the tributes to the late first President of Israel, and chief architect of the Balfour Declaration, represent the Jewish point of view in all its self-centredness (with the exception of Dr. Robert Weltsch's contribution on the years 1919-29), as was to be expected from the nature of their undertaking. Mr. Leonard Stein is not only anxious to do justice to all sides; he is a brilliant lawyer who is used to weighing and evaluating evidence as an end in itself. As a wise and experienced man he is fully aware how mixed human motives are. He is thus able to assess the right proportions of clear reasoning and muddled thinking, conscious determination and lazy carelessness, idealism and selfish calculation. He never grows lyrical, and seldom extols. Nor does he often denounce or condemn.

What strikes one at once in Mr. Stein's story is the fact that the Balfour Declaration was, as hinted before, the fruit of secret, almost private diplomacy in the strictest sense of the word (while the arrival of the age of open covenants openly arrived at was being heralded), and not the victory of a strong current of public opinion. The author recalls that towards the end of 1916 the (Zionist) British Palestine Committee sent a statement of its aims to some hundreds of eminent individuals in various walks of life. They had not been asked for any financial support but had been invited, if they agreed with the objects of the Committee, to identify themselves with it as patrons. Only about ten replies in all were received, of which half were purely formal acknowledgements, and of the remainder two expressed disapproval

[1] *Chaim Weizmann, a Biography by Several Hands*, ed. Weisgal and Carmichael, London 1962.

of the Zionist aims. Yet, there can be no doubt at all as to the genuineness and depth of the sympathy of such men as Balfour, Lloyd George, Smuts, Milner, Sir Mark Sykes, Lord Robert Cecil, C. P. Scott, Winston Churchill, Leopold Amery, all of whom played a role in preparing or in bringing to fruition (in the form of the British Mandate for Palestine) the Balfour Declaration. Zionism was one of those causes, to which most people pay little heed, but a sympathy for which can easily be aroused in the minds and hearts of certain men, when their attention is focused on it. It would, of course, be wrong to treat the subject as merely a case of winning and giving sympathy between individuals. It was nevertheless vastly important that in those years of prolonged negotiations the most skilful advocates had the ear of very responsive listeners. In spite of the vast differences in upbringing, social position, power and interests, the two sides, paradoxically as it may sound, spoke the same language, as we shall see.

The story of the Balfour Declaration as the history of Zionism and Israel in general offers a highly interesting lesson on the nature of political realism and unrealism. There was something highly unreal about the comings and goings of a few Eastern-European Jewish intellectuals who succeeded in obtaining access to British Ministers, about the memoranda exchanged between Ministers, Foreign Office officials and ambassadors on the future of Palestine, when the end of the greatest of all wars till then was still so far as not to be even within sight, and its outcome was still more than doubtful. The Allies were holding out by the skin of their teeth, casualties assumed unheard-of dimensions, and Palestine was still in Turko-German hands, without an Allied shot having been fired in its vicinity up to 1917. Any talk on the future of Palestine or Zionist claims could hardly signify more at the time than a way of keeping Foreign Office officials busy, when the war had cut down so much of their routine activity. On the other hand, war is a time when impossibilities of yesterday become the opportunities of tomorrow. Old, seemingly unchangeable facts and immovable realities are in a state of flux, and new forms struggle to emerge, while statesmen, uncertain of their own minds, are on the look-out for solutions and are often relieved and grateful to receive ideas from outsiders.

Everyone knew that the next Peace Treaty would entail a redrawing of maps and a rearranging of the fate of territories and populations, the like of which the world had never seen before, not even at Vienna in 1815 nor at the Westphalian peace negotiations in 1648, nor at Utrecht in 1713. Whatever the convictions held by this or that diplomat, everyone in the Christian world was conditioned by religious tradition or historic memories to feel that Palestine was a case *sui generis*, much as the Turks and Arabs might claim that there was no such entity as Palestine, and that the Holy Land was only the southern extension of greater Syria. The British statesmen around 1917, such as Lloyd George, Smuts, Balfour, Milner, Lord Robert Cecil, and others were perhaps the last of British leaders to feel no incompatibility between the challenge to build a better world for all men, and the urge to make, or rather to keep Britain great and mighty. It was the mission of the empire to undertake great deeds, which happily did good to both the world and Britain at the same time. The imperial nerve had not yet weakened. There was no need to feel apologetic. Instead of sounding like preposterous romanticism (return to Zion after 2,000 years) or unashamed imperialism (there was a settled Arab population in the land), the Zionist claim was calculated to appear to those trustees of the imperial destinies of Britain as far from implausible. It had the power to catch their imagination and fire their sympathy.

Mr. Stein shows that from Palmerston onwards there was hardly a British statesman who was not convinced that in some ways international Jewry represented a force which it was in the British interest to have as a friend. Using fashionable vocabulary I should lay great stress upon the image of Judaism and Jewry which hovered before the eyes of men like Lloyd George and Balfour, and was so utterly different from the Jewish image in the unspeakable nineteen-thirties and forties.

The attitude of a Balfour or Lloyd George to Jews was not,

as Mr. Stein reveals, free from ambivalences. There was in most of them a dose, if not of anti-semitism, at least of lingering contemptuous prejudice and distrust, which could on occasion find expression in the usual old time sneer. In the case of Balfour that ambivalence showed itself in highly sophisticated meditation upon the self-assertive dynamism of the Jews in finance and revolutionary activity, their rootlessness and their role of solvents in old established societies. The latest biographer of Balfour quotes a description of a party at the Sassoons at the close of the last century in which Balfour speaks of the "long, hot and pompous dinner—peopled with endless Sassoon girls" . . . "I believe", he goes on to say, "the Hebrews were in an actual majority—and tho' I have no prejudice against the race (quite the contrary) I began to understand the point of view of those who object to alien immigration."[1] None of them, however, would have any truck with any kind of Manichean racial and collectivist determinism. In some ways repellent to them the Jews were nevertheless likely to evoke in those men a sense of awe and puzzled admiration, and make their conscience uneasy. They appeared an extraordinary phenomenon, a great mystery. A unique fate weighed down their volcanic energies, or was diverting them into "bad channels". What a great destiny might be in front of them if their faculties could be released and canalised for good purposes!

The Zionist plea that after the Greeks had got their independence, the Italian nation had been reunited, it was now the turn of Jerusalem to be resurrected in the wake of Athens and Rome, fell on responsive ears. For if tribes, of whom one had hardly heard before, such as the Lithuanians, the Czechoslovaks and Estonians were to be granted free statehood, surely the Jews had as good a claim. Although suppressed and even persecuted, all those peoples without political independence had a soil under their feet, a cohesive territorial framework, whereas the teeming ghettos of the Czarist Empire were deprived of elementary human rights, while in the West the Dreyfus affair and the emergence of

[1] Kenneth Young: *Arthur James Balfour*, London 1963, p. 139.

anti-semitic mass movements in Central Europe had put a big question mark before the axiomatic assumption that inevitable progress was bound sooner or later to make the distinction between Jew and Gentile irrelevant.

Hostile comment can easily caricature the Zionist leaders as a bunch of smart lobbyists and manipulators. But they represented a mystique of compelling appeal.

"I foresee myself"—wrote Sir Mark Sykes in a letter to Sokolow on May 27, 1918, shortly before his death—"handed down to posterity as one of those enduring obscurities who did nothing in any way remarkable, yet whose names last for all time because they scratched their fleeting impressions on the Memnon at Luxor. Your cause has about it an enduring quality which mocks at time. When all temporal things the world now holds are as dead and forgotten as the curled and scented Kings of Babylon who dragged your forefathers into captivity, there will still be Jews, and so long as there are Jews there must be Zionism." The same romantic Catholic Tory had some years earlier resorted to all the stereotype sneers when speaking of Jews.

If they wanted to get something from Britain, the Zionists were also eager to give themselves to her. England stood very high in the esteem of Jews all over the world. Her enlightened treatment of the Jews; the visionary interest of men like Lord Shaftesbury and Palmerston in Jewish settlement in Palestine; the friendly attitude of Joseph Chamberlain; the strength of the biblical tradition in British life; parliamentary democracy rooted in respect for the human personality—all these, combined with her powerful position as the head of the greatest empire of all time, made Britain not merely a welcome ally (the Zionists in 1914-18 were not as pretentious as all that), but a much desired protector. The Zionist leaders would not exchange her for any other power, and were adamant, as we shall still see, in their opposition to all suggestions of a condominium of two or more powers or an international régime in Palestine. They never asked to put the term Jewish State into any of the drafts of the Balfour Declaration, although in internal discussions the question was raised. They were quite happy with the prospect of a predominantly Jewish Palestine under the British flag.

To Dr. Weizmann Britain represented civilisation and liberty *tout court*. The British connection was to him the cornerstone of his whole thinking, and when that began to crack and fail, Weizmann felt himself betrayed and lost his bearings. His usefulness was at an end, and the reins had to be seized by others.

A lecturer in Chemistry at Manchester University, who as yet held no official position in the leadership of the Zionist organisation, who had as yet no patent or indeed anything else to offer to the British Government, Weizmann was able as early as 1914 to impress Balfour as the "only statesman" (among Jewish leaders known to him) "a statesman of a powerful moral government". Weizmann was endowed with that most elusive quality, the natural authority and grace of a leader, whose leadership is not snatched by flamboyant appeal to mass emotion, or is slowly acquired through electoral exertions, patient scheming and waiting for opportunities, but is recognised instantly and submitted to without question. In the eyes of those disposed to look with awe upon Judaism, he was the embodiment, the personification of Jewry at its best. He was an idealist and sceptic; a visionary and severely practical; he seemed to read the thoughts and feelings of the most diverse people; he could be cosmopolitan, at home in every culture and milieu; and yet he was of a piece, a wizard from the East, rooted in folk-lore and proverb. He was an aristocrat, and yet was at his best when holding forth in colloquial Yiddish. He did not suffer fools gladly, but he could be courteous and charming. He had no qualms in jettisoning associates who were of no more use to him, and personal loyalty was not his strong side, yet he was idolised by the sophisticated no less than by the simple-minded. He seemed to carry all the sufferings of his race on his deeply furrowed face, and gave at the same time the impression of tremendous power, indeed majesty.

An unfriendly reviewer of Chaim Weizmann called him a supreme lobbyist. Weizmann's great strength was indeed in his ability to attune himself to every kind of listener and bring to bear upon him that aspect of Zionism which was most congenial or attractive to him. Weizmann was infinitely varied, because he was single-minded. He experienced his ideal so deeply and so richly that everything else in the world, in the words of Justice Frankfurter, was placed in relationship to and illumined by that central fact. Weizmann did not ask for a Jewish state, but for an opportunity to make one. It was not to be a ready-made gift—Weizmann was too hard-boiled to expect that. It was to be the fruit of exertions and the reward for merit. Weizmann did not believe in formulas and declarations as signposts for things to come, but not yet there. He was convinced that the definition was the act of recognition of things ripe or achieved. He was a chemist who would wait patiently for the experiment to yield results and believed not in short cuts. But as a chemist he was fully conscious of and was lying in wait for those moments of fusion, when things rapidly change from one state into another, for what is called in politics the hour of opportunity such as war and its aftermath.

Susceptible as a philosopher like Balfour, an imaginative romantic like Lloyd George or an imperialist like Milner may have been to the historic or human appeal of Zionism, more direct and more selfish interests were needed to quicken Platonic sympathy into readiness to take political action. Whether the vague good will predetermined the British statesmen's assessment of the concrete factors in a way beneficial to Zionism, or whether England first thought of her imperial interests, and then invoked the cause of Zionism by way of conscious or semi-conscious rationalisation will long be disputed.

The curious fact is that the idea of some sort of Zionist solution of the Palestine question, once the Holy Land had been seized from the Turks, occurred to different people independently at an early date (we do not speak of course of the single-minded Zionists who thought of nothing else). Others were easily won over as soon as the idea was broached to them. The Zionist leaders were astonished to learn in the course of their negotiations with British officials that as early as 1915 Herbert Samuel had circulated a Zionist memorandum among his colleagues in the British Cabinet. No one in the Zionist camp had suspected Samuel of any sympathy for or interest in Zionism. Sir Edward Grey's Zionist formulations and schemes embarrassed the assimilated Jewish leaders in the Western countries. (Asquith remained cool and contemptuous.) The "conversion" of Mark Sykes to Zionism is indeed the best example of how powerful the impact of Zionism could be on impressionable and imaginative minds. Sykes played a decisive part in planning Near Eastern policies. He was the British representative in the long drawn-out negotiations on the future of the Ottoman Empire, M. Picot acting on behalf of France. Idealism and *Realpolitik* became in his case indissolubly intertwined.

The British were above all interested in the security of the Suez Canal and the territories on the road to India. None of the major allies of Britain could be regarded as uninterested in Palestine. But whereas the Russians and the Italians, with all their interest in the Holy Places and the religious, philanthropic and educational institutions maintained in the Holy Land by their nationals or co-religionists, lacked the determination or the power to claim sovereign rights, France was a paramount pretender. The Crusades had been primarily a French venture and since then all Europeans are called Franks in Arabic. For centuries the friendship between the Most Christian Kings of France and the Sultans of Turkey, in common alliance against the Hapsburg Roman emperors of the German nation, secured special privileges for France in the Levant, and France was regarded as THE Catholic Power and Protector of all Catholic interests in the Holy Land. The Christian Maronite community in the Lebanon were the traditional *protégés* of France. The French had been promised Syria after the war, and a good case could be made out for Palestine, administratively a part of Syria in Turkish times, to be included in the Syrian zone, if on a somewhat special and different footing. The British connection with Palestine had in the past been very slender, and the French could be counted upon to take precautions to prevent the repetition of the Egyptian imbroglio of 1880, when they were ousted by the British newcomers from a country with which they had had close connections for generations and in which they had so many interests. The overriding fact, however, was that no French army could be spared for the Levant in the years 1914-18, and that the war was fought in that area, and Palestine was conquered by the British alone. The question arises whether the British needed Zionism as a pretext for not letting France have Palestine. Was it not enough that they were there to enable them to hold on to Palestine?

The Sykes-Picot agreement in the spring of 1916 carried out on paper another of those numerous partitions with which the history of that over-promised land is punctuated. The British were to receive—in addition to southern Mesopotamia—on the Palestine coast the ports of Haifa and Acre, whereas the strip of Palestine north of Acre up to a point near the head of the Lake of Tiberias was assigned to the French who were to get the coastal strip of Syria and the Lebanon, Cilicia, and still further north a triangular block of territory with its apex deep in Asia Minor. The territory south of the British Haifa–Acre region and the French zone bounded south by a line starting just north of Gaza, then running north of Hebron and ending at a point near the northern end of the Dead Sea, the so called "brown zone", was reserved for separate treatment as an international zone. Outside these areas there was to be an independent Arab state or a Confederation of Arab states, "under the suzerainty of an Arab chief", but divided into two spheres of influence, British and French. The special treatment reserved for the "brown area" was calculated to invite Zionist claims. Internationalisation, which would have meant a kind of Anglo-French condominium, was most unwelcome to the British—on that all British statesmen were agreed. The Zionist claims and their insistence on undivided British suzerainty could thus be of help to Britain in getting rid of French partnership. Similarly, once recognised in principle, the Jewish claim could be extended to the whole of Palestine, in which case Zionism could also assist the English in driving the French out of the northern strip which was promised to them. The Zionist and British interests thus coincided. The Jews, as said earlier, in any case preferred Britain as the protecting power. France was also believed to be bound by commitments to Arabs and the Vatican. France was untouched by any biblical mystique, was rather tainted by anti-semitism, and the French were feared by the Zionists for their proselytising tendencies. Besides it was a weaker power than Britain. In brief, France had little attraction to the Zionists.

Yet, it is fair to say that Britain, in undivided military occupation of Palestine and of much beyond it, could have found, if determined to hold on to the whole of Palestine, adequate reasons for staying there alone without the Zionists. Neither the British nor the French, nor for that matter anyone else entertained the idea of a separate Arab Palestine or of a Palestine incorporated into a larger Arab state or confederation of states. Welcome then as Zionist help may have appeared to the British in extricating themselves from an agreement which they disliked, it was not in itself decisive in causing England to identify herself with Zionism, as against the embarrassments and difficulties which such a course held out. There must have been considerations of a more positive gain that would ensue from pursuing a pro-Zionist policy.

Jewish sympathy for the Allied cause, especially in America, was thought very much worth having, firstly for the power the Jews were alleged to wield in the United States, secondly because the Jews had very strong reasons in 1914 to side with the Germans. The Jews had nothing but hatred for the Czarist régime, its anti-Jewish policies and Government-sponsored *pogroms*. They were strongly attracted by German culture, and grateful for the fair treatment of Jews, in spite of some social anti-semitism, by the Second Reich. Jewish leadership in the United States was still recruited from descendants of German Jews who came to America in the middle of the nineteenth century, while the masses were those poor people who succeeded in escaping from Czarist persecution. There were, however, arguments against using Zionism as a bait for world Jewish support. The rich and influential Jews in the West, in France, America, and especially in England looked with disfavour, and often alarm, and intense dislike upon Zionism. They feared that their Englishness or Americanism might be questioned. The whole conception of separate worldwide Jewish nationhood was abhorrent to them. Some genuinely considered Zionism as defeatist capitulation to anti-semitism, as an admission that Jewish equality and the rights of man may not be axiomatic and inevitable. Liberals and Left wingers resented the questioning or even the denial of the idea of progress allegedly implied in Zionist doctrine. To revolutionaries of all kinds Zionism appeared as political desertion or romantic escapism. The poetry of Zionism had no appeal to them, for they were under the influence of other mystiques. No one fought the idea of the Jewish National Home more bitterly than the Jewish member of the War Cabinet, Montagu, Secretary for India, and the official leaders of the Anglo-Jewish organisations, who at one moment seemed to have succeeded in nipping it in the bud. The Russian Revolution which brought down the Czar and proclaimed full civil equality removed the main cause for anti-Allied feeling among the Jews. It lent also some weight to the argument that the last stronghold of official anti-Jewish discrimination and active persecution having collapsed, there was no urgency in finding a national home for the Jews. With the rising tide of revolution in Russia, Jewish opinion became, however, important to the Allies for new reasons. The Russian will to fight was flagging, and it was thought highly desirable to galvanise Jewish enthusiasm for the *Entente* by a promise of support for Zionist aspirations. Two rivals were fighting for the soul of the Russian, and indeed Eastern European Jews in general, Zion and the Revolution, and it was believed that an open and spectacular demonstration of sympathy by the Western Allies for Zionism would wean away the Jews from the cause of world Revolution. The argument about the great Jewish influence in the revolutionary parties was, however, a double-edged weapon. It was calculated to evoke sharp anti-semitic reactions from quarters where there was no friendly disposition towards the Jews.

When all considerations are weighed, it becomes clear that while Platonic sympathy alone would not have sufficed to move British statesmen, no single utilitarian calculation, nor all taken together would have worked, had there been no *a priori* good will and positive sympathy. There is of course the argument that from the imperial point of view the British were interested in having in the Middle East a friendly and grateful client on whose loyalty they could rely. Such a long run calculation again depended on the evaluation of Zionism. Was it worth the risks run in regard to the other Allies and the Arab world? In this respect Zionist diplomatic skill was of perhaps decisive importance. Once they succeeded in winning over the British statesmen for their cause, the Zionists could make the most of it. There was little prospect that France or Italy or Russia could be persuaded to come out in open support of Zionism. But the Zionist leaders were in a position to make it very uncomfortable for them to appear as hostile to the Zionist aspirations and lag behind the British in friendliness for the Jews. Having extracted favourable statements from the other partners in the *Entente*, the Zionists could then, after getting to some extent the chestnuts out of the fire for Britain, come back and egg on hesitant British Ministers to adopt more determined attitudes. A word should be said about the United States in this context. By 1917 America was in the war, and no one needed worry that the Jewish citizens of the United States would not fight wholeheartedly for their country, especially after the fall of the Czarist régime. Furthermore, as Mr. Stein has shown, there was little sympathy for Zionism in the United States Government circles. The Secretary of State, Lansing, was distinctly cool, Colonel House, the President's confidential adviser, had little liking for Jews, although he admired Justice Brandeis very greatly, while Wilson himself was not in fact very interested in the whole business, often forgetting what he had said or had been said to him on an earlier occasion.[1] Far from prodding London, Washington had to be prodded by Brandeis and his friends not to remain

[1] Miss Deborah Barzilai of the Weizmann Archives has in the meantime placed at my disposal certain documents, notably a draft letter (not despatched) from Brandeis to James de Rothschild with a report on an interview with President Wilson on May 6, 1917, which necessitates some revision of Mr. Stein's views on this point.

behind Britain, who in such stark contrast to the later
nineteen-forties became the idol of the New York Jewish
masses in the closing phase of World War I. The Zionist
cause helped Britain in America. The pledge to facilitate the
building of the national home for Jews was calculated to
neutralise any purist objection that by seizing Palestine
Britain was pursuing a policy of annexations.

Nevertheless, the question arises: why in 1917, when the
circumstances did not particularly favour the Zionists, except
for the fact that British troops were actually conquering
Palestine (but also becoming aware of the existence of the
Palestine Arabs) was the British Government in such a hurry
to issue the Balfour Declaration? Mr. Stein shows that the
British were afraid that they might be forestalled by the
German Government, who—such was the rumour—were
about to publish a statement in favour of a Jewish national
home in Palestine. These fears were vastly exaggerated.
Although the German Zionists were being courted by the
Reich Government, Germany could hardly afford to offend
the susceptibilities of her Ottoman ally, the suzerain power
in Palestine.

II

And what about the Arabs? Were the British statesmen
unaware of the fact that in 1917 Palestine was inhabited by
650,000 Arabs and only 55,000 Jews? Did they take no care
to find out? Was there no one to draw their attention to that
disconcerting fact? And what was in the minds of the Zionist
leaders on this point?

The researches of Mr. Stein bear evidence how little that
factor weighed with the men responsible for the Balfour
Declaration, at least from what is known. With the exception
of Balfour, as we shall see, hardly anyone took care to think
out the problems and the implications of the Declaration to
the end. The general attitude, implicit or articulate, was that
the difficulties would somehow be ironed out or muddled
through. The idea of planting a minority of outsiders upon an
indigenous majority population, without consulting it, was
not calculated to horrify men who had worked with Cecil

Rhodes or promoted European settlement in Kenya, and Joseph Chamberlain who had offered Uganda for Jewish colonisation not so long before. National self-determination was taken to apply to European nationalities, but hardly to the peoples and tribes of Asia and Africa. The Mandates system foreshadowed a kind of "de-colonisation". Its authors were hardly motivated by a sincere wish to prepare the populations for freedom. They desired to obviate the accusation of violating the principles of non-annexation of former German and Turkish territories to which the *Entente* was pledged. The great wave of anti-colonialism and of imperialist abdication seemed still far off. It was, as Mr. Crossman has pointed out, the misfortune or the good fortune of Zionism to be caught in that uneasy interval between self-determination and de-colonisation.

But could one treat the Arabs of Palestine like Bantus or West Africans? Before World War I the West knew very little of the Arabs. The Arabs had been deprived by the Turks of political sovereignty for centuries and seemed to be sunk in deep slumber, either because their once glorious civilisation had spent itself or because it had been sterilised by the Turkish blight. The Arabs were not considered an identifiable political factor before 1914. They were "a population". In many minds they were just bedouins who might have their discontents, which could be utilised, but whose tents could be shifted from place to place as in the days of the patriarchs; hardly a rising nation on the way to national unity and independence.

In his recollections called *Tour of Duty* (published 1946) Sir Stewart Symes, who spent a lifetime in the Middle East, served as Assistant Director of Intelligence at Khartoum in the years 1909-12, as Private Secretary to the Sirdar, and Governor-General (1913-16), and in the years 1917-19 was attached to the Staff of the High Commissioner in Egypt (G.S.O.L., Hedjaz Operations), saw seven years' service in Palestine (1921-8), and finished as Governor-General of Sudan (1934-40), recalls that "as the great war approached its climax, it became clear to many of us that the arrested movement for Egyptian independence would be resumed at the first favourable opportunity and at a much accelerated tempo. Few of us at that time anticipated that Nationalist agitations, playing on real but minor grievances, could evoke latent and centuries-old antipathies of the Fellahin, anti-government and anti-foreigner, to swell the volume of the movement and create the semblance of a united people."[1] And insofar as in the course of 1914-18 the national aspirations of the Arabs assumed the character of a positive political factor, and began to impinge upon the Western mind, and the thought of possible trouble between Jews and Arabs began to gnaw at some observers on the spot, British statesmen did not find it difficult to brush aside these worries. There was, in the first place, the principle of distributive justice. If the Arabs were going to get unexpectedly so much, the Jews, who had suffered so much more and to whom the Christian world owed so vast a debt, were surely entitled to obtain so little in comparison. The scheme might inconvenience the local Arabs, but measured in relative terms the injury that would be caused to the Arab world as a whole was not considered, from the point of view of distributive historic justice, to be too heavy a price for the redress of so old and deep a wrong, and for the restoration of an ancient nation of possibly great promise. "Arabia for the Arabs, Armenia to the Armenians, Judea for the Jews"—was the slogan voiced by Lord Robert Cecil, certainly no cynic.

Furthermore, a good many people, and among them T. E. Lawrence, looked upon Zionist colonisation as a lever of an imminent semitic, or indeed, Arab renaissance. "The Zionist thesis intruded at this point"—writes Symes. "Ought not Jewish genius, exercised in every kind of human aptitude, to be engaged upon the task of a semitic renaissance? Could not the masters of monetary exchange, of science, and the arts, become political brokers between the Western and a revivified Near-Eastern civilisation? Might not a Jewish haven securely lodged in the new Arab body politic raise the latter's status and enhance its significance? It was a pseudo-philosophic concept (plus strategic considerations, of course!) of this nature, conceived as an act of constructive statesmanship

[1] Stewart Symes: *Tour of Duty*, London 1946.

which appealed to many great and generous minds—
Lord Balfour's amongst them. There was a practical synthesis in the idea, for, on a lower plane of analysis, it could
be argued that Arabs' and Jews' characteristics, their
strength and weaknesses, were often curiously comple-
mentary to one another. In such a golden perspective the
Palestine question might properly be regarded as the *gage
d'amour* of a great alliance: the suggestion that it might also
entail the excision of a pound or more of Arabs' territorial
flesh was dismissed as monstrous."

Arthur Balfour had the courage to face the problem
squarely. In a memorandum of August 11, 1919, on the
future of Syria, Palestine and Mesopotamia, Balfour points
out the contradictions between the letter of the League
Covenant and the policies of the Allies, who "got themselves into a position so inextricably confused that no really
neat and satisfactory issue is now possible for any of them. . . .
In Palestine we do not propose even [as was done in the case
of Syria—J.L.T.] to go through the form of consulting the
wishes of the present inhabitants of the country. . . . I do not
think that Zionism will hurt the Arabs, but they will never
say they want it. . . . So far as Palestine is concerned, the
powers have made no statement of fact which is not admittedly wrong and no declaration of policy which, at least
in the letter, they have not always intended to violate. . . .
The four Great Powers are committed to Zionism. And
Zionism, be it right or wrong, good or bad, is rooted in age-
long traditions, in present needs, in future hopes, of far
profounder import than the desires and prejudices of the
700,000 Arabs who now inhabit that ancient land. In my
opinion, that is right. What I have never been able to understand is how it can be harmonised with the declaration
[Anglo-French declaration of November 7, 1918], the
Covenant or the instructions of the Commission of Enquiry."
"In any Palestinian plebiscite"—Meinertzhagen in his
Diary quotes Balfour as saying—"the Jews of the world must
be consulted." "Palestine"—Balfour told Brandeis according
to Justice Frankfurter—"presented a unique situation. We
are dealing not with the wishes of an existing community

but are consciously seeking to reconstitute a new community and definitely building for a numerical majority in the future."

It is only pertinent to add that unshaken as he remained in his support for Zionism, Balfour evinced little enthusiasm for the idea of a British Mandate over Palestine. He would have preferred America to hold the baby.

Lloyd George quotes in his diary (April 20, 1917) the answer he gave to the expostulations of the British Ambassador in Paris about the difficulties a Zionist policy was calculated to encounter from the Arabs and France: "we shall be there by conquest and shall remain, we being of no particular faith and the only power fit to rule Mohammedans, Jews, Roman Catholics and all religions . . ." "There is nothing to suggest"—remarks Mr. Leonard Stein, himself a life-long liberal, and three times an unsuccessful parliamentary candidate of the Liberal party—"that Lloyd George ever wavered in his robust belief that Great Britain could take all the difficulties in her stride."

Mr. Stein quotes what he believes to be an authentic record of an exchange in the Eastern Committee of the War Cabinet (December 1918) as given by Lloyd George in his *Treaties*.

"General Wilson: . . . It lies between us and the Americans.

Lord Robert Cecil: There is not going to be any great catch about it . . . because we shall simply keep the peace between the Arabs and the Jews. We are not going to get anything out of it. Whoever goes there will have a poor time.

General Smuts: It would affect Jewish national opinion, and nationally they are a great people.

Lord Robert Cecil: They are likely to quarrel with the Protecting Powers.

General Wilson: If well-handled, I do not think so.

General Macdonough: I suggest the most important thing in the consideration of Palestine is . . . its being, as Mr. Balfour says, the home of the Jewish people and, therefore, interesting the whole of the Jews all over the world."

Viewed in isolation as a clash between Jews and Palestine Arabs the conflict of rights was insoluble. It looked different when world Jewry and the Arab world as a whole were confronted, with mankind called in to arbitrate. Weizmann and his Gentile friends searched for openings which could lead to a deal with the Arab world.

In a note dictated for Sir Stewart Symes's benefit in 1916, and published by Symes for the first time thirty years later in his book, T. E. Lawrence says: "The real imminence of the Palestine problem is patent only to Feisal and the Sherifians. He believes that we intend to keep it to ourselves, under the excuse of holding the balance between conflicting religions, and regards it as a cheap price to pay for the British help he has had, and hopes still to have. He has no idea at all that any of us ever dreamed of giving it to the Jews. Dr. Weizmann hopes for a completely Jewish Palestine in fifty years, and a Jewish Palestine, under a British façade for the moment. He is fighting for his own lead among the British and American Jews: if he can offer these the spectacle of British help, and Arab willingness to allow Jewish enterprise free scope in all their provinces in Syria, he will then secure the financial backing which will make the new Judea a reality. . . . Weizmann is not yet in a position, as regards Jewry, to make good any promise he makes. In negotiating with him the Arabs would have to bear in mind that they are worth nothing to him till they have beaten the Turks, and that he is worth nothing to them unless he can make good amongst the Jews. . . . As soon as Feisal is in peaceful possession of this area the effendi class, the educated class, the Christians and the foreign elements will turn against him. His movement is a popular one, and his supporters are the peasants under the village sheikhs, the tribes under the tribal sheikhs, and the poor Moslems of the towns. If the British and American Jews, securely established under British colours in Palestine, chose this moment to offer to the Arab state in Syria help

1. against the Syrian autonomous elements,
2. against the foreign railways, ports, roads, waterworks and power companies,

Sherif Feisal would be compelled to accept the help, and with Anglo-Jewish advisers could dispense with the effendis and buy out the foreigners. This would give time for a development of an Arab spirit in Syria from below, and might be preferable to a Syrian-Effendi régime." This vision of an Arab-Jewish monarcho-democratic alliance against feudal and alien exploitation is quite startling.

The negotiations and exchanges between King Feisal on one side, and Weizmann and Frankfurter on the other, were attempts in that direction. But of course it was not in the power of the Jews to prevent Feisal's expulsion from Syria by the French or to help the Hashemite family to retain a United Arab kingdom outside Palestine, and save them from being dispossessed by the late Ibn Saud. Both Arabs and Jews were the victims of the discrepancy between declaratory, general principles and the failure to evolve any machinery for their realisation—a failure which frustrated so many excellent intentions of the peace-makers at the end of World War I. The Age of Keynes and the New Deal had not yet arrived, and the League of Nations lacked the spirit, the resolve and the instruments for carrying out international decisions. Except for some rudimentary attempts to exercise international control over opium and other dangerous drugs traffic, to grant aid to refugees, the League never evolved any schemes and agencies for sustained and positive international action, as U.N. has done against all the odds. The League of Nations Mandates Commission was nothing but a talking shop, where elderly gentlemen, mainly former colonial governors, airily discussed reports submitted to them by the mandatory governments and petitions or complaints by other interested parties. Except for the extremist Revisionist-Zionist wing no one even envisaged the possibility that the League of Nations, as keeper of world conscience and international government on the way, could be called upon to assume direct responsibility, evolve a plan, provide the means, appoint the executives for bringing to fruition an internationally supported settlement. It occurred neither to the Jews nor to the British that the mandatory power entrusted with the task of carrying out the Balfour Declaration should adopt a policy of five- or ten-year plans on the Soviet or Rooseveltian model. Such a course would have been regarded as putting too heavy a burden upon the British Government, as too direct an identification of Britain with Zionism, although of course planning of that nature should have been designed to blunt the edge of the Arab-Jewish antagonism by making practical provisions for the Arabs. *Laissez-faire* was still the dominant creed of the day and the Jews themselves were passionate believers in self-help, in "Auto-emancipation" in the spirit of the famous pre-Herzlian brochure by J. L. Pinsker. Self-reliance, voluntary adhesion, the very fact of "doing it themselves" were thought to be integral parts in the fulfilment of Zionism. The famous break between Weizmann and the American Zionist leaders under Brandeis occurred soon after Britain took over the Mandate precisely as a result of such divergent approaches. The Americans claimed that the political conditions having been secured, the colonisation of Palestine by Jews should be regarded from then on as a field for free enterprise, while Weizmann realised that Palestine being economically a very doubtful proposition and bristling with political difficulties, there was no escape from some forms of collective planning and public enterprise.

The Jews in Palestine were left face to face with the colonial servants sent to Palestine from Whitehall with the vaguest instructions, and precious little consistent guidance. The solemn utterances of the great leaders in London, whether expressions of sincere faith or flights of oratory, appeared irrelevant, if not vexatious and calamitous mischief to the officials on the spot, harassed by Jews who seemed to them insistent and arrogant and by sulking or rebellious Arabs; sent to govern, and yet all the time fearing to lose, and indeed often losing grip on the situation; with each of the two contending groups offering allegiance not to the government of the country, but to causes which recognised no boundaries, and were diametrically opposed. However lofty the far flung and distant visions of the great statesmen in the metropolitan capital, the man on the spot more often than not sympathised with the Arabs and disliked the Jews. Few officials went to Palestine as anti-Jewish, but many left it as anti-semites, because dormant, deep-seated prejudices found a powerful irritant on the banks of the Jordan. The Arab case was simple and self-explanatory, the Zionist aims were complicated and sounded aggressive. The Arab spoke of facts and rights, the Jews talked of claims and aspirations. Nor did the Jews in the 1920's appear powerful and determined enough to inhibit all opposition. The Zionist mystique had won the hearts and minds of the majority of the Jewish people, certainly of the most generous spirits, but it would be an exaggeration to say that this victory manifested itself before 1933 in a mass stampede to Palestine, braving all difficulties, oblivious of any personal and utilitarian considerations. "History"—says Engels in a purple passage recently quoted by E. H. Carr—"is about the most cruel of all goddesses, and she leads her triumphal car over heaps of corpses, not only in war, but also in 'peaceful' economic development. And we men and women are unfortunately so stupid that we never pluck up courage for real progress unless urged to it by sufferings that seem almost out of proportion."[1]

The Zionists were by no means of one mind as to the desirability of unregulated mass immigration, because many of those who were as anxious to build a perfect society as they were bent upon securing a refuge for the persecuted, preferred selective immigration designed to bring to Palestine in the first place the most zealous and most steadfast devotees of the ideal of the Kibbutz. That attitude may in some cases have been rationalisation of an unacknowledged disappointment. Still, it did count for something.

The Zionist policies towards the Arab question should be viewed in this context. Was there ever any chance of solving the problem by an Arab-Jewish agreement, with or without the help of the mandatory power? Did the Zionists hope for an agreement and work for it, or did they ignore the Arabs altogether, being prepared to ride roughshod over them? It is all too easy to pass total condemnation upon Zionism on this point. But that would not be the attitude of a historian.

[1] E. H. Carr: *What is History?*, London 1962, p. 75. Letter of February 24, 1893 to Danielson in Karl Marx and Friedrich Engels: *Correspondence, 1846-1895*, published 1934, p. 510.

Propagandists and partisans attribute to those whom they like skill, to those whom they dislike ruse. Their friends are resourceful, their enemies unscrupulous, the former earn praise as dynamic, the latter are branded as imperialist aggressors. When you approve of someone, he is an idealist, when you disapprove he becomes a selfish nationalist. Your own foreign conquests become commitments, the dependencies of others are subjugated countries; your own old established interest is law and morality, the uprising of the have-nots are to the haves immoral flaunting of laws and treaties.

Anti-Zionists, Arabs and their friends, can see nothing in Zionism but a conspiracy to steal a country from another people and to dispossess its inhabitants. If the Zionists wanted to found a home for a homeless, persecuted people, why had they to do it at the expense of the Arabs in Palestine? The Zionists saw only one country to which history and sentiment could give them any claim, and that was Palestine. The world was not empty, and they certainly had no right to trespass upon the territory of any other people. There is no answer in the mouth of the historian, any more than of the moralist, why innocent people are called to suffer and foot the bill so that aims extraneous or even injurious to them may be achieved. Any war is a case in point. A fair-minded Arab scholar came closest to the truth when he said that the Zionists had no evil intentions towards the Arabs, they just had none, preferring not to think of them. But this is only a half-truth. Some Zionists were so self-centred and self-righteous that Arab resistance appeared to them as nothing but perversion or wickedness, and Arab guerrillas as bandits and assassins. Many consciously or unconsciously sought to ease their conscience by attributing to the Arabs a greater dose of original sin than that possessed by any ordinary people. Others harped all the time on the material benefits, the higher standard of living which Jewish colonisation was calculated to bestow upon the Arabs. Leftists put all the blame on the feudal elements among the Arabs, and pinned high hopes on the progressive forces with whom they were sure to find a common language. Weizmann belonged to none of them. In his memorable evidence before the United Nations Palestine Committee Weizmann defined the position as he saw it in a way all his own: this was a problem which you could solve only along the lines of least injustice. Equal justice to both was impossible. One could express that attitude by quoting the reply Dr. Johnson gave to the objection that he could not be both at the same time, an upholder of the absolute sanctity of authority forbidding any form of disobedience to it, and a good Christian extolling the resistance of the early Christians to the pagan Roman Empire: the emperors of Rome had every right to persecute the early Christians, and the early Christians had every right to seek martyrdom.

Early in World War II Berl Katznelson, a man of immense moral authority, who twenty years after his death still continues to be venerated as the guide and conscience of the Israeli Labour movement, formulated his views on the Arab question in the following sentences:

"There can be no doubt that the Jewish state means full rights for the Arabs [literally 'the fullness of rights']. No Arab will be dispossessed, no Arab will be expelled. No Arab will [have to] leave the country against his will. We shall certainly not prevent him from leaving the country if he so wishes, we shall even help him in that. It is fair to assume that there will be many transfers [of population] in Europe, at the end of this war. We have still to see what Czecho-[slovakia] will say about the Sudeten Germans: will they leave them [where they are] or ask them to bestir themselves and move elsewhere? After all that has happened to us in the world, and all that has happened to us here, in this country [Palestine] since 1936, we are entitled to say: we want to rule in this corner. Indeed not to prejudice anyone's rights, not to injure the rights of any worker, anyone's right to a job [in the civil service] and the like. All rights will be respected. But the task of *ruling this country* [italics in the original]: problems of immigration and settlement—things upon which our very fate depends—in all these we will not submit to others; these matters belong to us as of right."

Apart from ultra-nationalist romantics who had visions of

some apocalyptic upheaval, with general groaning and gnashing of teeth, and therefore would not bother about what would happen to any particular individuals or groups in the event, the majority of Jews would have endorsed Katznelson's statement at the time. Perhaps because they were afraid to probe too deeply into the matter, consciously they certainly believed that the Jewish state would have no need and no reason to harm, dispossess or expel the Arabs, for there was room for both peoples. . . . But if they chose to go . . .—no doubt many Jews, and officers of the Israeli army, were not disinclined to see in the mass escape of Arabs in 1948 a matter of free choice, and if not actually taking steps to expel them, did nothing to stop the exodus of the Arabs. It could so easily be interpreted as a part of a vast historical transformation, a heaven-sent, unexpected and radically simple solution of a most difficult problem.

Fine, too fine, as the distinction between the granting of full rights to the Arabs and the insistence on undivided and supreme rights on the question of Jewish immigration and settlement may sound, it was not a hypocritical and self-righteous twist in the minds of those who upheld it. The whole question of Jewish statehood turns on this point.

With the exception of the Revisionist-Zionists under the Mazzini-like Jabotinsky, who formed themselves into a separate group in the twenties, and then broke away from the Zionist organisation on this very issue in the thirties, and out of whom the Irgun Zvai Leumi emerged in the forties, the Jewish state did not become a mystique till the idea was launched by the Royal Commission report, in its plan for the partition of Palestine into a Jewish and Arab state, in 1937.

Before that time most Zionists, although the most important canon of their ideology was a brochure under the title *Judenstaat*, were curiously inhibited on this point, as *mutatis mutandis* were Social-Democrats about the Revolution. Fully aware that the majority Arab population was against them, they were not so anti-democratic as to wish for a minority to rule the majority, as in South Africa. They demanded the opportunity to become the majority through immigration, colonisation, industrial development, scientific progress, educational and other activities. Early enough the Jews of Palestine formed a network of self-governing institutions, something like a state, within the State of Palestine, and an outpost of the exterritorial Zionist world-state. It was for a long time not taken for granted by everyone that when the Jews had become a majority Palestine must become an independent Jewish state. Some of the qualms and hesitations that many Jews, among them convinced Zionists, felt up to the very minute of the establishment of the State look quaint today. Apart from the inhibiting Arab factor (which made some people ask for a bi-national state or for Dominion status within the British Empire), there was a widely held vague view that a state, with all the paraphernalia of statehood, army and police, and its ethos of power, was fundamentally at variance with the traditions of a community, which though no longer exclusively a Church dedicated to the service of God, was still held to owe allegiance to some impersonal calling, and could not be guided by selfish interest or its own wilful views alone. Those who held that opinion were convinced that the Jewish constructive achievement, especially the Socialist nature of the experiment, would shine more brightly if uncontaminated by the evils of domination and coercion. Not only would the Arabs not be subjugated that way, embarrassment would also be spared to those diaspora Jews who feared the spectre of dual loyalty. At all events, the question, besides being highly inopportune, was not really pressing up to the middle thirties. As late as 1932, the ratio of Arab and Jew was neither alarming to the Arabs, nor very encouraging to the Jews. As to the British, though under the impact of Arab riots in 1929 the Labour Government made in 1931 an attempt to put a permanent brake on the progress of the Jewish National Home, the policy was soon given up. Jewish immigration and colonisation could still be, if not stimulated, at least grudgingly tolerated.

III

By 1933 the Jews were overtaken by a storm which, growing in momentum from year to year, indeed from month to month, soon assumed the character of an Apocalypse. The atmosphere changed overnight. The Jews found themselves subject to increasingly more compulsive and irresistible pressures, while an array of formidable forces was taking up positions against them.

It would be difficult to imagine today the shock which world Jewry received, when one of the foremost countries in the world annulled by a stroke of the pen the rights of Jews as equal citizens. In a sense that formal denial of equality, of something that had been considered as absolutely self-evident and unalterable, was worse than the brutalities committed by Nazi thugs or the summary dismissals of Jewish professors and musicians. Jews were resigned to social anti-semitism, to being barred from a good many positions. They were not unused to savage outbursts, and occasional *pogroms*, in brief to the discrepancy between formal equality and disabilities in fact. But no one could have envisaged that a modern state could by law abolish Jewish emancipation and turn the Jews into a pariah group outside the national community, and that civilised powers instead of ostracising such a state would be falling over each other in courting its insolent rulers who never tired of pouring scorn upon the allegedly most sacred values of Western civilisation. While utter disillusionment, wounded pride and desperate need converted overnight hundreds of thousands of Jews to Zionism, which appeared tragically vindicated by history, a wave of anti-Zionist Arab nationalism was just then culminating (in 1936) in an anti-Jewish and anti-British armed revolt in Palestine, supported by the Arabs outside, as well as by the Nazi-Fascist powers.

In the meantime, while Jewish needs grew desperate, their image shrunk. From a force of incalculable promise and compelling moral stature as well as potent influence twenty years earlier, the Jews were turned into a mass of hunted and haunted beings; even to the humane a standing reproach and irritant, instead of a crying challenge to world statesmanship and humanity's conscience. Britain was just then in the throes of a paralysing loss of self-confidence in face of the defiant dictators, expressing itself in a decline of the will to rule and the capacity to take bold decisions. When the Royal Commission, sent to Palestine in the wake of the 1936 Arab revolt, came to the far-reaching conclusion that the Mandate had proved unworkable, and that in view of the nature of the Arab-Jewish conflict as a clash of mutually exclusive rights, Palestine must be partitioned into a Jewish and an Arab state, the British Government could not find the courage and strength to cut the Gordian knot. It adopted a policy of temporary and vacillating makeshifts, and on the eve of the outbreak of World War II came out with the White Paper which—by stopping immigration and prohibiting land purchase and settlement by Jews in large areas of Palestine— seemed to foreshadow a Jewish ghetto in an Arab state, a little over twenty years after the Jews had been promised a National Home, authoritatively interpreted as a Jewish state.

By the end of the war the Jews were maddened by despair. Their state of mind, and the actions resulting from it, assumed the dimensions of a revolutionary, indeed apocalyptic uprising, so elemental as to defy the usual standards—"*on ne fait pas de procès aux Révolutions*".

It was not only the suffering that defies the imagination, and not only the plight of the survivors of Belsen and Auschwitz who had nowhere to go or could not be induced to go back to graveyards. It was the *prima facie* inexplicable fact that millions went to their death without resisting, after devilish cunning had previously by degrees taken away their strength and their will to live by systematic starvation, every possible humiliation and inconceivable brutality. There was then also the unspeakable experience of lawlessness turned into law. A whole race had been delivered into the hands of assassins who could do with it what they liked, on the sole condition of bringing about its annihilation. In the utter loneliness and defencelessness the marked victims had no court to appeal to, no judge to ask for redress, no authority to protect them against abuse and arbitrariness. They were surrounded "by the apathy of the civilised world", while refugee ships were being turned away from the shores of the promised land and their wretched passengers driven to mass suicide: the inevitable end of a journey, with no end, in sub-human conditions. On top of this then came the cruel disappointment with Ernest Bevin's policy on the morrow of the famous Labour Party Conference resolution, which *au fond* embarrassed the responsible Zionist leaders, because it went further than they thought advisable and practicable, and they therefore feared a rebound: "Let the Arabs be encouraged to move out as the Jews move in", for "there is surely neither hope nor meaning in a Jewish National Home unless we are prepared to let Jews, if they wish, enter this tiny land in such numbers as to become a majority. There was a strong case for this before the war. There is an irresistible case now after the unspeakable atrocities of the cold and calculated German Nazi plan to kill all Jews in Europe."

In the light of the unprecedented catastrophe the question of Jewish statehood changed character. The Jews in Palestine became obsessed with the conviction that they were doomed to the same fate as their brethren, unless they became masters of their own fate, for the world's justice could not be relied upon; and if they were to perish, they would go down fighting, for they must make good the failure of the millions of martyrs to fight. Without political power all achievements gained by so much effort in Palestine would be in vain, as they would all be turned to dust in a state dominated by a vindictive Arab majority. It was no longer a question of a refuge for the homeless survivors alone.

Here was perhaps the greatest failure of Ernest Bevin, a failure which reveals his severe limitations as Foreign Secretary. Whatever wonderful qualities the Labour leader was endowed with, he lacked a sense of history, and the massive imponderables were beyond his ken. I can still remember Winston Churchill exclaiming, to passionate thumping of the Despatch Box, that the Rt. Honourable Gentleman did not even begin to understand the Palestine question, a world problem that went back a thousand, two thousand, nay three thousand years. And the Foreign Secretary thought he could treat the Jews as Mau-Mau in Kenya or bandits in Malaya. Bevin's excursions into philosophy of history, his disquisitions on the meaning of a national home and national freedom; his repeated references to the position of Welshmen and Scots and to freedom of religious worship; his private utterances that his trade union experiences had taught him to wear down the sides in an industrial dispute till they were ready to accept any terms— are enough to show that Bevin failed to understand Arab nationalism no less than the Zionist mystique. He had nevertheless the *naïveté* or the conceit to stake publicly his political career on the solution of this problem. Bevin was certainly not a conscious anti-semite from the start. Unconsciously prejudiced or not, he was not particularly interested in the Jews and their problems, although he was on occasion quite helpful to the Zionist cause before and early in the war. Bevin had his share of vanity, which was fed by success, adulation and flattery throughout most of his career. In most cases he was allowed to have his own way sooner or later. In 1945 Bevin was for the first time faced with a problem which baffled, and in the end defeated him. To his robust common sense the whole question seemed simple at first. As time went on it began to overwhelm, ensnare and crush him, blows being hammered upon him from all sides: terror in Palestine, displaced persons camps, refugee ships heading for the shores of Palestine, American Jewry, Truman, Winston Churchill. Bevin lost his bearings, and just played for time, in the hope that something would turn up. In the meantime he was giving vent to his exasperation in invectives against the Jews who were "pushing to the head of the queue", and in sneers about the New York Jews and the United States President. As Mr. Abba Eban correctly remarks, he missed his chance by refusing the 100,000 permits of entry to Palestine, recommended by the Anglo-American Committee of Enquiry and demanded by Truman: "The irony is that if this friendly inclination had been put into effect the problem would have lost its unendurable tension, and it is doubtful if the State of Israel would have arisen. Mr. Bevin was destined to be Israel's George III, the perverse and unwilling agent of her independence." To the pious Jews it seemed as if God had hardened the heart of Pharaoh.

In retrospect it is difficult to be harsh upon a British

Foreign Secretary reluctant to have an enfeebled, war-weary, empire-weary Britain force upon the Arab world a policy to which they were implacably opposed. But it meant letting the Jews down. Bevin does not stand condemned for despairing of a solution, pulling out of Palestine and handing over the issue to the United Nations, a course which Winston Churchill was urging upon incredulous or deaf ears at an early stage. He aggravated the situation beyond repair by stratagems and makeshifts, and grave insincerities which earned him the bitter resentment of the Jews, and no gratitude from the Arabs. When he finally took the matter to Lake Success, he probably believed in the expert opinion given to him, according to Lord Attlee, by Field-Marshal Montgomery, that the Arabs would throw the Jews into the sea. He expected that when that operation had begun, the Jews would implore the British to come to their rescue and restore law and order, and then lie down under British protection.

A far-reaching change was taking place from 1939 onwards in Jewish leadership. As a nineteenth-century Jewish liberal and intellectual, Weizmann was a profound believer in the rule of law. He hated, it would be more correct to say despised, violence, arbitrariness, lawlessness. To him war was abomination, a sign of mankind's immaturity. Weizmann was fond of telling amusing Yiddish anecdotes which showed how incomprehensible the very phenomenon of war was to the Jew of the old type, for instance the story of a Jewish recruit who after being put for the first time in the trenches hears firing from the other side and cries out "Madmen, what are you doing? People are here!" Weizmann was also deeply impressed with the invincible might of the British Empire, and desperately fearful that the moral case of Zionism would be tarnished by terror, and the tender, weak plant of the Yishuv (the Jewish settlement in Palestine) would go up in flames, if the Jews were to go on defying the might of Britain. I can still remember his utter bewilderment, the horrified amazement in his eyes and voice, when listening and replying in closed conclaves to speakers urging active resistance, and the use of violent means against the British:

"Are you mad? This is un-Jewish. It is crazy!" Every new outbreak of terror, the assassination of Lord Moyne, the blowing up of the King David Hotel, the hanging of the two sergeants as a reprisal for executions, was another crucifixion to the old humanitarian. In this anguished attitude Weizmann was out of tune with the Jewish masses, having besides lost his usefulness as a leader long before, when the British for good or bad reasons had come to the conclusion that Zionism was no ally, and only a burden. Weizmann was swept aside. Up to the late thirties the Yishuv had been as pacific and as law-abiding as its leader, and *havlaga* (restraint) was the proclaimed and, with few exceptions, observed policy in the face of Arab attacks in the later 1930's. It was soon ushered into the ice-age, and "madness" started creeping in. Things unthinkable a little while ago began to lose their horror, to look plausible, then practicable, then necessary, in the end inevitable. Weizmann, who had followed the growth of Palestine Jewry from its infancy and was naturally full of desperate anxiety lest a misfortune befell it, underestimated its vitality and strength as an independent and self-reliant factor, while failing to understand the tremendous force born out of despair. The lessons of Cyprus, Algeria, Kenya were still to come, and Weizmann never liked to remember Ireland. The leadership was taken over by a man who at that hour expressed Jewry in the same way as Winston Churchill spoke the voice of England in 1940. While Ben-Gurion still kept the door of negotiations and legal arguments open, the initiative largely passed to the underground organisations and the terrorist groups of various hues. Yet the latter were ultimately no more than a catalyst, and effective control remained all through in the hands of Ben-Gurion—a pattern followed in many movements of national liberation.

It will long be disputed which factor was the most decisive in bringing about the Jewish state in 1948—the entrenched strength of the highly organised Jewish community in Palestine, the terrorist underground, the solid front of American Jewry, the United Nations sanction or military victory over the Arab armies. In so far as the United Nations decision in favour of a Jewish state in a partitioned Palestine, and then the surprise recognition of it by President Truman (after the United Nations, and especially the United States had got cold feet about it) were of paramount importance in according a legal status to the new state, Weizmann's role in obtaining them was decisive. There was a measure of poetic justice in that re-enacting of a part played by Weizmann in World War I. But it was also a token of his greatness. He was not an unreserved enthusiast for the Jewish state idea in earlier years, but in 1947-8 the chemist realised that this was the moment of fusion, and that it was now or never. Not for a moment did he waver in his conviction that notwithstanding all the odds, the opposition or scepticism in the outside world, and the gravest doubts among some of the Zionist leaders themselves, the State must be proclaimed there and then. He felt instinctively that in that state of conflict and tension any other solution meant throwing the issue back into the melting pot, in fact conjuring up chaos. The mounting wave of anti-colonialism and de-colonisation would have made a Jewish state quite impossible a few years later, when the tide of horrified and guilt-ridden sympathy for the survivors of the Nazi holocaust would have ebbed away. And nothing but another massacre could have forced the Jews to accept the status of a permanent and defenceless minority in Palestine.

Triumph and failure: on the morrow of his second greatest achievement Weizmann, proclaimed President of Israel, practically blind and a dying man, became in the words of Mr. Crossman the prisoner at Rehovoth, a *roi fainéant*, without any power. Nor has the victory of the cause to which he had given his life been a fruit without any of the bitter taste to the movement he had led. Resolute and purposeful, Israel is immensely proud of being a master in its own house, as far as any country, except the United States, the U.S.S.R., China (and Albania) can be truly sovereign nowadays, and it has perhaps sometimes been too eager to reassure itself and others of the fact. The "normalisation" of the Jewish position from that of a ghetto to an independent member of the family of nations is, however, mocked by the hermetically sealed frontiers of the neighbouring states, just as the joyous sense of homecoming of exiles is marred by the hundreds of thousands of Arab refugees across the border. The Jews in Israel are in the ambiguous situation of the last of white settlers in Asia, after the European imperialists and colonisers had made their exit from the two continents. They form the only State in the world to be put by its neighbours into a kind of quarantine (ghetto) and denied the very right to exist. Israel is pathetically anxious to redress the balance by making the Asian and African nations accept it as a friend and as one of the nations which have wrested their independence from an imperialist power (*pace* the Balfour Declaration and the British Mandate), and is passionately eager to share with them the experiences and lessons of nation building.

Christopher Sykes: *Crossroads to Israel*, London 1965, was unfortunately published too late for me to comment upon it in this essay. It is, however, an important work in this context.

8

Experiment in Utopia
The lesson of the Israeli Kibbutz

THE ISRAELI KIBBUTZ is widely regarded as the most original and most remarkable social institution evolved by the Zionist settlers.

The Kibbutz has now been in existence for over fifty years, and from the very small and uncertain experiment in the Jordan valley half a century ago, the Kibbutz movement has grown into a network of several hundred settlements, with a total population approaching the figure of 100,000, dispersed among units which in size range from well over 1,000 members to a few dozen. Some of the older Kibbutzim can boast of flourishing industrial undertakings, besides beautifully cultivated fields and orchards, whereas in the Negev young settlements are engaged in a desperate struggle to wrest some crop from an arid soil in a treeless wilderness.

The revolutionary idealistic resolve of a handful of men and women in the early century to create a society where there would be no "mine" and no "thine", and no one would be forced to join and stay or forbidden to leave, and all decisions would be reached by general consent—has hardened into reality, which the grand-children of the first pioneers take for granted as a natural way of life, notwithstanding individual departures.

It would be wrong and foolish to maintain that nothing has changed in the Kibbutz over a period of over fifty years, which has witnessed such vast transformations in the world at large, and particularly so in Jewry and in Palestine. Yet, it is still substantially the same institution. Both its sameness and its evolution over the decades deserve to be examined not merely from the point of view of the role of the Kibbutz in the history of Zionism leading up to the establishment of the State of Israel, but also as a lesson of wider and general significance. After all, not one of the numerous experiments in Utopia has ever been successful for any length of time, except when buttressed by deep religious conviction as in the case of monasticism, or maintained by coercion from above as in the case of Soviet Russia and China. Sooner or later such communal settlements were rent by strife and ended in failure. Normally the reason was not economic but psychological. Old Adam reared his ugly head, the acquisitive urge and the craving for personal self-assertion proving themselves more potent in the long run than the conscious pious determination to share everything on equal terms and co-operate with others in a spirit of enthusiastic solidarity. Once the malaise set in, the objectively most favourable circumstances were unable to stop the rot.

Has the Kibbutz really achieved a lasting success; and if so, what can its history teach us about human incentives? To what extent does it vindicate the Socialist view that in changed social conditions the idealistic appeal to conscience will suffice to induce man to exert himself on behalf of the community? What can upholders of market economy, who pessimistically claim that only the fear of hunger or of the whip, and conversely the prospect of personal gain are likely to move man to make an effort, learn from the Kibbutz experiment?

It is still too early to pronounce final judgement on the Kibbutz either as an unqualified triumph or as a sad disappointment. The time has certainly come for drawing up a provisional balance, because the forces at work, although far from having solidified for good, are clear enough to gauge their direction and potency. In order to do justice to the phenomenon as a whole, we have to delve a little into the early history of the Kibbutz. The origins of the Kibbutz are to be found in a mixture of theoretical teachings and of practical necessity. An idealistic disposition was made effective by special and concrete circumstances; and from grappling with hard realities by way of trial and error, men with a hankering for generalised and systematic thinking were led on to universalise their immediate experience.

Many a national movement in modern times believed that national liberation was to be a prelude to a spiritual rebirth. In the struggle against a foreign invader or for national unity patriotism was synonymous with self-sacrifice and the subordination of selfish considerations to an impersonal goal. A comforting theory laid all blame for social evils in the community at the doorstep of the alien oppressors, and native exploiters were branded as reactionary, feudal or capitalist henchmen and stooges of the imperialist powers. National brotherhood triumphant was sure to inaugurate the reign of social justice. And thus in the present century national movements in Asia and Africa tend to identify themselves as Socialist or Communist, just as 100 years earlier European and American nationalism gathered under the banner of democracy and liberalism.

The urge to invest their nationalist ideology with social and ethical aims was particularly strong in Zionism. There was the prophetic tradition to which even the most secularised Jew cannot feel indifferent, and which finds expression, among Jews alienated from formal religion, in Socialist loyalty, philanthropic activity or dedication to learning. Although Zionism was a secular movement aiming at full and free self-expression under the protection of a national state, its roots were religious and it neither could nor would shake off the past, that is to say the history of a dedicated confraternity called upon to embody values, which are at variance with selfish utility here and now.

Zionism emerged as a force in Central and Eastern Europe at a time when Socialist ideologies, which in the West had already spent their impetus as movements of Messianic fulfilment, were having their strongest appeal to the oppressed and discontented of the Czarist and the other two empires. The heir of Russian populism, the Social-Revolutionary party, was deeply affected by social Utopianism, which in its Fourierist form had gained quite a few adherents in Russia in the mid-nineteenth century. The blend of abstract Utopianism and the myth of the Russian *mir* produced the idealised vision of a communal way of life, in which labour is a religious duty, one owns or rather holds on behalf of the community only what one is able to till with one's own family and where the spirit of solidarity is strong enough to dispense with all forms of coercive government and hierarchical arrangements. The West stood condemned for its selfish individualism, based upon the Roman concept of private property as absolute and exclusive possession and its offspring the spirit of murderous capitalist competition. Russia shall be spared all that, and it will be given to her to effect the passage from *mir* to socialism by leaping the phase of capitalism.

Left-wing Zionism deplored the contamination which Judaism experienced through its close ties with capitalist corruption. It felt the need to purge itself of the poison of Mammon, urban civilisation and selfish materialism.

The new Jewish society in a reborn Palestine was to be primarily a community of tillers of the land. Moreover it seemed also imperative on national grounds to create a Jewish peasantry and a Jewish working class, for otherwise the Jews would not be able to achieve that balanced social structure which was the condition of any healthy body politic, especially where everything had to start with settlement and colonisation—indeed from scratch. A Jewish Palestine was unthinkable as a society of colonial planters and capitalist city dwellers living on the toil of non-Jewish peasants and workers. The very fact that the Jews were about to begin from nothing in a country soaked with the ancient prophetic tradition was a challenge, and perhaps a guarantee that they would succeed in avoiding the mistakes of other societies which had let themselves be drifted by circumstances and inertia, instead of acting on conscious resolve. There was to be a leap from Babel to Utopia. National aspirations and social idealism were thus beautifully blended. Idealism appeared to be a practical necessity.

There was a general conviction that individual labour, especially the physical effort devoted to the redemption of the land, was a patriotic act, besides being an act of Socialist realization. Many believed that ultimately the way to real national liberation was through Socialist forms, while national emancipation was a condition of a Jewish Socialist society. Yet, it is far from certain to what extent the founders of the first Kibbutzim knew what they were doing, and whether they were really convinced that they were laying foundations for a lasting social institution. To a large extent the first experiments were in the nature of expedients arrived at under the impact of circumstances, although not un-influenced of course by doctrinal tenets, to mention only the ideas of the sociologist Professor Franz Oppenheimer, the century of whose birth was recently observed in Israel.

The intellectual town dwellers who had resolved to become agricultural labourers could not very well compete with native cheap labour. The harsh conditions; the nature of the soil, rock or swamp; the shortage of water; the absence of tools; the lack of any previous experience of agriculture—all these factors were calculated to daunt the most determined pioneer from setting out singly and on his own. To this we have to add reasons of security and the need to belong. In brief, it was imperative to band together in order to share good and bad fortune, to form a society in a new environment, for that was the essence of Zionism; not merely the betterment of one's own individual lot.

Whatever was in the minds of the Fathers of the Kibbutz when making their first steps, the Kibbutz soon assumed enormous significance as a social achievement, and no less as a national myth. The best of Jewry went into the Kibbutz, and hundreds of thousands of young Jews all over the world were brought up in veneration of that institution. The Kibbutz emerged as a model for all forms of Zionist activity in and around Palestine, since it offered a wonderful synthesis of individual disciplined self-reliance and a remarkable ability (and enthusiastic readiness) for voluntary collective effort. This incidentally was the secret of the Jewish achievement in Palestine as a whole, and of the Israeli victory over the combined Arab armies. As a result of centuries of despotic rule, the Arabs had not in the past developed any tradition of self-government and voluntary joint endeavour.

The Kibbutz was a school of character, a centre of Hebrew culture, a military outpost on a dangerous frontier, an experimental agricultural station, soon a seat of industry, above all a way of life and an enlarged family. The members of the Kibbutzim were dedicated men and women, but they were also deeply conscious of the admiring gaze of millions of Jews (and non-Jews) and intensely conscious of their duty to serve as an example and inspiration.

By way of ironical paradox it was the emergence of the State of Israel, to the establishment of which the Kibbutz made a signal contribution, that administered the Kibbutz a blow from which it has not yet recovered.

The State has created a new myth, that of the State. It came into being and gave in turn birth to a whole set of overriding compulsions. A violent shift occurred from the small brotherhoods of the elect, pledged to an exalted type of existence, to the rough, sometimes heroic, occasionally squalid, very spectacular, and at the same time immensely exacting realities, in the face of which no squeamishness was possible. A new scale of values and priorities imposed itself. The State, furthermore, took away the cream of Kibbutz's manhood, because it needed the best human material available, and the finest supply was to be found in the Kibbutzim. So many of the leading figures in Israel, including the present Prime Minister, half the Cabinet, a large proportion of members of the Knesset (Parliament), outstanding generals, ambassadors, heads of the Civil Service, directors of public services and national enterprises hail from the Kibbutz. They still go "home"—to the Kibbutz—for week-ends now and again, and on such an occasion proudly serve as waiters in the communal dining-halls, or do the washing-up in the kitchen, since these jobs require no continuity or specialised concentration.

A breeding ground of builders of the State, the Kibbutz as such played only a very minor part in the tremendous effort of ingathering of exiles since 1948. The Kibbutz was never designed for indiscriminate mass membership, but for an *élite*, who have the vocation and are identified with the Kibbutz *Weltanschauung*. Before admission one had to pass a period of noviciate. While the Kibbutz was neither able nor willing to break down all barriers and be swamped by new-comers, the new immigrants on their part evinced little enthusiasm for the Kibbutz. The survivors of concentration and death camps in Nazi Europe longed for privacy in the midst of a self-contained family. Many of them had not had the time to receive the ideological preparation for life in a Kibbutz. The immigrants from the Orient were not respon-sive to the mystique of the Kibbutz, since in North Africa and in the Middle East the clan is a rudimentary form of social organisation, and there is no tradition of loyalty to abstract causes, apart from religious allegiance. From having thus served as spearhead, the Kibbutz suddenly found itself on the margin of the great events, as if by-passed and almost forgotten in the bustle and noise produced by the milling of enormous crowds. The relative numerical strength of and the distinct part played by the Kibbutz in shaping society at large declined very sharply.

As could have been foreseen, Israel has developed into an industrial and technological society and a very highly urbanised country. Agriculture has reached a saturation point, and even if the Negev is one day made to blossom it is doubtful whether a further extension of agriculture would be economically worth while. The Rousseauist–Tolstoyan glorification of rustic simplicities sounds in the present circumstances hollow sentimentality, almost reactionary. Similarly the idealism of university graduates forsaking their studies in order to join a Kibbutz and work with their hands is not calculated to evoke admiration in an age of rapid automation and in a country with an abundance of unskilled labour over-supplied by Oriental and North African immi-grants. The scale of values has changed. A single individual who would work out a device to harness solar energy for industry or to turn sea-water into water fit for drinking and cultivation would perform a pioneering feat which the efforts of thousands and thousands of Kibbutz members in the fields could not equal. The virtues of ascetic renunciation are no longer *en vogue*, and all emphasis is placed all over the world on increase of production and high output. Once premium is set on the latter, egalitarian distribution ceases to be an ideal. The incentives employed by both Capitalist America and Communist Russia, and inevitably all other countries, including reluctant Israel, run counter to Kibbutz values.

The State of Israel is a highly institutionalised country, while in pre-state Palestine the Jewish state on the way was maintained by a whole nexus of volunteer groups, with the Kibbutz in the forefront. This was for instance true of the underground Jewish army, the Hagana, as of the terrorist organisations. At present in the face of the multitude of State agencies with their coercive powers, the individual has lost his sense of urgency and the previously so vivid feeling of being as it were personally responsible for the national endeavour in its various aspects. The Kibbutz is no longer called upon to serve as a military outpost, since there is an army, and what with State planning, with public works sponsored by the State and central controls, the Kibbutz is no longer seen as single-handed redeemer of the desert; and the private sector of the economy grumbles at what it regards as unfair competition by an artificially pampered Kibbutz industry.

Can mortals go on for long serving as examples of virtue, without being admired or at least enjoying approval? It has been said about Leon Trotsky that he was prepared to jump into fire for the revolution—on condition that the whole world looked on. And Voltaire two centuries earlier opined that nothing was more annoying than being hanged anonymously. But we may as well quote Chesterton's startling dictum that nothing fails like success.

The Kibbutz has significantly contributed to the State of Israel, and having successfully fulfilled that mission, was left with a large part of its *raison d'être* gone. The question therefore arises: has the Kibbutz been an episode called into being by an emergency situation, the preparation for a great break-through, which demanded maximum mobilisation and self-dedication; or has the Kibbutz enough inner resources to maintain itself as a permanent form of life and social organisation even in ordinary times, without coercion, without a semi-religious Messianic creed, and with no world public present to approve and admire?

The Kibbutz has also prospered economically. It is hardly now a sacrifice to belong to a well established Kibbutz. As a result much of the old ascetic puritanism has gone, and the conservative instincts, love of privacy and craving for comfort have been asserting themselves at the expense of the more communal forms. Things unheard of some twenty years ago have become commonplaces in the Kibbutz: a private radio set, a tea service and facilities for private entertainment and hospitality in a family's own living quarters. In olden times a tea-pot to oneself would have been decried as heresy. All eating and drinking and entertaining had to be done in common in the communal hall. And one could hardly have called one's shirt one's own. Whether this trend may lead further to a dissolution of common ownership and communal living in favour of some looser form of co-operation no one can tell.

The Kibbutz experienced a period of grave malaise in the first years of Israeli statehood. More veterans were leaving than new recruits joining the Kibbutz. The Kibbutzim were also rocked by bitter ideological quarrels, which made in some cases old companions come to blows and caused secessions from and splits in old established settlements. These quarrels had absolutely nothing to do with concrete immediate issues impinging upon daily existence, but with points of doctrine such as the evaluation of the phenomenon of Titoism or social realism in the arts. Observers claimed that these ideological storms were a symptom of unresolved psychological tensions and general malaise.

There is reason to think that in the last few years the situation has stabilised. The exodus has slowed down and bitter strife has been assuaged. But even the optimists could not claim that the Kibbutz has resumed its old momentum and that its membership is growing, and new Kibbutzim are cropping up. The shortage of new recruits on the one hand and economic expansion on the other have compelled the Kibbutzim to engage hired labour in growing numbers. This is causing grave doctrinal difficulties since nothing could be more alien to the original spirit of the Kibbutz than employment of hired workers, and the enjoyment of "surplus value" produced by them. The fundamentalists staunchly reject any compromise on the subject such as sharing of dividends or special help to the families of the employees, but their purism appears reactionary in the face of inexorable economic developments.

Professor Martin Buber has summed up a few years ago the achievement of the Kibbutz movement as "no failure". He did not go so far as to call it a success.

9

Who is a Jew?

SOME TIME ago a most unusual *cause célèbre* before the Supreme Court of Israel created a considerable stir among both Jews and Christians.

The litigant was a Carmelite monk of Polish-Jewish origin. Brother Daniel was born and bred a Jew, and had a heroic record of rescuing Jews from massacre, while serving in the disguise of a *Volksdeutscher* as a Gestapo interpreter. Fleeing for his life one day, in danger of being detected, Ruffeisen, as his real name is, found refuge in a Carmelite monastery. There, after some time, he embraced the Catholic faith and took the vows of a Carmelite monk. At the end of the war, he went to Rome and at his insistent request was eventually given leave by his superiors to join the Carmelite monastery on Mount Carmel in Israel.

Brother Daniel sued the Israeli Home Secretary, who incidentally happens to be the leader of one of the religious parties, for refusing to grant him Israeli citizenship in accordance with the fundamental law of the ingathering of exiles—a piece of legislation probably unique in history— which grants to any Jew who chooses Israel as his home citizenship upon his arrival. The Minister was quite prepared to offer Brother Daniel naturalisation as to any non-Jewish resident who meets the necessary requirements, but not automatic citizenship, since by conversion to Christianity Ruffeisen had—in the Minister's view—ceased to be a Jew. The monk refused the concession, insisting that he was a Jew and a convinced Zionist, and therefore entitled to be treated as such.

By a majority of three to two, the Court upheld the

278

Minister's ruling. Of the latter two, one judge gave a firmly dissenting opinion, while the other took up a somewhat intermediary position.

The majority decision of the Supreme Court paid tribute to the personal qualities and fine record of Brother Daniel, and acknowledged the enormous difference between a Church presided over by Pope John XXIII and medieval papacy in its darker hours. The Court nevertheless refused to recognise Brother Daniel as a Jew. It did that not on religious grounds, for paradoxically from the strictly doctrinal point of view a case could be made out that, in spite of his conversion to Catholicism, the monk was still a Jew, but for national-historical reasons.

By taking the formal step of dissociating himself from what has for centuries formed the essence and represented the universally recognised identity of Judaism, the monk had contracted out of the Jewish nation. His subjective sentiments, however deep and sincere, cannot alter that objective fact, for Judaism was a historic totality which must be taken for granted, and cannot be redefined by every individual on every new occasion.

The dissenting judge voiced the opinion that a Jew is simply a person who feels and defines himself as such. This on the one hand individualistic and on the other secular-nationalist view, may be regarded as a strong reaction to that inexorable racialist determinism which in the days of Hitler left to a person of Jewish ancestry, whatever his religious or other affiliations, literally no avenue of escape.

The fifth judge stated that personally he would be prepared to recognize Brother Daniel's claim to be a Jew, but in doing that he would find himself at variance with prevailing convictions. The business of the Court was, however, to give voice to the sense of justice obtaining at large, and not to be ahead of public opinion. What the judge seems to have wished to convey in this was that as yet religious identity was the essential prerequisite for all claiming to belong to the Judaic entity, but in due course Israeli realities were bound to evolve a new focus or new foci of Jewish self-identification. It may then become possible for a Jew to choose his religion as freely as he chooses his philosophical system, and still be a Jew.

The case of Brother Daniel brings into relief a tremendous paradox. Here we have a group which for millennia was held to be and was often forced to be the most stubbornly clannish and exclusive of entities, and yet at the end of some 3,500 years it is still impossible to define who does and who does not belong to it. Indeed, a few years before Brother Daniel went to Court a coalition government in Israel collapsed on this very issue. The then Prime Minister, Mr. Ben-Gurion, turned in despair to leading religious and lay thinkers in world Jewry for their views, but the answers only deepened confusion.

A new *cause célèbre* has recently blown up in Israel to bedevil the situation still further. As if to add special symbolism, the trouble came to a head in the city of Nazareth, of all places.

Mrs. Rina Eitani was a very active and dynamic member of the local municipality council, representing *Mapai*, the governing right-wing Labour party. In spite of the fact that there is a nation-wide coalition alliance in Israel between *Mapai* and the Religious-National party based (as we shall see) on a give-and-take arrangement and on an "equitable" division of spoils, the relations between the representatives of the two parties on the local Nazareth level were rather strained; and Mrs. Eitani made herself unpopular with the other party by opposing a special subsidy to a religious kindergarten. Mrs. Eitani is an immigrant from Germany. She had suffered under the Nazis, had braved the British ban on immigration to Israel in the early post-war period, and arrived in Israel by smuggling herself across the frontiers and illegally entering into the Jewish National Home. She then served with distinction in the Israeli army, and in all her later activities displayed intense Israeli-Jewish patriotism. When tempers in Nazareth became frayed, a rumour spread that Mrs. Eitani was born of a non-Jewish mother, had never become converted to the Jewish religion, and therefore was not really a Jewess.

The Orthodox activists got busy. The local Home Office

official in charge of birth and death registration, who as
a matter of course (the result of the spoils system) is a
member of the Religious-National party, was anxious to
have documentary evidence. He therefore despatched an
enquiry to the German Record office about the racial origins
of Mrs. Eitani's mother, and he received the information for
which he was panting. He immediately requested Mrs.
Eitani to return her passport—because she had obtained her
Israeli citizenship under false pretences (automatically, as
a Jewess, on the basis of the law of ingathering of exiles),
whereas she was not, after all, a Jewess at all. Furthermore,
her Jewish marriage was also invalid. Since there is no civil
marriage in Israel, she was bound to live in sin—unless she
went through a formal ceremony of conversion—which
again the Rabbis were most reluctant to perform, claiming
that the conversion would not be prompted by genuine
conviction.

No one could have invented a more embarrassing and a
more intractable affair. The very idea of an Israeli-Jewish
official taking advantage of Nazi records on "Aryan" and
"non-Aryan" ancestors evoked feelings of deepest revulsion.
It then became known that the "Aryan mother," far from
abandoning her non-Aryan husband in the hour of danger,
had shielded him from the worst that could have befallen
him, and had identified herself with his and her children's
Jewish loyalties. As in the case of Brother Daniel there was
something here which the Jewish past had never or hardly
ever known: a person with a doubtful claim to being called
a Jew, and with another (and, in worldly terms, better)
alternative before him, opting consciously and voluntarily
for Judaism. If the non-Jewish blood of the mother was an
insuperable barrier, surely here was a case of biological
racialism overriding spiritual content and freedom of
choice. And the panacea of religious conversion, even if
granted by the Rabbis, smacked too much of coercive
pressure.

The country is now torn by controversy and no solution
is as yet in sight.

It would be difficult to imagine a more complex, more

insoluble and indeed more poignant problem than the question of religion and State in present-day Israel. Although seemingly affecting only Jews, or still more precisely Israeli Jews, the issues involved touch upon some of those basic dilemmas which go to make up the human condition. Ancient exclusive loyalties rooted in the deepest, one may almost say desperate convictions, are pitted against overwhelming forces of change and sweeping innovation. A battle is fought between the urge for free individual self-expression, and the "grantedness" of a concrete, most sharply contoured historic totality. What are the legitimate limits which the heritage of all the ages may set upon the sovereign right of the generation here and now to fashion its life?

The Jews—who are they and what are they? It is doubtful whether a question so formulated allows for a single, unambiguous answer. It was one thing to be a Jew in the centuries of faith, another in a secular environment in the West. It is not the same thing in a pluralist society as it was in countries of warring racial groups in Central and in Eastern Europe. And it certainly is quite a different matter to be a Jew in the State of Israel. Surely there must be a Rabbinical view on that? Yes and no. The Rabbinical doctrine wavers between (and rather tries to combine) two criteria, the religious and the racial (or national). Anyone who professes the Law of Moses, was born into the Jewish faith or adopted it, is a Jew.

But a Jew by race who has lost his Jewish faith and jettisoned all religious practice does not cease to be a Jew, for anyone with a Jewish mother by creed or race is a Jew. A person born of a Jewish father but of a non-Jewish mother is not acknowledged as a Jew, for you can never be sure about paternity. Some wits delighted in thus pointing out that the grandson of Mr. Ben-Gurion was strictly speaking a *goy*, since Ben-Gurion jr. married an English Gentile girl, whereas Mr. Khrushchev's grandson was a Jew, since the Soviet leader's late son had married a Jewess. Even a baptised Jew could in certain contingencies still be considered a Jew, for instance in family matters, but he could claim no religious

rights as a Jew. This may perhaps appear to be a case of
heads I win, tails you lose. The position could be best
formulated by saying that a Jew is a person of the Jewish
race or religion, who has not formally embraced a non-Jewish
religion, no matter whether he observes his own or does not.
Blood (the Jewish mother) or adoption of the Jewish faith,
which in the circumstances has always been tantamount to
a decision to share a common fate, are decisive for being
counted a Jew; creed or rather change of faith for being
counted out, since till the spread of Nazi racialism adoption
of a non-Jewish religion had been an act of abjuring the
common fate: the contingency of what was originally a tribal
religion and then became a community of fate. For an example of such a state of affairs we would have to look to the
Greeks in the Ottoman Empire. Greek race and Greek
orthodox religion were absolutely inseparable in face of the
Moslem Turk. No Greek would be considered a Greek after
his conversion to Islam. In the case of both, Jew and Greek,
their situation of beleaguered cities made apostasy to the
dominant religion-nation appear an act of highest treachery
and base selfishness. And it would be difficult to determine
what was more potent in this, the deep sense of exclusive
superiority or the desperate fear of extinction.

The cases of Brother Daniel and Mrs. Rina Eitani are two
of the numerous instances which keep driving home to the
Jews in Israel and elsewhere the fact that in their new
independent State the most ancient of religions and the most
ancient of peoples are faced by an unprecedented Church
and State problem, and one of a peculiar kind.

The Law of Moses is claimed by the Orthodox to be not
merely a guide to individual salvation, but to embody the
constitution of a polity. Just as religion and nationhood were
inseparable in Judaism, in the same way the religious code
and State legislation could not but form one totality. Although the conscious appeal of the Orthodox is to the biblical
and Talmudic past, the concrete continuity invoked by them
refers really to the sectarian existence of the Jewish communities in self-imposed or enforced isolation on the margin

of society for the last 2,000 years of Diaspora history. They are simply unable to conceive that in ancient days pre-exilic Jewry was a nation, comprising godly and ungodly people—and that there had been heterodox and even secular trends in Judaism, but their voices had been suppressed by the priestly scribes and compilers. When a Talmudic scholar recently discovered that in the second century there were Hebrews who gambled on horses, worshipped Aphrodite, prayed to Greek gods, coveted other men's wives, dodged bill collectors, and concocted ways to "become invisible," he expressed himself "shocked and terrified that there existed a kind of Jew like this—one who deals in charms and horses, and kills. . . ." Apart from the question of the relevance or applicability of Pentateuch laws, Talmudic decisions and ghetto practices in a modern state, there is of course the question of enforcing them upon the recalcitrant.

However fervent their protestations of principle, few of the Orthodox go so far as to envisage the enthronement of the whole Torah and nothing but the Torah upon all spheres of life and upon all and sundry in Israel. The few unyielding fundamentalists have solved the problem by refusing to recognise the State of Israel altogether and settling down as a little hermetically closed, sullen Kingdom of God, in the midst of a pagan state. They know they cannot impose their convictions on the State. Nor will they bow to its writ. The Zionist State is altogether the fruit of sinful pride to them. Instead of waiting for the promised Messiah and the miraculous intervention of God, self-willed infidels rose to bring about something which God alone could do, and had promised to do.

The breathtaking, not to say comic, paradox in the attitude of the *Neturei Karta* was revealed to me when I was visiting that quaint slum quarter. I got into a conversation with an eight-year-old girl who would not or could not speak a word of Hebrew, only Yiddish. When I asked her why she spoke no Hebrew, her reply came like a shot: "I do not want to be a *goya*!"

There are various shades of opinion among the more

moderate elements of Orthodoxy. The common denominator is the claim that although individual consciences may not be forced, there is the paramount duty and necessity to preserve a Jewish public visage of the State of Israel. This is insisted upon not so much on religious as on national-historical grounds. Some confusedly deny that personal faith in the nature of individual assent is required for the imposition of religious observances on the public, since laws and regulations are enforced by the State without every person being expected to believe in them. Others, oblivious of the Protestant and rationalist heritage, maintain that the Law of Moses, like the medieval established Church, has absolute objective validity, independent of personal conviction. Still, restrictions on public traffic on the Sabbath day become binding only if passed in the form of law by the Knesset, in other words, as State enactments; the state of Israel is explicitly and formally based upon the sovereignty of the people (and not upon the Law of Moses and his successors). There is no written Constitution, because the legislators very much feared a controversy on this very subject.

The same person who will, however unenthusiastically, observe even an irksome State regulation for reasons of expediency, will revolt against it, if it is motivated by religious reasons unacceptable to him. More generally the non-believers are, as hinted before, asked by the Orthodox to comply as a form of national duty. A Jewish state is unimaginable without embodying historic patterns of immemorial antiquity which have preserved the identity of the Jewish people and constituted its distinct historic personality. The non-believers are being urged not only to avoid giving scandal and entreated to spare the deep susceptibilities of believers, they are above all implored not to split the nation. Civil marriage and divorce laws for instance would do precisely that, since the religious would not be able to intermarry with the offspring of civil marriages, or rather with the offspring of persons divorced by civil divorce and remarried who in the eyes of the Law are bastards, with whom no Jew can be joined in wedlock. But the most telling argument and by which even determined secularists among the nationalists cannot help being shaken is the one pointing to the Jews in the Diaspora. In the teeming Eastern European ghettos, with their rich, varied and compact Jewish civilisation, it was possible for a Jew to be an atheist and yet to be at the same time an ardent Jewish nationalist in language, culture, political and social interests. In surviving atomised Jewry in the West, the only focus of Jewish self-identification is the synagogue. Any lowering of barriers by way of secularisation of life in Israel would remove those checks and inhibitions which keep Westernised Jews from intermarriage and total assimilation. On the morrow of the most murderous persecution the survivors are haunted by the fear that Judaism may melt away under the benevolent sun of tolerance and equal opportunity. Hitler is thus, indirectly, the author of that intractable religious-national situation, which may become quite impossible if—as is so ardently desired by Zionists—Soviet Russia lifts the ban on emigration of her Jews to Israel. The Jewish State would then be flooded by tens of thousands of Jews whose marriages and births have no legitimacy in the eyes of the Rabbinic law. Whether the Rabbis will devise some religious solution (and it is at present difficult to see what they can do in the matter), or whether the sheer numbers will force a secular solution, no one can predict.

Where is one, once more, to draw a line between the rights of the whole and the imprescriptible freedoms of the individual in this grave dispute? The underlying differences of principle are probably unbridgeable. Is Judaism something given and granted, a Law and a tradition, and are Jews men and women who obey that Law and carry on that tradition? Or is Judaism the sum total of the lives, activities, aspirations and ideas of men and women of Jewish stock in the past, in the present, and in the future? To be a Catholic or a Moslem is to conform to the former pattern. A Frenchman or Dane are presumably what they are by simply being.

The Jews are and are not unique in that fusion of religion and nationhood. In a certain sense all societies in the Middle

Ages were in the first place confraternities of servants of the Lord. It would not be far-fetched to consider the process of secularisation to which all peoples have been subjected, as a gradual transformation of religious communities into nations. Nationalism is in the first place an aspiration to full untrammelled expression of all the potentialities immanent in the ethnic group. The fear of sin restricts the interests and activities of the pure to the exclusion of all that threatens single-minded service of God.

The process of secularisation in Europe has lasted for centuries and is not yet complete. Jewry and the ancient civilisations of Asia and Africa have suddenly and violently been swept into the battle between ritualistic traditions and the solvent forces of rationalism and technology: and the strains and stresses are thereby made graver. Although rooted in religion and history and actuated by the dream of restored ancient glories, Zionism was all the same a movement for secular national liberation, indeed very much a movement for the substitution of a national existence for a sectarian way of life. Some of its earlier prophets voiced distinctly Nietzschean accents engaging in an almost pagan glorification of life and resolutely condemning the ethics of the humble and weak. They would no longer bend their heads as they had done in all their history, but raise them high.

National self-assertion is of course bound to result in a quest for and then an apotheosis of distinct historic symbols and myths, including those of the national religion, as we can observe at present even in Africa. (Mention need only be made of the libation to the gods with which President Nkrumah of Ghana was greeted by Ghanaian students of London University, when he alighted from the plane which brought him last summer to the Commonwealth Prime Ministers' Conference—something unimaginable only a few years ago!) But although some ardent Zionists were led that way to a return to religious practice, most of the Zionist prophets and theoreticians, brought up in the liberal atmosphere of the nineteenth century, gave very little heed to the place of religion in their future state, apart from conventional insistence on religious freedom and inattentive assurance of respect for ancient traditions. The Orthodox wing of Zionism had little effect on the general movement, for it feared secular nationalism and had deep pious qualms about forcing the hand of the Almighty.

With the emergence of the State of Israel the Jews began to realise to their dismay the intractable nature of the problem.

For 2,000 years the Jews had been a sect based upon voluntary adherence. The rabbis had no powers of coercion, except those occasionally granted to them by the non-Jewish State for fiscal or other reasons. Only those in the last analysis obeyed the rabbinical writ who so wanted. There were of course ecclesiastical sanctions, but a Jew who was prepared to brave them had already to all intents and purposes left the fold. Where all are unanimous, there is no problem of coercion and freedom. In present-day Israel we have believers and non-believers, but the rabbis enjoy powers of coercion over all given to them by the State. This, of course, is aggravated by the fact that the Jewish religion lays so much emphasis upon external rites and practices, being really a way of life designed to erect, for reasons of self-preservation, a high fence between the faithful and the world around them.

A sectarian group concerned mainly or even solely with its own survival and the preservation of an exclusive tradition, unwilling or forbidden to accept commitments outside its narrow sphere for fear of contamination and disintegration, found itself overnight faced with all the wide-flung challenges, tasks and responsibilities of a modern industrial and technological state. The religious leaders were totally unequipped to cope with these new realities and had to resort to all kinds of makeshifts and stratagems of an ingenuity which is at once exceedingly clever and at the same time childishly naïve. Instead of being apologetically on the defensive, the Orthodox are paradoxically growing more and more militant (and the numbers seem to be increasing). The reasons for this are twofold. There is a desperate quest for national identity among the younger generation of Israel, on the morrow of the establishment of the State and against the worldwide setting of declining ideologies and general disillusionment. And the memories of the holocaust continue to haunt. There are on the other hand powerful institutional factors encouraging Orthodox militancy. As is well known a Jewish rabbi has no charismatic powers such as are attached to Apostolic succession and the power of sacraments. He is merely a learned man employed in a certain job. Judaism has no doctrine or even tradition of a centralised ecclesiastical organisation, because for one thing the Jews are a people of priests. There has been no supreme ecclesiastical authority in Jewry since the Sanhedrin has ceased to exist. Not official function, but the authority of superior learning and piety gives the ultimate sanction. It has thus happened very often that the law was laid down by a saintly learned layman in a God-forsaken townlet in Lithuania who held no rabbinical office, but whose decisions no chief rabbi of a great country would presume to question. The chief rabbinate is altogether an institution unknown to Jewish law, and in those countries where it exists, it came into being as a matter of administrative convenience. Not a sovereign power once more, but moral authority was obeyed in Judaism. And various people (and communities) would bow to different authorities. In Israel today the rabbinate is rapidly developing into a firmly institutionalised and centralised Church imposing an exacting discipline on its members and facing the general body of laymen as a distinct power. This is not a religious development, but ironically enough the outcome of the emergence of the State. The latter has given rise and legitimacy to an established Church. A peculiar political constellation has in no small measure contributed to this development. Israel has proportional representation, and no party can muster a majority in the Knesset. One of the more outspoken leaders of the governing Right-wing labour party, Mapai, is quoted to have stated that the Orthodox parties were "cheaper" coalition partners than the other factions. They have no particular views on economic or social problems, or special foreign policies. They will accept any line on these matters so long as their religious demands are met.

It may be doubted whether such a state of affairs is calculated to help true religion or is likely to raise moral standards. The Orthodox parties are naturally led to measure their success by the extent of encroachments upon the lives of the secular population, sincerely believing themselves to be labouring for the glory of God. There is no other record with which they can face their followers.

On the other hand the lay parties do not stop to remember that they are making political bargains involving matters of conscience and fundamental principles. And since the battle is waged at least on that level, on imposition of external forms and not on winning souls, it becomes a matter of make-believe, of going through the motions, not to say hypocrisy, without regard to inner conviction. This does not mean of course that the convictions of the truly observant lack depth and force. There are signs of an incipient Church and State struggle on the medieval model.

The other day the luxury trans-ocean liner *Shalom* was launched by the Israeli Government in conjunction with private companies. It was originally planned to have two kitchens on the ship, one adapted to the Jewish dietary laws (all official institutions, the army, Knesset and almost all hotels keep only a kosher kitchen), and another kitchen for those, and of course among them non-Jewish passengers, who wish to have cream with their coffee after their meat meal. The chief rabbinate immediately vetoed the plan. This was not just a formal statement of condemnation. The chief rabbi refused to give his authorisation to the kosher kitchen, and without such an imprimatur the faithful would not eat from it. The rabbinate in the first place expressed horror at the very idea of a Jewish ship providing food that was not kosher. On this they would not listen to utilitarian arguments such as needs and wishes of Gentile passengers, or to democratic vindications of freedom of choice as a basic principle. But the rabbis went further, and in this they really conjured up shadows of medieval papacy. They would not grant authorisation to the kosher kitchen, since one could not trust people who were prepared to run a non-kosher kitchen to be scrupulous in observing the dietary laws in the kosher kitchen. And indeed hotels have been refused the rabbinic imprimatur unless they undertook not only to maintain a strictly kosher kitchen but pledged themselves to prevent smoking, dancing, music and similar such things on the Sabbath day or mixed bathing in the swimming pool on ordinary days. From this there is only one step to a certificate of general moral conduct. The rabbis may be right in taking the view that the imprimatur is not a strictly mechanical or technical matter. But in that case they would be setting themselves up as judges and rulers of the State, claiming the right and power to pronounce a person worthy or unworthy, and thus free or forbidden to engage in certain economic or other activities impinging on religious life. If stretched far enough there is after all nothing that does not do that. It would, however, be rather incongruous to exact inner assent when granting permits, but deny its relevance when imposing restrictions.

Centralisation in the State leads to centralisation in the established Church, but the inescapable result of such a parallelism is a clash of temporal and spiritual powers. This was recently manifested again in a matter of far-reaching economic significance. For centuries ritual slaughter of animals was a powerful lever in the hands of the Jewish communal organisation in general, and the rabbinate in particular. It made possible a form of control upon all believers and helped to give reality to, and to finance the institutions of Jewish self-government. In the midst of an inimical population and in face of restrictive laws the Jewish religious and lay authorities gradually evolved a considerable amount of internal legislation designed to combat unfair practices and harmful competition, and to protect the poor and the needy, and also to prevent the Jewish name and security from being put in jeopardy by irresponsible or offensive behaviour of Jews towards non-Jews. Control of ritual slaughter, involving the power to suspend it, to regulate prices and employment in the industry as well as to organise the supply of meat, was, as said, one of the most effective means of putting teeth into the regulations of Jewish self-governing institutions. Law and custom combined to accord to these powers and practices the character of a traditional religious prerogative vested in the rabbis.

But what was a natural and to a large extent a desirable mechanism of self-defence or instrument of self-government in the situation of a persecuted isolated group in the midst of a hostile word, becomes monopolistic privilege in a Jewish state, a derogation of State power, a means of establishing and perpetuating restrictive practices, and from the point of view of dissidents, a coercive measure of social-economic significance because of the higher price of meat of ritual slaughter.

A violent clash occurred recently between State and rabbinate when the latter invoked and tried to apply its traditional powers in regard to a newly opened co-operative abattoir in the southern part of the country on the ground that it was its duty to forestall any possible contingency that might threaten the principle of *Kashrut* in all its purity or to endanger the livelihood of the religious employees of the industry in other parts of the country, although no objection at all could be raised against the arrangements obtaining in the new establishment and its marketing practices, at the present moment. For a while it seemed that a headlong medieval-style collision between the two powers was inevitable. The meat co-operative in question brought its case before the Supreme Court asking for an *order nisi*. Rabbinical spokesmen declared that they would neither appear to plead nor accept the Court's ruling. In the last moment a compromise was patched up.

There are different rites in Judaism, in the first place those of the Western reformed or conservative (but not Orthodox) synagogues, and then diverse rites are observed by certain Oriental Jewish communities, not to speak of course of agnostics. But this fact is brushed aside by the rabbis and the spokesmen of the Orthodox parties with the argument that watered-down Judaism has proved to be a road to apostasy and that any concessions from the most rigid standards to non-observant people or religious dissidents would lead to adulteration of ritual purity and true believers would be made to commit, unwittingly, sin.

Israel is caught in a vicious circle. Where so much stress is put on external ritual, a religious struggle is bound to degenerate into a tug-of-war for power, and power naturally seeks to assert itself in an institutional manner. Where arms clash, the whisper of humble faith or the silent meditation of contemplative reverence cannot be perceived, and when passions are aroused, the most uncompromising on the opposite sides come to the fore.

Israel is faced in this way with a "two cultures" problem all of its own. The Orthodox are growing more and more self-centred, sensing everywhere dangerous solvents and thin-ends-of-wedges—whereas the secular are developing a distaste for the peculiarities of the Jewish tradition, and a rootless and often shallow hankering for cosmopolitan values and modes. Indeed the cleavage is becoming very apparent in the different styles of expression of the protagonists. The observant cling to ancient idiom, quaint Rabbinic forms of speech and antiquated metaphor with theological references and overtones. The Hebrew of the secular is often a wholly unidiomatic verbatim translation of ideas and terms from foreign languages. Secular nationalists accuse the Orthodox of using religion as an opium for nationalism. To this the latter reply that the very distinction between religion and nationhood, implicit in the secular argument, in itself represents a mode of thought wholly alien to Jewish tradition, indeed a form of apostasy. The religious claim that without faith in Divine promise and the idea of a divinely chosen people, the Jewish claim to Israel would lack foundation, and the Jews would appear as invading imperialists. In their turn the secular have raised archaeology to the dignity of a national religion. The Orthodox again and again go back to the argument that neither Jewish martyrdom nor the survival of the Jewish people against all the odds can be explained otherwise than by direct and special providence. To this a secular thinker is wont to reply with an amusing anecdote. When the cause of the Allies in the last war was at its lowest ebb, the Polish leader General Sikorski came to a famous Hassidic Rabbi and enquired of him how in his good wisdom the war could be won. "There are two ways of winning this war," the holy man reflected. "What are they?" asked the General, and sat up most anxiously. "One is to win it by a miracle. The other to win it in a natural way." "What would be the natural way?" the General asked. "To win it by a miracle," replied the Rabbi. "And what, then, would be the miracle?" wondered the General. "To win it in a natural way," said the Rabbi.

Why not cut the Gordian knot by a separation of Church and State? Although the demand is being voiced, the prospects for such a solution seem at the moment very remote. Whether out of exasperation on being badgered by his secular colleagues, or because he knew he would be forcing them to the wall, an Orthodox member of the Cabinet formally proposed this solution at a recent Cabinet meeting. The secular Ministers were quite dumbfounded and could hardly hide their alarm. For indeed when you come down from abstract formulas to concrete arrangements, it is difficult to see in what way, apart from the introduction of civil marriage and divorce, matters would change from what they are to-day. Jewish religion is so intertwined with Jewish lore, and religious tradition is so deeply and all-pervasively embedded in Jewish history and national myth, that out of fear lest the younger generation brought up in secular homes become totally de-nationalised, a secular Minister of Education some years ago introduced into the school curriculum obligatory teaching in what is called "Jewish Consciousness". It, in fact, amounts to lessons about Jewish religious beliefs, rites, practices, and liturgy, in addition to the teaching of the Bible and Talmud. It also appears inconceivable that a Jewish state would declare its "neutrality" towards Jewish religious holidays, dietary laws, the Sabbath rest day, etc., if only for reasons of expediency— and in order to spare believers very grave hardships and even terrible conflicts of conscience.

The Jewish religion may paradoxically be facing its supreme test precisely in the Jewish state, and the problem of Jewish identity may prove even more intractable in the Jewish National Home than in the countries of dispersion. The idea of the sanctification of life in its totality through a refusal to admit any distinction between theory and practice, social ethics and individual morality, religion and politics, has a different meaning in a voluntary sect without powers of coercion from that in a state with an established religion.

It is one of the ironies that the Jews have everywhere in modern times advocated if not separation of Church and State, at least the rights of private conscience, and called for the secularisation of politics and political life, if for no other reason than the difficulty of enjoying full rights in the type of Christian state defended by old-fashioned conservatives. The danger inherent in this incongruity has alerted American Jews. Thriving upon and deeply committed to the principle of separation of Church and State, and like the American society at large very diversified from the religious and other points of view, the members of the largest and most powerful Jewish community of all time are bound to feel very apprehensive at the sight of a society, in whose fortunes they feel so deeply involved, seeming to revert to forms which they thought happily discarded for ever.

In this respect the Orthodox in Israel may be achieving the very opposite of what they were so anxious to secure. Instead of erecting a dam to the forces of assimilation, they may be estranging and discouraging those whom they wished to save. Similarly the struggle to make the Torah rule supreme may prove the surest way to unchain a real *Kulturkampf*, a thing which Mr. Ben-Gurion is quoted to have said he feared more than the Arabs, the U.S.S.R. or China, and more than an economic collapse.

Another danger is looming in the distance. The insistent emphasis upon the identity of religion and nationhood, involving the coercive imposition of patterns of life and behaviour, may prove too grave a strain on very many Jews, especially in the West, who are imbued with liberal notions about religion as being a matter between God and the individual, the human kind and eternity, excluding the intermediary entity of tribe and nation, and rejecting any idea of a chosen people as an expression of tribal arrogance.

It is too early to tell how this clash between the logic of history and the logic of reason is going to be resolved.

IO

Lewis Namier

I WAS PRIVILEGED to know the great historian Sir Lewis Namier, and to enjoy his friendship for some twelve years before he died in 1960. The more I got to know this strange combination of scholar and man, of English gentleman and East European Jew, the deeper grew my admiration—which was characterised by awe, fear, and occasionally irony. There was the historian of phenomenal erudition, whose knowledge of various cultures and languages, and whose mastery of several disciplines, led Sir Ernest Barker to compare him to Lord Acton. Further, there was the pioneer and founder of a school of historical scholarship who earned that rarest of distinctions—having an "ism" affixed to his name in his own lifetime. There was also the man of culture and imagination whose words—spoken or written—were charged with the meaning achieved by individual observation and richness of expression. But above all, there was Namier himself.

If he was a monumental figure, there was also something infantile about him. His fondness for the saying of a philosopher, a deceased colleague, that the idea that man ever grows up is a childish notion, often made me gaze at him enquiringly. He was a tall man, sparely but powerfully built, and he talked as if it was natural for him to make himself heard and for others to listen. His egocentrism, which was proverbial, came partly from the familiar self-absorption of the artist who innocently rides roughshod over the feelings of those around him, and partly from deep-seated problems that robbed him of flexibility and real assurance. He had a strong sense of mission, and yet was pathetically in need of

296

approval. But praise, in turn, would again give him pain—the embarrassed pain of the perfectionist who feels he is unworthy and lives under false pretences. Any stimulus, friendly or adverse, could evoke an exaggerated response in the man, and throw him off balance. Thus his affection and warmth would almost submerge those whom he liked, but he was capable of the most implacable, indeed paranoic, hatred.

But beyond the meaning of Namier's behaviour, there was the deeper meaning of his character, one that was reflected in his work as it was in his life. In the Introduction to his second major work, *England in the Age of the American Revolution* (1930), there is a revealing passage on the role of landed property in the growth of English liberty. After a rhapsodic reflection on the social significance of the stately homes of England throughout the ages, Namier concludes as follows: "The relations of groups of men to plots of land, of organised communities to units of territory, form the basic content of political history; social stratifications and convulsions, primarily arising from the relationship of men to land, make the greater, not always fully conscious, part of the domestic history of nations—and even under urban and industrial conditions ownership of land counts for more than is usually supposed. To every man, as to Brutus, the native land is his life-giving Mother, and the State raised upon the land is his law-giving Father, and the days cannot be long of a nation which fails to honour either. . . . There is some well-nigh mystical power in the ownership of spaces—for it is not the command of resources alone which makes the strength of the landowner, but that he has a place in the world which he can call his own, from which he can ward off strangers, and in which he himself is rooted—the superiority of a tree to a log."

Then, suddenly, and for no apparent reason, the flow is interrupted by a powerful *cri de cœur*: "Only one nation has survived for 2,000 years, though an orphan—my own people, the Jews. But then in the God-given Law we have enshrined the authority of a state, in the God-Promised Land the idea of a Mother-Country; through the centuries from Mount Sinai we have faced Eretz Israel, our Land. Take away either, and we cease to be a nation; let both live again, and we shall be ourselves once more."

These two passages express Namier's two most deep-seated emotions—an agonised, envious love of historic England, and a tormented passion for Zion; or one may put it more abstractly—the outsider's need for roots and the wanderer's yearning for an anchor.

These passages were written in the 1930's—when a Central European Jew would curse Hitler by asking that God might make him a Polish Jew without a passport, and when almost every part of the world was considered as a possible refuge for Jews or as a possible site for a Jewish state, except the repeatedly promised Jewish National Home. However, Namier's reaction was not merely a temporary response to the Jewish fate in the 1930's. The intense interplay between the need for roots and the yearning for an anchor was a constant that determined not only Namier's character as a man and his work as a historian but also gave a further dimension to the meaning of his life. There is a famous remark of Keats that the story of a man of any worth is a parable, and may thus serve as an allegory. Namier's "story" richly bears out this notion. Unique as his life was, it also can be seen to represent the lesson of the Jewish predicament in modern times, specifically of those talented and ambitious young Jews from Eastern Europe who tried to take by storm the new, alien places they had come to in the West, and who had to pay a heavy price in spiritual torment for their brilliant successes.

Namier's fate was to be always and everywhere an outsider, a resident alien rather than a full-fledged citizen and participant. His parents were landowners in Eastern Galicia, and their deepest aspiration was to enter the Polish Catholic nobility. They hid from the boy the fact of his Jewish origin. When at the age of nine he learned the secret, he experienced a shock whose effects he would continue to feel throughout his whole life. He was filled with bitterness against the parents who had deceived him, and his suppressed rebellion against them was full of potent implications for the future theoretician of conservatism and the poet who celebrated the glory of the traditions that are passed on from father to son. This sense of not belonging fully—neither to Judaism nor to Catholic Poland—was further intensified when he met with the refusal of his Polish friends to accept him, in spite of the burning Polish patriotism he felt at the time. It was, indeed, the experience of overhearing anti-semitic sneers at his parents' desperate attempts to elbow their way into the Polish gentry that eventually made him a dedicated Zionist.

England was kind to him when he arrrived in London in 1908 after a spell of Vienna and Lausanne. He stayed for a while at the London School of Economics, attracted by the Fabianism of its faculty, even though the Fabian temper was so different from the romantic nationalistic socialism of Pilsudski's Polish Socialist party. He then went to Balliol College at Oxford. Balliol, in those days very fashionable, was the recruiting ground of British cabinets and diplomacy, and enjoyed the patronage of one of its most illustrious sons, the Liberal Prime Minister Herbert Asquith, later Lord Oxford. In Oxford, Namier (or Bernstein-Namierowski, as he then was) hob-nobbed as an equal with young men who were to become famous, like T. E. Lawrence and Arnold J. Toynbee. Among his Jewish contemporaries at the college was Leonard Stein, future secretary of the World Zionist Organisation and president of the Anglo-Jewish Association. (His lately published *History of the Balfour Declaration* is likely to remain the definitive study of that much-debated document which contains in a few lines the most controversial and vaguest promise of all time.) Another Jewish contemporary was Leonard Montefiore, of the famous Anglo-Jewish patrician family, a rather shy though witty man, almost cynically apologetic but at heart zealous in his work for non-Zionist Jewish causes.

Bernstein-Namierowski must have seemed an exotic and overbearing figure to the Fellows and undergraduates of the college. On one occasion, when they as yet hardly knew each other, Namier appeared at the door of Stein's rooms, and announced in his heavy accent: "I have come to discuss with you the Jewish question." Similarly in the course of a visit to the Montefiores' country home, young Namier sitting down one morning to breakfast announced that he intended to open a discussion of the problems of the Jews in Rumania. Upon which Mr. Claude Montefiore, the fastidious and wealthy scholar and theologian, editor of the Synoptic Gospels, abruptly barked out at his guest: "Now, Bernstein, you will eat your egg, and there will be no discussion either of Rumanian Jews or any other subject." Dr. Toynbee remembers how Namier would regale him and those who would care to listen with the intricacies of the nationalities struggle in the Austro-Hungarian Empire. From the start he had to dominate others by acting as their teacher and mentor because he was incapable of feeling accepted simply as a member of whatever group he was in.

In 1914 Namier volunteered for the British Army. He served for a time in the Foreign Office Intelligence Service, and was brought to the Versailles Peace Conference to advise on the problems concerning the old Hapsburg Empire, Poland, and Eastern Europe generally. There is reason to believe that he played some part in the rejection of the Andrassy note—a last attempt to ward off the dissolution of the Hapsburg Monarchy through a separate peace with the Allied Powers. Although he was listened to on questions relating to the future of Poland, it is not true, as some Poles and above all the anti-semitic Roman Dmowski claimed, that Namier initiated the Curzon Line scheme. It is true that he was against the inclusion of the territories inhabited by a Ukrainian and White Russian population into the new Poland: an arrangement which, while it flattered the Polish ambition to undo in part the 1772 partition, became an incubus upon the artificially inflated body of the new republic.

The years following World War I were exceedingly difficult in both his personal life and scholarly career. He did not turn at once to an academic career, but tried his luck in business, representing British firms in Vienna and then in the United States, without much success. (He needed the help of friends to complete his first book, which he wrote as a private scholar.) His first marriage turned out disastrously, and ended in divorce. These miseries were followed by years of solitude and study and were acutely unhappy ones.

One outlet he found was his Zionist activities, into which he threw himself with devotion. However, the leaders of the Zionist movement, and still more the delegates to the Zionist congresses, viewed him with suspicion. He did not belong to any of the factions, his ways were strange. His pedantic insistence on the niceties of formulation and protocol, his close contacts with the English world, his lack of flexibility, and finally his unclear religious affiliations made him appear as an outsider to the ordinary Zionist from the pale, someone to be appointed but never elected, a useful technician but not a representative. For a time he served as political secretary of the Zionist executive, but his deep wish —in which he had the support of Chaim Weizmann—to be elected member of the executive was never fulfilled. On one occasion two renowned Zionist leaders pulled him up sharply by reminding him that he was no more than a secretary and should know his place.

It was as a volunteer backroom boy in the kitchen of history that Namier made his contribution to the Zionist cause. He and Mrs. Blanche Dugdale, the niece of Arthur Balfour, were the chief draftsmen of the Jewish Agency. The infinite pains Namier would take to eliminate a superfluous word or to dig up the most telling and most idiomatic adjective became a legend, and a source of much mirth. However, Namier also played a considerable role as go-between in obtaining the Ramsay MacDonald Letter, which in fact cancelled the Passfield White Paper of 1930. Thanks to his friendship with Professor Coupland, the author of the famous 1937 Report of the Peel Commission (the first official British document to bring up the idea of a Jewish state in a partitioned Palestine), Namier was able to exercise a direct impact on matters of high importance.

For a time he served as deputy to Weizmann on the Anglo-Jewish Committee for Refugees from Germany, and took part in the struggle against the anti-Zionist notables (or "barons" as they were sometimes called) of Anglo-Jewry. On the eve of World War II, Namier returned to

active Zionist work on a full-time basis. Criticising Weizmann for his feebleness, he took a militant stand at the St.
James's Conference which resulted in the publication of the
ill-fated White Paper of 1939. A British patriot, he nevertheless insisted on the need of a forceful and even threatening
policy toward His Majesty's Government.

The Jewish world and the Zionist masses knew little of
Namier's work, and this lack of recognition weighed heavily
upon the historian-diplomat. Apart from his devotion to the
Jewish people, Namier relished political action, a trait not
uncommon in historians. Theodor Mommsen, for example,
could never forgive either himself or the German people for
his not having become a statesman. It is a moot point whether
scholars of this type take up historical research and teaching
as a substitute for making history or remain in the academic
field (with occasional forays into the world of politics)
because they cannot overcome their inhibitions.

In any case, Namier's Zionism was of a special kind. It was
above all a passionately sentimental reaction to the humiliations inflicted upon the Jewish people in the last generation.
His essays of wrath and pride on the Jewish question are
among the most moving of all Jewish writings. But for all its
intensity, Namier's Zionism had little connection with Judaism. He knew no Hebrew literature, he hated the Jewish
religion, especially the religious parties in Zionism. He kept
aloof from the ideological struggles between the various
Zionist factions, although he had a definite predilection for
the labour leaders. Namier's Zionism was political, untouched
by any cultural Ahad-Haamism. It was a romantic nationalism in the tradition of Mazzini and Pilsudski—the vision of a
historic break-through conceived in Messianic terms. He was
too conditioned by the spirit of Polish patriotism to rule out
military means for the achievement of Zionist ends. In later
years—sophisticated as he was—he would proudly wave a
newspaper which praised the Israeli infantry as the best in
the world and which prophesied that the Israeli army would
be in Damascus twenty-four hours after the start of hostilities,
if another war were to break out.

One day while staying with him I began to lament the lost

glories of the Mount Scopus landscape, to which he remarked that he had never set foot on the former campus of the Hebrew University. I expressed astonishment that he had never found time in the course of his numerous trips to Jerusalem to visit Mount Scopus before the road to it had fallen into Arab hands. "I would not shake hands with traitors," he said. "Traitors?" I murmured with raised eyebrows. "Well, Magnes," came the reply.

Once Namier was asked by a friend of his youth, a Gentile Polish historian, whether he would settle in Palestine after the Jewish state came into existence. "No," he answered, "I would not be able to feel at home there. Everything will be rough and ready, with no roots, with no organic cohesion, so provisional. No, I could not."

It was a typical remark. Lewis Namier was considered by many an incurable snob. Not only was he always seeking the company of the well-born, but he never tired of talking— both to those who were interested and those who were not— about his intimate contacts with dukes and lords, and about his week-ends in the great ancestral homes of England. With what delight Namier would roll off the names of all the members of this or that clan, the dates of their marriages across the centuries, the vicissitudes of one or another family estate. Yet to me, at least, none of this sounded like bragging —partly because of Namier's way of treating his own person and all that affected it as somehow of objective significance, and partly because of the deep romantic strain in the homage he paid to aristocracy. Other great Jews—among them Benjamin Disraeli and Ferdinand Lassalle—have displayed the same pathetic longing for ancient lineage. This is the way of some outsiders, who always sit on the edge of the chair, trying to experience a moment of communion with the "unbought grace" of the deeply rooted and the self-assured, those who have never known the need to present credentials.

Namier was much less eager for friendship with those famous for their intellect than he was for intimacy with men and women whose names could be found in *Burke's Peerage*. With them he met on a plane where the question of competition did not arise. In their eyes, he was a kind of glorified jester whom they genuinely admired and liked, and they appeared to his imagination—as they had to Disraeli's—as living symbols. Not that such exceptionally shrewd and penetrating men as Namier and Disraeli were unable to see through this duke or that marquis and realise that he was after all a dullard. In their heart of hearts both men, capable of exquisite irony, would even mock their own passion as climbers. But in every aristocrat they saw the values which he was supposed to represent in all their splendour—the idea of nobility and chivalry, the chain of generations. Furthermore as outsiders weighed down by the sense of squalor attendant upon the struggle for recognition, these two Jews of genius and heart yearned for a loftier reality above and beyond their concrete circumstances. No wonder that Namier and Disraeli became the greatest poets of the glory of British aristocracy after Edmund Burke, who indeed belonged to it as little as they.

Namier's historical research may be classified under four headings: the social-political structure of England in the eighteenth century, the 1848 revolutions, the twilight of the Hapsburg Monarchy, and the international crisis leading up to World War II. His writings under the first heading are concerned with the stability of a society with deep historic roots and an unshakeable sense of continuity. Under the second heading, he explores the discrepancy between the ideological will to total revolution and those forces and habits which resist change and in the end prove their superiority. Under the third and fourth headings, he finds lessons in decline and fall. It may be said that all four enquiries are variations on one and the same theme: cohesion versus disintegration.

To this extent, Namier's work, like that of every great historian and true artist, was also a veiled spiritual pilgrimage and even a way of working out a personal predicament. But however strongly subjective the imprint may be, the work must nevertheless retain objective significance. Thus the first question to ask is what is objectively novel about Namier's contribution? What does "Namierism" stand for? The best answer is provided by Namier's masterpiece, *The*

Structure of Politics at the Accession of George III, which was published in 1929 when he was already past forty.

In this book Namier broke away from the prevailing Whig interpretation of English history which presented the struggle between George III and the opposition as a stage in the perennial conflict between liberty and tyranny. According to that view the Court lacked the power in the second part of the eighteenth century to challenge the authority of the Commons in open battle, and it therefore resorted to intrigue and corruption in an attempt to drain the parliamentary system of any real content. The results were not late in coming—the weakening of fibre lost Britain the American colonies. Namier decided to eschew any attempt at another panoramic view of the political scene, and resolutely ignored accepted categories such as ideology, party, general tendencies inherent in the march of history, or socio-economic determinism, which are so often merely a cloak for prejudice and the refuge of lazy or fuzzy minds. Instead he embarked upon a fabulously microscopic examination of the composition of the successive Houses of Commons under George III: where did the M.P.'s come from, what was their family background, into what families did they marry, what and how much did they own, what was their education, what schools had they attended, who were their friends, what prompted one or the other to take up politics and stand for Parliament, in what ways did each one get elected? Namier followed up this investigation with questions on the circumstances of the emergence and of the fall of governments, the process of crystallisation of parties, groups, and factions, and other such matters. He even went so far as to consult graphologists about the handwriting of an obscure eighteenth-century squire, and he would discuss the utterances, the lapses, and the style of a Hanoverian politician with a psychoanalyst. This method of research came to be called the biographical method, and was adopted for the great collective *History of Parliament* which Whitehall and Westminster initiated and over which Namier was invited to preside.

The picture which emerged from Namier's examination of

the eighteenth century was of a political system run by a network of powerful families, with the help of followers, or rather retainers, who were dependent on them. From this point of view the Court was only one of the great families, although the most important. Its ways and means of obtaining support were not appreciably different from those used by the territorial magnates, except, of course, that royal patronage exceeded in scope any rewards that even the richest aristocrat could offer. On the other hand, the King could claim with a good deal of justification that he, if anyone, embodied the national interest, while the noble clans represented only their own self-interest.

On the face of it Namier may seem to arrive at a rather cynical conclusion: the governance of a selfish oligarchy without any idealistic aspirations. But that was not what Namier meant to convey. What was to him most important was that the tradition of political independence, of a direct and active share in local and national government which the nobility and gentry succeeded in preserving for centuries became a model to all classes of the nation. English liberty, then, was not the result of an uprising against existing institutions, but the concomitant of the assurance and stability which removes all fear of arbitrariness on the part of government or individuals. The monopoly of the ruling classes was not destroyed in one blow but rather the privileges and powers of the aristocracy were gradually extended to all. Class after class, as it were, won its spurs. Further, in England, immunities, privileges, liberties, and political rights were rooted originally in the ownership of land. They constituted one of the ingredients—alongside others—of the family patrimony, as inviolably the hereditary possession of the landowner as the chattel or the house or the land itself, and thus they were not something conceded by the legislator that could also be withdrawn. They were property pure and simple. Hence their strength and permanence.

Namier has one further reason for viewing the land as the matrix of liberty. For him, it is the focus of integrated ways and habits which make the man who lives by them feel self-assured and firmly fixed. Otherwise, outside the organic web of custom, man is a lonely and weak creature, hesitant, swayed by many conflicting influences, and a prey to tyranny.

From these premisses Namier reached a somewhat disconcerting conclusion for an orthodox Zionist. He condemned the nationalist movements inspired by the idea of the unity of language and race—that is to say, those movements which rested on a personal instead of a territorial basis. Too conscious of the English example—which has hardly any relevance to conditions on the European continent, especially Central and Eastern Europe—Namier attacked linguistic nationalism as a pernicious solvent which destroyed the social-political cohesion that had crystallised in the dynastic empires over the course of centuries. Societies were turned into hordes, clusters of groups into human dust. Since it was impossible to separate the interlocked races who made up the mixed population of these empires, the national conflicts which began to break out in Central and Eastern Europe around 1848 assumed the character of racial wars being fought to the death. In that atmosphere, charged with hatred and warlike postures, the tender plant of liberalism could take no root. And the drama came to an end in World War II in race massacre, mass expulsion, and, at the very least, in the transfer of millions of people from one country to another.

The cry "away from Namier and Namierism" was raised two or three years before the historian's death. Critics began to point out the weaknesses of Namier's method. One-sided, certainly, was his concentration upon political history, in spite of his strong awareness that politics is a function of social realities. Namier was not interested in economic transformations or social structure or class struggle in themselves. His concern was with how politics are made. In this respect the corrective offered by him remains important: a country is run not by the masses or classes or great individual leaders, but by closely interlocked groups of men. Namier set out to portray through the biographies of individuals a group mind and a political style.

The most telling objection against Namier was that he

took the mind out of history, that by dwelling too much on how and by whom intrigue is consciously or unwittingly cooked up, he forgot the existence of great causes that stir men's minds and hearts, and of leaders who are able to inspire and, when endowed with vision, to impose a pattern on generations. There is some substance in that criticism, but it seems to me that one issue is wrongly put. In a certain sense Namier was in fact obsessed by the question of the role of ideas in history to the point of its having a tragic meaning to him. He was haunted by the mysterious discrepancy between conscious ideas and unconscious urges in the hearts of men and masses, between the image we have of things and what things really are. Far from denying the potency of political and social ideologies, he was frightened by their power to disturb, and he was inclined to regard them as the neurotic symptoms of a society, as traumatic visitations. Experiences of early childhood dominate men for all their lives like demons: instead of adapting themselves to a given concrete situation, men cannot help going again and again through the motions which had been summoned up by that earlier fateful situation. The French people could not shake off the trauma of the French Revolution for over a hundred years. Although objective conditions would have frustrated any attempt to restore feudalism even in its mildest form, the left never ceased to dread the restoration of the *ancien régime*. And although the revolutionary volcano of 1793 had been extinct for a long while, the right saw in every insignificant riot the spectre of the Red Terror coming back, and out of this mortal fear came the bloody massacres of 1848 and 1871.

Namier sums up his viewpoint as follows: "Human society is not an organism capable of unconscious growth; at every stage thought and theory intervene, more often impeding than promoting readjustments imposed by circumstances and achieved in practice . . . a neurotic, according to Freud, is a man dominated by unconscious memories, fixated on the past, and incapable of overcoming it: the regular condition of human communities. Yet the dead festering past cannot be eliminated by violent action any more than an obsession can be cured by beating the patient. History has therein a 'psychoanalytic' function; and it further resembles psycho-analysis in being better able to diagnose than to cure."[1]

How else is one to explain the attacks of collective madness that sweep a nation—for instance, the "Great Fear" that swept France in 1789, to which Namier liked to refer; or the strange vacillations of popular sentiment towards heroes and creeds—if not by psychological projections or displacements, and the externalisation of unresolved inner conflicts? The organic cohesion of historic continuity is the most constructive factor, whereas ideas act as solvents or as paralysing forces, and any attempt to transform "the way of life of a nation, its *mœurs*, by an act of will or an edict . . . [is] . . . expressive of intellectual hubris. . . ." For Namier, the ideologue lacked the saving wisdom of self-knowledge; he was duplicitous and dangerous: "self-deception concerning the origin and character of his seemingly intellectual tenets enables him to deceive others; the intensity of the hidden passion sharpens his mental faculties and may even create the appearances of cold, clear-sighted objectivity."[2]

In Namier's later years, of course, a traumatic memory of nazism and bolshevism was always at the back of his mind, but there was also the suspicion that recourse to ideas is an expression of some neurotic choice. He believed in "instincts and modes of thinking much deeper and much more cogent than any conscious reasoning." Characteristically Namier concluded his essay on "Human Nature in Politics" (a review of a new edition of Graham Wallas's famous book of the same title) with an aside against those who since the end of World War II have been complaining of a "tired lull" and the "absence . . . of argument on general politics". To him this absence "seemed to betoken a greater national maturity", and he could "only wish that it [might] long continue undisturbed by the workings of political philosophy". The best state of affairs is characterised by a situation in which "practical solutions are sought for concrete problems, while programmes and ideals are forgotten by both parties".[3]

If all attempts at consciously directing the flow of events

[1] *Avenues of History*, London 1952, pp. 4-5.
[2] *Personalities and Powers*, London 1955, p. 2.   [3] *Ibid.*, p.7.

are doomed to frustration and impotence, are we to conclude that history is propelled by predetermined and uncontrollable forces? In one place Namier gives a blood-curdling answer to this question. "Those who are out to apportion guilt in history . . . judge the collisions of planets by the rules of the street traffic, make history into something like a column of motoring accidents, and discuss it in the atmosphere of a police court. But whatever theories of 'free will' theologians and philosophers may develop with regard to the individual, there is no free will in the thinking and actions of the masses, any more than in the revolutions of the planets, in the migration of birds, and in the plunging hordes of lemmings into the sea."

Namier's achievement and reputation as a historian did not win for him the regard he most desired, and his academic career was marked by much the same frustration and disappointment that attended his work as a Zionist. After the publication of *England in the Age of the American Revolution*, he was given the chair of Modern History at Manchester University, which he held from 1931 to 1953. He never grew attached to Manchester; his heart was set on returning to Oxford, which he loved in the spirit of Cardinal Newman or Matthew Arnold. However, Oxford continued to keep him out. When the Regius Professorship of Modern History fell vacant in the late forties, there were rumours that Prime Minister Attlee did not appoint Namier because he would not have a scholar who was both a Zionist and a Tory. However, what is more likely is that Oxford, like Cambridge, though fond of eccentrics, is frightened of men who do not converse at ease but instead hold forth and grant audiences. Namier's manner was such that the faculty of Oxford could feel no more comfortable with him than could his Zionist colleagues.

Yet in the end this lonely and neurotic man won his fight for acceptance, and some measure of peace and happiness came to reward his years of toil and torment. Namier was invited to give the Romanes Lecture, the highest of the honours that Oxford can bestow; and shortly after Harold Mac-

millan's election as Chancellor of the University, he awarded
his old friend an honorary doctorate. Namier's second wife,
the former Julia de Beausobre, brought joy into his life. A
daughter of the Russian gentry and deeply committed to the
Greek Orthodox Church, she had suffered in Soviet prisons
and concentration camps; her first husband had been executed by the Soviets, and her only child had died in prison
(an experience movingly described in her book, *The Woman
Who Could Not Die*). To her Namier symbolised the people
chosen by God for some mysterious calling, like the Russian
people. It is possible that her influence accounts for Namier's
having begun to believe—or having tried to persuade himself to believe—that Christianity was nothing but a kind of
Jewish protestantism, and that Jews should forget all
animosities towards Christians and become proud of their
offspring. (Curiously, this was also Disraeli's conviction.)

It may well be that the most solemn moment in the closing
phase of his life was Namier's address to the Modern History
seminar at the Hebrew University in Jerusalem, when he
came for the last time to Israel in connection with a scheme
for the publication of the Weizmann papers. It was one of
those exhilarating spring days, before the khamsins from the
desert have tarnished everything with that dusty brown
colour and when in a riot of Van Gogh sunshine every rock
seems to be bursting with flowers and every hill calls
hosanna. The reception hall of the Sherman building was
packed with teachers and students. Lewis Namier rose to his
feet. His voice trembled and tears rolled down his cheeks as
he began with the Hebrew "If I forget thee, O Jerusalem,
. . ." It was not a lecture in the ordinary sense. Without a
scrap of paper in his hand he gave us his testament as a
scholar, recalling his early beginnings, his later successes and
failures, issuing warnings, giving advice and encouragement
to the young. The words were simple, but the things he said
came straight from his deepest personal experience. One felt
an intimation of the tremendous seriousness of the historian's
quest, and one was touched for a moment by the majesty of
life, when wisdom becomes indistinguishable from goodness
and the same as beauty.

Index

315